EXPERT OBEDIENCE TRAINING FOR DOGS

EXPERT OBEDIENCE TRAINING FOR DOGS

SECOND REVISED EDITION

Winifred Gibson Strickland

MACMILLAN PUBLISHING CO., INC.
New York

Library of Congress Cataloging in Publication Data
Strickland, Winifred Gibson.
Expert obedience training for dogs.
1. Dogs—Training. 2. Dogs—Obedience trials.
I. Title.
SF431.S8 1976 636.7'08'87 76–1875
ISBN 0–02–615020–4

First Revision 1969
Seventh Printing 1975

Second Revision 1976

Macmillan Publishing Co., Inc.
866 Third Avenue, New York, N.Y. 10022
Collier Macmillan Canada, Ltd.

Printed in the United States of America

for my daughter Susan

The author and her daughter Susan at home with some of their German Shepherd dogs.

Acknowledgments

Grateful acknowledgment is made to the American Kennel Club for permitting me to reprint their *Obedience Regulations* in this book, and to quote from them a few times.

A special thank you to my husband, Ross Carson, for his line photographs.

CONTENTS

FOREWORD TO THE SECOND REVISED EDITION

This is the second time I have revised this book, and both revisions are a result of drastic changes in the American Kennel Club Obedience Regulations. Judges and handlers should be pleased with the new regulations as they are clearly defined and thoroughly explained. The new format for the advanced work makes training and handling in shows easier.

Handlers who have used my training method since it was first conceived will notice no change in the calm, gentle manner that is my style. Nor will they notice any change in my basic training formula or any laxity in my constant striving for perfection. However, it will be very apparent throughout this revision that anyone who applies my training method correctly, in its entirety, will have, in the shortest possible time, a highly trained dog capable of winning Obedience titles with high scores.

At this writing I have earned 86 AKC Obedience titles myself; these include 36 Companion Dog titles, 30 Companion Dog Excellent titles, 16 Utility titles, and 4 Tracking titles. I have trained hundreds of dogs for other people and many of these have won Obedience titles when shown by their owners. Thousands of handlers and instructors have attended my Obedience classes and clinics and have gone on to show their dogs and/or to instruct classes back home.

During the one period in my life when I had the time to devote most of my weekends to showing dogs, I had the National Obedience Champion and Runner-up for five consecutive years with three different dogs. At this time I was also showing them in Conformation, judging AKC Obedience Trials, raising two litters of puppies a year, and raising two children.

Since that time I have not competed for any National "Top Dog" awards, but have continued to train and show dogs just to earn their Obedience titles. A trained dog, particularly a Utility dog, is a joy to own, so I train all my dogs to some extent. The fact that I have won forty perfect scores of 200 points each, and that all the dogs whom I have trained, handled, and shown in the past twenty-five years have been "in the ribbons" 99 per cent of the time gives you an idea of the quality of my work. I often wonder what would have happened if I had given each dog a little more time instead of following so many other pursuits.

I wrote a much-needed training book for handlers and instructors called *Obedience Class Instruction for Dogs—the Trainer's Manual.* It is the only book of its kind and has become very popular with Obedience enthusiasts. Scores of people have written training articles for magazines from knowledge gleaned from this book. It will be a rich source of information for many years to come.

In the past ten years I have become very active in breeding German Shepherds. Hundreds of people had been asking me to write a book on German Shepherds, so I took three years of my time to write *The German Shepherd Today*. I invited James Moses to collaborate with me on this. This very comprehensive breed book has also become a "best seller" and its success is very gratifying after all the work I put into it.

I never suggest a training procedure unless I have completely analyzed and perfected every detail involved, and have personally and thoroughly tested it in actual show competition. As all avid Obedience enthusiasts know, there is no experience like handling dogs in Obedience trials. It quickly separates those who make false claims from those who can prove their theories.

Some people who just own one or two dogs derive a great deal of pleasure from showing them until the dogs are too old to work. In time, many of these dogs become "top workers," substantiating the old adage that "practice makes perfect." It is much easier to train and show one or two top dogs for ten or more years, than it is to train and show two or three new dogs each year and consistently win with them. So little time can be allotted to the new dogs that their training must be faultless.

This past summer I trained, handled, and showed three of my German Shepherds who, without failing, earned their CD's, and CDX's with 14 First Place Awards out of 18, were "in the ribbons" every time, and had several Highest Scores in Trial while competing against the current "top dogs." All three each earned their two titles from scratch in about three months, and each learned the Utility exercises in five weeks. Routine training like this proves my method is undeniably sound, and to many, unbelievably fast. You will enjoy training dogs when you try it.

WINIFRED GIBSON STRICKLAND

FOREWORD

In 1941 there arrived on the Obedience Trial scene a reserved, infinitely patient young woman who was, within the next decade, to gain international renown for herself and the dogs she trained and handled. Now, after many years of experience both with her own dogs and those owned by others, Winifred Strickland is sharing her *Expert Obedience Training for Dogs* so that her own successful methods may aid others to attain training titles in the shortest possible time and with the faultless precision necessary to win top scores.

There have been many good trainers and handlers since Obedience Trials were adopted in 1936 by the American Kennel Club. However, none has attained the records of Winifred Strickland's dogs, nor have other trainers received continual acclamation of their dogs' eagerness and willingness to work. Top scores and mental attitudes both were gained through methods of training that employ the magic of praise, patience, understanding, and respect by the trainer-handler for each dog's individuality.

The joy with which the Strickland dogs always work emphasizes the fact that no force training is employed; the dogs work because they have been taught to enjoy learning. Gay, willing workers can be yours, too, if you will follow the methods explained in detail in this book.

So successful has Winifred Strickland been that her methods, thoroughly tested by her and proven so successful by her enviable record, have been adopted by many Obedience advocates who, as a result, have themselves been most successful. None, however, has attained her great over-all record, compiled prior to her retirement from extensive showing in 1955.

Up to that time Winifred Strickland had earned the greatest record in Obedience history, and many of these records still stand.

For five consecutive years three of the German Shepherd Dogs Mrs. Strickland trained and handled were named Top Obedience Dogs of the Year in the United States. In 1952 and again in 1954 while showing two dogs at the same time she captured Top Obedience Dog of the Year and runner-up. Four dogs have been trained through the Tracking title by her. One German Shepherd dog earned all his degrees, including tracking, in the record time of five months, three weeks with an average score of 199, for which he received a special award. Another earned his CD, CDX, and UD in exactly five months with an average of 195.

We mention these achievements and records of 231 First Awards, 91 Highest Single Scores, 68 Highest Combined Scores in Show, 35 Perfect Scores, citations from various clubs, including the German Shepherd Dog Club of America, Inc., for service to the breed and the Verein für Deutsche Schaferhunde for outstanding success in training, and numerous honors from dog magazines to point out that the methods presented in this book have succeeded hundreds of times.

Winifred Strickland's approach to training and handling gave Obedience Trials a much-needed lift in the late '40s and early '50s. The team of immaculate handler and well-groomed dog working almost as one gave other handlers a goal of perfection at which to shoot; thus many tried to emulate her performances. This writer described one such performance in 1951, after watching *this* Obedience artist at work at the Obedience Trial Specialty of the German Shepherd Dog Club of America, Inc. We quote: "However, highlight of the day was the perfect 200 score earned by Winifred Strickland's ever reliable Margelen's Chieftain (Topper). Topper and his handler-owner work with a precision and mutual understanding attained in few dog-owner combinations. Watching this team is a thrill, although the observer may miss the merit of the work because of the ease with which the exercises are complete. Topper and his owner are to be complimented by German Shepherd Dog advocates for bringing before the public the precise work of an Obedience Trial dog, while at the same time displaying the rapport and complete understanding which is needed to put Obedience Trial exercises to practical use."

Readers will find that *Expert Obedience Training for Dogs* will do more than any other book on the subjects covered to assist them in attaining faultless performances at Obedience Trials, *and* practical obedience away from the show ring.

JANÉ GAWTHROP BENNETT
Editor of the *German Shepherd Review*

EXPERT OBEDIENCE TRAINING FOR DOGS

1

Should You Own a Dog?

This may seem like an impertinent question, but the sad truth of the matter is that some people are not fit and do not deserve to own a dog.

The Society for the Prevention of Cruelty to Animals handles approximately five hundred stray dogs per month in any small city. Many are purebred dogs that have been picked up as strays, or have been left at the shelter. Here, then, is concrete evidence that there are hundreds of people who should not own a dog.

Certain people will buy a female because they think she will be cheaper than the male. This is generally true where mediocre stock is sold. The buyers claim they have no intention of breeding her, but just want a pet. However, when the so-called pet comes in season, they rush out to find any stud dog of the same breed, with an owner who will accept a puppy in exchange for a stud fee. That settled, they proceed to sit back and wait for a large litter of puppies to sell. The pattern is always the same. The mother is never fed properly, although the owner expects her to feed and look after her puppies without extra rations. The puppies are sold as soon as they can walk, and no precautions are taken to inoculate them against distemper or hepatitis. If the puppies are not sold within seven weeks, the owner panics and either gives them to the local humane society or sells them to a pet dealer. In many cases the whole litter is sold to a pet dealer for a few dollars apiece. After one or two litters the bitch becomes emaciated from lack of care and the owner is ready to sell her or give her away. Here is the type of person who is not fit to own a dog. People like this do absolutely nothing to promote the breed; instead they are responsible for bringing ill-bred, undernourished, inferior puppies into the world.

Then there is the couple that buys a pet for their children. The puppy is turned over to the children, and the parents feel they have done their part. They have no interest in dogs themselves, but have bought the puppy solely to amuse their children. Although he is fed regularly, he never gets a balanced meal, but exists on scraps. After a month or two the children lose interest in him and the puppy grows up completely undisciplined. The owners let him roam, and eventually he becomes a public nuisance.

Consider these facts if you are contemplating the purchase of a dog. You must give him a well-balanced diet if you want him to be healthy. He

Below: Margelen's Chieftain, UDT (Topper), National Obedience Champion 1950, 1951 and 1952, and Hussan vom Hans Kilmark, UDT, National Obedience Champion 1953 and Runner-up 1952 and 1954.

Above: Alf vom Kroppelberg, UDT, National Obedience Champion 1954.

must have permanent distemper and hepatitis inoculations. He will need a rabies shot when he is six months old.

If you have neighbors, you should fence in your back yard so that the dog can get plenty of exercise on your own property. A dog needs as much love and attention as a child.

Think twice about getting a dog "just for the children." It will mean that you will not only have to train the dog, but, what is harder, you will have to train the children to respect the dog's rights. Children should be taught to be gentle with dogs. They should not be permitted to pick them up by their legs or carelessly drop them. They should be taught to walk around the dog and not step on him thoughtlessly. The dog should be permitted to eat in peace and should not be teased when he wants to sleep.

Parents have a wonderful opportunity to do a little character building when they introduce a puppy into their home. It is a pleasure to watch children grow up with a dog when they have been taught to be kind and considerate of the dog's feelings. Encouraging a child to help take care of a dog is fine, but it should not be the sole responsibility of the child unless he or she is over twelve years of age. Even then, the child will need supervision and guidance from the parents. It is the parents' responsibility to see that the dog is fed, sheltered, and trained. Children who learn to take loving care of their own dogs and, in many cases, train their own dogs become very fond of all animals. Thus a child's love for his dog will often awaken other virtues in him. On the other hand, children who are permitted to torment, tease, or needlessly neglect their dogs will become so hardened to cruelty that they may someday turn their vindictiveness upon their fellow man.

My daughter wanted a dog of her own for many years, but I refused to let her have one until I was certain that she would train and take care of him herself. It would have been simple to give her one, since I raise pure-bred German Shepherds and we have a large place in the country. Whenever she begged for a dog of her own, I would tell her which dog I would give her if she trained and took care of it for three months. She never lasted out the trial period. I knew that if I helped her to train the dog it would become attached to me and it would no longer be her dog. I have taken dozens of dogs of various ages that seemed fond of some member of my family, but when I started training them they lost all interest in everyone else. I did not want this to happen to Susan, for it would have been a crushing disappointment to her.

Then, when she was thirteen, she became seriously interested in training. I gave her a ten-weeks-old German Shepherd puppy of show caliber. She gave the puppy all the love and attention he should have, and trained him faithfully under my guidance. She earned his Companion Dog title with progressively high scores. She was glad she waited until she was mature enough to appreciate a dog.*

Dogs are fun to own. Their antics are a constant source of entertainment, their companonship can dispel any thoughts of loneliness, and their loyalty and devotion to their master are unparalleled. All this becomes fact and not fancy when you care enough to treat a dog like a member of the family.

* Since that time she has trained dozens of dogs successfully and has become one of the top Obedience handlers in the country.

2

Choosing a Puppy

Every puppy has so much appeal that it takes all the will power you command not to succumb to his charms. Any breed of dog can be irresistible as a puppy, but when full grown may not be exactly suitable for your needs or taste. If you are undecided about the breed of dog you want, it is a good idea to go to a dog show and get acquainted with all the various breeds.

If one particular breed appeals to you, speak to a breeder and find out its characteristics, virtues, and limitations. You will see it shown in the Conformation Classes where dogs are judged for beauty, structure, and gait. The dogs that place in the ribbons are usually good representatives of their breed, and you should keep their appearance in mind later on when you are selecting your pet. You may also watch your breed shown in the Obedience Classes where the dogs are judged for their ability and intelligence. Almost all the different breeds can be successfully obedience-trained and shown in American Kennel Club licensed Obedience Trials. Many Obedience enthusiasts have become interested in training their own dogs after watching an Obedience Trial at a dog show.

When you choose a particular breed, consider the following—its overall characteristics, personality, general behavior pattern, temperament, size, required amount of care, and acknowledged intelligence. To get a clear picture of any breed, study a sound, normal animal. You can make the right decision only after observing a true representative of the breed. There are good and bad individuals in all breeds, so be sure the one you choose is sound, physically and mentally. Sex is also a matter of choice, since both male and female are equally intelligent and affectionate. Give either sex a good home with care and personal attention, and the response will be the same.

I knew for many years which breed of dog I wanted, and as soon as I was in a position to give the dog the care it needed, I bought one. I chose a German Shepherd Dog because I had wanted one since I was a little girl. I had seen all the movies in which they were featured, and read everything printed about them. I was greatly impressed by their courage and intelligence as well as their noble appearance and size. I spent many hours planning what I would teach my dog someday. I have never regretted my choice.

At about the same time, good friends of mine chose a Miniature Poodle for its size, appearance, and gaiety. They wanted a dog that did not shed hairs, and one that they could carry. They did not mind the extra expense involved in getting it clipped every six weeks. They have been just as happy as I am. Choose your breed to suit your taste. If you buy a certain breed because the Joneses have one, you may end up giving it to the Joneses.

Once you have made up your mind what breed of dog you want, go to a reputable breeder. He can show you his breeding stock and some young dogs so that you will have an idea what your puppy will look like when it is mature.

Hussan when he was eight weeks old

If you are interested in training and showing your dog in Obedience Trials, be selective in your choice of a kennel. Many kennels breed dogs for intelligence and physical soundness as well as for temperament and conformation. These conscientious breeders have spent considerable time and money in developing a strain that is way above average in intelligence. Only superior dogs are used for breeding purposes, and these highly trained dogs can be traced back five or more generations.

I know from personal experience that this is true, for here at Wynthea we have developed a strain of show dogs that is remarkably intelligent and sound in every way. By selective breeding, these dogs are consistently expert at scent work and tracking, and all display an amazing ability to jump effortlessly and fluidly.

There is nothing quite so wonderful as a sound, healthy puppy that delights you each day with proof of its intelligence. You will probably have your dog for at least ten years, so choose one that will be a joy to own.

It doesn't cost you any more to buy a puppy that has generations of selective breeding behind it. So many people who decide to get a dog rush out and buy the first cute puppy they see because it is a bargain. Most of these bargain puppies require medical attention and special diets to keep them healthy. Later they have countless training problems because the dog turns out to be below average in intelligence or unsound in temperament.

The first thing you will notice is the puppy's temperament. If it comes running to greet you, wagging its tail, it is a pretty good indication that it is sound. If it stays back and tries to run away from you when you approach it, it is probably shy. Shy dogs do not make the best pets or Obedience workers. It takes the most expert training and patience plus endless hours in building up the dog's confidence in himself and the world to obtain satisfactory results. The dog will grow up giving strangers the impression that it has been beaten by you or his former owner, when in fact he is, frankly, neurotic. The quiet puppy who approaches you will be easier to cope with than the extrovert who is the boss of the litter. The latter will always be trying to keep one step ahead of you, and you will need a great deal of determination and experience to master him.

Your puppy should give the impression that he is well fed; he should have a glossy coat, healthy skin, and clear eyes. He should be sturdy, alert, and unafraid. When you buy him, ask for a copy of his pedigree, a record of the inoculations he has had and those he needs, and inquire about a proper diet for him.

Determine if the litter has been registered with the American Kennel Club. If it has, the breeder will give you a registration slip to fill out and send to the American Kennel Club with a small fee, which will enable you to have the puppy registered in your name. If not, be sure to get the necessary information needed to register your puppy on the day you take him home. You will need the sire and dam's registered names and numbers, the date your puppy was born, and the name of the breeder. If the sire of your puppy at birth was owned by someone other than the breeder, you will need his signature. Do not put off obtaining this information. The breeder may move away or die, and it may be difficult, a year or two later, to trace your puppy's ancestry.

You should be able to get a purebred puppy for about two hundred dollars if you just want a pet. If you are interested in a puppy that is a show prospect, be prepared to pay more.

A purebred puppy is sold as a pet when it does not quite measure up to the standard for that particular breed. It may be overshot (the top teeth may protrude over the lower), or it may have another fault that would prevent it from becoming a champion. You could, nevertheless, own a purebred dog with good bloodlines that might make a name for itself in Obedience or become a happy addition to your family.

3

Choosing a Name for Your Puppy

When choosing a name for your puppy, try to find one that is original. If you don't, you may find yourself doing a Long Sit exercise with your dog in a ring while next to you a handler is doing the Recall with *his* dog using the same name as yours. This can be confusing to say the least.

Remember that when you register your dog with the American Kennel Club you cannot use more than twenty-five letters for its name. I think it is nice to include the dog's call name in the registered name so that everyone will become familiar with it. For instance, if I wanted to call a dog Hussan I would include it with my kennel name. For example: Hussan of Wynthea. It becomes less confusing later on when the dog is well known. The call name will be easier to use if it is only one or two syllables. The name should not rhyme with any of the commands, such as "Neal, heel," or "Day, stay." Keep it distinctive, and the dog will not be confused.

Here are a few suggestions:

AMBER	BARNEY	CANDY	DANNY	EASTER
ANDRÉ	BART	CAPTAIN	DAVID	EDO
ANDY	BERNICE	CHIEFTAIN	DEIRDRE	ELMER
ANNETTE	BERRY	COOKIE	DIANE	ELSIE
ASTA	BRANDY	COUNTESS	DINAH	ERIC

Fancy
Flaxe
Flint
Fran
Freda

Gaby
Gary
George
Gerry
Ginny

Hans
Hansel
Happy
Harry
Holly

Ilsa
Inca
India
Ingo
Ingrid

Janette
Janice
Jill
Jimi
Joni

Karen
Karl
Karol
Kimmy
Kris

Ladd
Lana
Larry
Lori
Luke

Mandy
Maple
Mark
Mickey
Mister

Naida
Nanette
Nero
Nina
Noble

Odon
Oka
Opal
Oscar
Otto

Pat
Patience
Paul
Perry
Polly

Qazak
Quacker
Quail
Quantum
Questor

Raven
Rita
Robin
Rocky
Ruby

Sally
Sammy
Simon
Slim
Sunny

Terry
Tiger
Timm
Tucker
Tula

Uca
Udall
Ufa
Ugric
Ulan

Varro
Vaux
Vega
Vera
Verdun

Waco
Wilbur
William
Wotan
Wyatt

Xanth
Xenon
Xeres
Xerus
Xylan

Yamin
Yankee
Yola
Yolann

Zena
Zeus
Zorn
Zulu
Zyggy

When to Start Training Your Dog

It is important to you as a new owner to know when to start training. You have just bought a new puppy, have paid what seemed to you a good price, and you feel that he deserves the best care and training that you can give him. Naturally, you wonder when you should start training him, what you should do first, and how you should go about it.

You will hear all sorts of conflicting stories, words of advice from friends, and a barrage of warnings from well-intentioned souls who all have one thing in common—they are self-appointed experts.

The training program I am outlining in this book is simple and direct, and covers all phases of training from housebreaking to the most advanced exercises. It discusses all the problems that will crop up sooner or later. The only thing it will not cover is the human element. If you wish to achieve success in training your dog, stick to the method of training described in this book and ignore any outside attempts to try something else. By switching from one method to another and then back again you will break the perfect harmony and consistency necessary to achieve success. My method is highly successful and well proven; this is owing primarily to the fact that I am consistent in my training from the very first lesson throughout the advanced work. Praise, reprimands, tones of voice, and gestures should remain consistent. From the moment you buy your puppy to the day he receives his Utility degree, your method of handling him should be the same. As you advance from the preliminary training to the more formal training, your dog should know what to expect if he does well, or if he misbehaves. The whole period of training should proceed smoothly and harmoniously. The degree of success that you achieve can be measured by your own ability to follow instructions carefully.

A well-trained dog does not become so accidentally. It takes careful planning, close adherence to details, and the patience to progress one step at a time. If you start training your dog when he is between twelve weeks to six months of age, he should be fully trained when he is fourteen months old or less.

Your puppy can start his training as soon as you get him, that is, any time after seven weeks of age. People may tell you that you will break the dog's spirit if you start training him so early. Naturally, you are not going to start with scent discrimination or any other advanced work at this tender age. Would you expect a child in kindergarten to learn algebra? You merely give the puppy his training in simple stages, remembering at all times that he is a baby. If the lesson is short and pleasant, the puppy will retain it.

Let your puppy live in your home, and don't be afraid to love him and pamper him. You won't spoil him by doing so. You can train him not to be destructive, or bite, or be rough or noisy. If the puppy has his own toys, it is easy for him to understand that he is allowed to chew only these or a beef bone. Since puppies must chew, especially when they are cutting their second teeth, give them toys or beef bones. The large hard rubber balls make excellent toys. Puppies also enjoy soft squeaky toys, but once they start to tear them apart, throw them away, or your puppy will swallow the small pieces. In fact, some puppies seem to have a penchant for swallowing anything from stones to razor blades. If you have noticed your puppy eating a variety of stones or litter in your yard, give him a dose of Phillips' Milk of Magnesia every two weeks until he gets over the habit.

Don't allow the puppy to bite or to be rough. It will become a habit, and will be hard to break later on. If he persists in jumping up against you, catch him in the chest with your knee, and after he has lost his balance two or three times he will stop. Follow through immediately by calling him back to you and petting him while he is standing still. He should not be discouraged from greeting you. He jumps simply to attract attention, so the act must be accompanied by something unpleasant. If you get in the habit of bending over to pet your puppy before he gets too close to you, he will soon learn to stand quietly. Don't be timid about bumping your knee into his chest. One or two good jolts will break this bad habit where dozens of futile attempts will make no impression whatever. This method will work with either a puppy or a full-grown dog.

Don't step on your puppy's toes when he jumps up on you. You may step too hard and break his toes. Imagine how you would feel if someone tried to step on your bare toes.

If you plan to show your dog in Obedience, and you want to win with him, my advice is to make a companion of him. The dog that you keep by your side, that will work for you always just for the joy of pleasing you and being with you, is the dog that will win consistently.

5

Care and Grooming

I am not going to delve too deeply into the subject of general care. I will cover those phases which I feel are of extreme importance to the person owning a pet. If you are interested in training your dog, you are undoubtedly concerned about his welfare. A dog in good health and top condition will respond much more readily to training than one neglected by his owner. Any dog shown in Obedience Trials should be shown at his best. He does not need to meet the breed standard, but he should be a shining example of good care and grooming.

You have the opportunity to mold an even stronger bond between your dog and yourself by this evidence of loving care. He will respond with a full measure of devotion.

The benefit you both derive from this daily ritual is twofold. Aside from the obvious benefit to your dog's health and appearance, you can learn to employ the first subtle approach to training. In other words, you can train your dog to understand simple commands without him becoming aware of them, for his attention will be centered on the actual act you are performing—bathing, brushing, combing, etc. Take these moments to understand your dog better. To train him successfully you must understand him thoroughly, his moods and reactions, and this is a splendid opportunity to do so.

Cleanliness is as important to your dog's general health and well-being as a good diet. Your dog should be brushed or combed every day. Even though it may appear unnecessary, it still should be done. Dust particles, skin scales, and dead hair accumulate and make the dog want to scratch to get rid of them. If he scratches, he may do so too vigorously and break the skin, thus leading to skin infections. If you give the dog a sensible diet and groom him every day, his coat will acquire a high gloss that is beautiful to behold.

Make it a practice to do this every day at the same time. By doing so it will become a good habit, and when it becomes a habit, you will not consider it a chore.

If you are grooming a puppy, start by having him sit in a corner. Press down on his rear to make him sit, and then quickly brush his neck, shoulders, and chest. If he gets up, caution him with the command, "No, sit," in a pleasant tone of voice. When the brushing is finished, have the puppy stand, and show him how to do this by supporting him with your hand under his stomach. Then quickly brush him again to center his attention upon the act. Brush his back, sides, and hindquarters. If he moves, caution him to "Stand"; and then pause and say, "Stay."

The puppy will learn quickly what is expected of him, and he will absorb the four words, "No," "Sit," "Stand," "Stay." By the time you are ready for formal training you will have accomplished a great deal. When the puppy responds nicely, talk to him and praise him for his good behavior in a pleasant tone of voice. If you have to correct him, change your tone of voice, speak firmly and with authority, but do not raise your voice. Use any of these commands whenever it is necessary so that the puppy will really understand their meaning, and be quick to show him what any command means. This applies to mature dogs as well.

Dogs do not need many baths in the course of a year. Still there may be times when it is necessary. If they should soil their coats, whether in winter or summer, give them a bath. Small dogs do not present a problem, since they can be washed indoors with little or no trouble. The important things to remember in washing any dog are to RINSE HIS COAT THOROUGHLY with clear water, dry it just as thoroughly, and make sure that he is warm and away from drafts.

In my new home I have a special room where I groom my dogs. They have their own bathtub that is raised up off the floor so that I won't have to bend over to wash them. Two cement steps have been built against the far end of the tub so that the dogs can step into the tub. There is a telephone shower attached to the wall and this is just the greatest thing for bathing dogs that I have ever seen. It is a glorified hose attachment that resembles a telephone and when it is not in use hangs up out of the way like a phone. The hose is made of flexible chrome tubing to match the rest of the fixtures.

I bathe my dogs one at a time, and since German Shepherds are too heavy for me to lift, I have taught them to step into the tub. I did this by lifting their front paws into the tub, saying, "Hup," and then lifting their hind legs in. With a little urging I soon had them stepping in themselves by just saying, "Hup." Of course I praise them a great deal, letting them know the instant they start to get the idea that they really are clever. I believe in being extravagant with praise.

I get my dog's coat completely wet with the shower, then I pour a mild shampoo lightly over all of him except his head. If your dog has a skin problem, use Phisohex, as it will get him very clean, combat skin problems, and make the coat glossy. I have never had a dog with a skin problem of any kind when I used this. Then I spray my dog lightly and rub his coat vigorously until I have worked up a thick lather that penetrates the fur. Last of all I rinse him thoroughly with the shower to remove all traces of lather. I wash his head and face with a damp sponge.

If you have a problem with fleas or ticks you can get rid of them, or prevent your dog from becoming infested with them, at the same time you are giving him a bath. Either get a tick solution from your veterinarian or make up one yourself. I buy a product at a garden-supply center called Sevin, which is a powder used to combat garden insects. Add about one

Joll steps into the tub.

teaspoonful of powder to a cup of tepid water and mix thoroughly until the powder is dissolved; then pour and mix this into a gallon of water. This will be enough for five or six large dogs, depending upon the thickness of the dogs' coats. It will penetrate better when the dog's coat is wet.

I have my dog lie down flat on his side and pour a little solution over him, patting it in with my hand to be sure it goes right down to his skin. Then I have him turn over so that I can do his other side. I make sure to get some solution around his neck, below his ears, and in between his toes, for ticks go for these areas. It is absolutely untrue that "every dog has fleas." It is only true in the cases where his master is negligent.

Winter or summer I rub the dogs as dry as I can, using plenty of towels. The toweling also serves to bring a beautiful sheen to their coats. In summer I make them run by playing ball; the heat from their bodies dries their coats faster. In winter I keep them indoors until they are completely dry.

After you remove the excess water with a towel, comb your dog so that his coat will be neat. If your dog has a short coat, finish grooming him by rubbing the towel over his coat to make it lie flat and smooth. Later, when the coat is dry, brush it with a clean brush. A daily brushing will keep his skin healthy and his coat glossy.

Check your dog's ears every week to be sure they are clean. If they are not, wipe them out very gently with a piece of cotton moistened lightly in alcohol. If you see that the inside of the ear is red and swollen, take your dog to your veterinarian. Many dogs seem to get a fungus disease in their ears at certain times of the year. Some dogs are bothered with ear canker; others need your help to get rid of excess wax that hardens. If your dog is scratching his ears constantly and shaking his head he may have ear mites; have your veterinarian check him. If you are alert, you can catch these things in the beginning when they are simple to cure.

Your dog's toenails should be clipped regularly depending upon the type of exercise he gets. Dogs that run on cement do not need their nails cut as frequently as those that exercise on grass. When using a nail clipper on your dog, try to cut off just the portion of the nail that extends beyond the quick. If you should happen to cut off too much nail and it bleeds, do not get upset. Stop the bleeding by holding a piece of cotton soaked in cold water on the nail. After the nails have been cut, file them off smoothly with a dog file or a file from your workbench. If you have made a nail bleed, do not file it for several days. Some dogs object strenuously to having their nails cut but do not object to having them filed. Hold the nail firmly between your two fingers as you file with the other hand. To file it down fast, go sideways, then, to finish it off smoothly, file in one direction away from the paw.

I have found that the simplest way to cut a mature dog's nails is to do it while he is lying on his side. Have your dog sit; then pull his front paws out from under him, saying, "Down." When he is down, roll him over on his side and gently scratch his stomach. When he is relaxed go ahead with the clippers or file. If you talk to your dog while filing his nails, he will probably go to sleep and make your task a simple one.

Your puppy will begin to cut his second teeth when he is about four months old. The second teeth, or permanent teeth, will force out the baby teeth. The puppy should be given beef bones to help him with this process. Occasionally, the second fanglike teeth have trouble coming in straight because the baby fangs are in the way. If this should be the case, you should try to loosen the baby teeth when you are playing ball or tug of war with the puppy, as you could do it at this time without antagonizing him.

Hard rubber balls or bones make excellent teething toys. Raw beef marrow bones are the best, as they will not splinter, and the puppy will spend hours licking the marrow out of the bone. You might find one or two baby teeth on the floor, but the puppy will swallow most of them. This will have no ill effect upon him.

A young puppy is able to keep his teeth clean and white until he is nine months old, if he has not been ill. At this time, if you clean the teeth at two-week intervals the tartar will not harden. Moisten a piece of cotton in water, dip it in baking soda, and rub each tooth clean. If your puppy's teeth are already caked with tartar pry it off with a tooth scraper which you can obtain from any pet store. Your dog will not object to having his teeth cleaned if you are very gentle with him and do not stick your fingernails or scraper into the gums or pinch his lips.

There are as many well-balanced diets for dogs as there are different opinions on the subject. The following is the diet I give my own dogs, and is a wholesome diet for any breed.

A puppy that is eight weeks old gets four meals per day. Two of these are milk meals made with powdered milk. The other two meals consist of small puppy biscuits (softened in hot water) and then mixed with a small amount of raw ground beef. To this I add a good vitamin powder. When the puppy is nine weeks of age I omit one of the milk meals. I now add one chopped hard-boiled egg to the milk meal. Some dog food companies make an excellent dry food especially for puppies that is highly nutritional. Our puppies love the taste of it and never seem to get tired of eating it.

When the puppy is six months of age I discontinue the milk meal and give him two meals per day. The hard-boiled egg is added to the morning meal. If the puppy doesn't object you can now start feeding him kibbled dog biscuit instead of the puppy food. The amount of food you give your dog will vary according to the size of the dog. Raw vegetables are very good for dogs. Some of my dogs are particularly fond of raw carrots, cabbage, and potatoes.

Before closing this chapter I want to mention one source that can raise havoc with a dog's health. Almost every puppy has worms. The litter should be wormed by the breeder when they are three weeks old and again at five weeks. Have your puppy's stool checked for worms every month for the first six months and then every three months until he is two years old. This is of the utmost importance: worms can rob a dog of all the nourishment that you are giving him, and can sap his strength and vitality literally as you watch. If you have the slightest suspicion that your dog has worms because of poor coat, finicky appetite, sometimes a ravenous appetite, or loose stool, have him checked immediately. By means of a flotation test in which the worm eggs in the stool float to the surface and are then examined under a microscope, the veterinarian can determine what type of worm is present. It can be roundworms, hookworms, or whipworms. By taking a blood test the veterinarian can determine whether your dog has heartworms. If heartworms are not detected in the early stages, they can prove fatal to the dog. Heartworms are found in areas that are heavily infested with mosquitoes. Keeping your dog in a screened enclosure or spraying him with a mosquito repellent will help. If your dog has fleas he may get tapeworm from them. If you should look at a fresh stool and notice small white segments in it that look like rice, it means that your puppy has tapeworm. In administering medicine to rid the dog of worms the most important point is to be careful to follow your veterinarian's advice.

Not long ago I bought a puppy that was alert, lively, and sturdy. He gave every indication of being in good health: he had clear eyes, clear skin, and a glossy coat. The puppy had a good appetite and his stool was normal. When I arrived home I isolated him until I had had his stool checked. I was surprised to hear from my veterinarian that he had a very bad infestation of roundworms, hookworms, and whipworms. If I had not been naturally cautious, the puppy would have gone unchecked and the worms would have eventually ruined his health. What is even worse, he would have infested my whole kennel if I had not isolated him until the veterinarian had checked him. All my other dogs might have become infested with worms because of this one puppy.

6

Housebreaking

Housebreaking is the first lesson your puppy must learn. You can teach him in any time from two days to three weeks. The length of time it takes usually depends upon your determination to put up with the inconvenience of watching him constantly. A concentrated effort over a few days on your part is better than any sporadic method that may last for months. A puppy should be let out the first thing in the morning (try to sneak up on him before he wakes up), after each meal, after each nap, after he has been playing, and the last thing at night.

When you get your puppy home, give him a bowl of water; and when he has had all he wants, take him outdoors so that he can relieve himself. Wait until he does, then praise him and take him back indoors. Thereafter, when you let him out, take him back to the same spot and give him some command such as "Hurry up." Use the same words each time so that the puppy will associate the act with the words. Months or years later, if you travel with your dog, he will understand what you want when you tell him "Hurry up" in a strange place.

It is best to teach your puppy to go outdoors, but if you should prefer to break him on newspapers, start him off in one room with newspapers covering the whole area. When he gets used to soiling the papers, probably in two or three days, gradually reduce the area until only one square of newspaper remains. The puppy will still go over to it. This arrangement will work at night for the puppy who is trained to go outdoors in the daytime. For this little fellow, wait until he is reduced to one square of newspaper for several nights, then do not put any down. Try to get up earlier than your puppy does each morning, and he will soon learn to wait for you to let him out.

If your puppy makes a mistake, be sure to clean the spot thoroughly with soap, water, and ammonia. If there is any odor left, the puppy will feel it is permissible to return to the same place. When he soils the floor in your absence, take him over to the spot, saying in a disgusted tone of voice, "What did you do? Shame. Go out." Then be sure to take him out so that he will connect the misdeed with the act of being put outside. If he should make a mistake in your presence, rush him out immediately saying, "No. Shame. Go out." Besides being trained, he will learn the word "out." Eventually he will look at the door and whine if he needs to go out or if the word "out" is mentioned.

Puppies entirely broken to newspapers sometimes refuse to go outdoors when they get a little older, and when you yourself are tired of this whole procedure. If this is the case, take a soiled newspaper outdoors, and when your puppy decides to use it, slip it away from him. Once he has soiled the ground, take him back to the same spot each time.

It will help with the puppy's training if you take his water away from him at 5:00 P.M. If you notice him circling the floor and sniffing it, he probably wants to go out. A very young puppy has difficulty going through the night without relief. If he should get up during the night and soil the papers, don't scold him. The average puppy is anywhere from twelve to fourteen weeks of age before he can go from 10:00 P.M. to 6:00 A.M. comfortably. For the older puppy that is slow in going through the whole night, tie him to your bed; if he should have to relieve himself, he will whine and ask you to let him out. Another method is to tie him to a radiator or some stationary object, with a four-foot leash or light chain. A puppy rarely soils his bed, and this prevents him from straying far enough to feel comfortable.

The fastest way to housebreak a puppy during the night is to tie him to your bed. If he has to do his business, he will either whine or jump up against the bed to tell you. You should take him outdoors on leash, tell him to "Hurry up," then praise him when he goes and bring him back indoors again. He will gradually learn to wait until you get up. I always housebreak my puppies this way and they rarely ever make a mistake in the house.

If your puppy soils a rug, wash the area immediately with warm soapy water, and rinse thoroughly with clean fresh water. Then apply a good brand of rug shampoo, which is available in a spray can. The soiled area has to be covered with the foam which should be rubbed into the rug with a clean cloth and left to dry. Later the spot should be vacuumed. By cleaning the area this way there should be no telltale spot. Dog owners who have wall-to-wall carpeting in their homes will appreciate this foamy rug cleaner. A soiled area left uncleaned is an open invitation for a puppy to soil again, even though he was punished earlier for his mistake.

Summing up, the simplest way to housebreak your puppy is to watch him constantly for a period of at least two weeks, and take the time to take him out whenever necessary.

7

Should a Top Obedience Dog Live in Your Home?

Some people feel that if a dog lives in the home, he will be spoiled for the precision work needed to win high scores in Obedience competition today. Their argument is that if the dog is kept in the kennel, he will be so glad to see the handler that he will work more enthusiastically. A good number of handlers kennel their dogs for just this reason. I do not agree with this cold, insensitive approach to training your dog. I have known a good many handlers who leave their dogs on the bench at a show in the morning and purposely keep away from them all day with the hope that the dogs will be happier to see them on their return and work better in consequence. But this method of training results in no bond between the dogs and their owners. The dogs are trained only for Obedience competition and cannot be called obedient dogs in the true sense of the word. A properly trained Obedience dog who is still a pet in the home will obey his owner's commands all or almost all of the time.

I can offer three excellent examples of my theory that pets make the best Obedience dogs. My three German Shepherd males, Topper, Hussan, and Arry were all pets who lived in my home and were with me constantly. They were my constant companions and would follow me all day from room to room or accompany me on errands. If I was gardening, each would carry something I needed—a tool, a pail, or a basket. If we went to the grocery store they would each carry packages into the house from the car. They were true companions in every sense of the word, and made life much more fun for all of us. Yet each became the Top Obedience Dog of the United States and among them held the title for five consecutive

The author with Joll, Bar, and Randy.

years. They worked in the show ring with the utmost precision and had consistently high scores including twenty-eight perfect scores. What is most important, they enjoyed every minute of it.

These three were males but of different ages, yet they loved one another and would eat from the same dish. They would invariably lie down at my feet, and rest their heads on each other. As each joined the family, he was taught to be friendly to the others. They were loved equally and for themselves, and felt so secure and happy that they never found any cause to fight.

Topper was two years old when I bought Hussan, and although Hussan was only six weeks of age, Topper was very gentle with him. In the weeks and months that followed, Hussan was a bundle of energy, but Topper was always tolerant with him. I was very careful to give them an equal share of affection and praise. If Hussan was naughty he was promptly scolded. A trained dog such as Topper would not understand it if a new dog was permitted to get away with misdemeanors. When the scolding was over I would pet Topper and say, "But you were a good boy." He seemed to understand.

Hussan was two years old when Arry, who was also two, was brought into our home. Arry was an aggressive dog, very self-assured and fearless. He was very rambunctious and had every intention of bossing the other two dogs around. Whenever he tried to assert himself in an unpleasant way such as growling whenever the other dogs came near him, or pushing them aside in order to get all the attention for himself, he would be tapped on the nose and scolded. He soon learned that it was more fun to be gentle and friendly. In just a few days they were all playing outdoors together having a wonderful time.

If you introduce a second dog into your home, insist that he behave himself. Don't do anything to make either dog jealous of the other. If you handle the situation sensibly and show no impartiality there will be no misunderstanding.

During the past ten years I have bred and raised German Shepherds. All the dogs that we keep for ourselves are trained so we generally have about ten dogs in the house. They are of different ages and both sexes and they all get along together very amiably. The oldest male is the boss and the other dogs realize this instinctively. He never has to prove his leadership beyond a quiet growl or a fixed stare. Since dogs communicate with each other by thought transmission no other outward signs are necessary. Even though the house dogs might change from one week to the next, there is a definite pecking order and it applies according to the age of the dogs. The older dogs are always encouraged to be very tolerant of the youngsters, and the puppies are taught not to pester the older dogs. It is easy to keep peace among so many dogs if you treat them as individuals and respect their rights.

So by all means let your puppy or grown dog live in your home with you, and never fear to love him and play with him. By making a companion of your dog you are cementing a bond between you and him that will last a lifetime. It does not mean that, because you keep him with you, your dog will be spoiled. He will learn much more quickly if you are there to encourage him along the right path.

8

Preliminary Training

Teaching Your Dog Not to Bite

Never allow your puppy to bite or become obstreperous. This sort of thing will become a bad habit, and be hard to break later on. I have said this earlier, but I repeat it now. If he bites your hands, give him a sharp tap on the nose with your fingers. He will probably yelp, but he needs this lesson as early in life as you can give it to him. A puppy that is allowed to nip and bite becomes very bold and aggressive as he grows older. Then when he gets to be over a year old, the harassed owner takes him to a professional trainer to be tamed down. Such dogs present a problem to both their owners and society in general. It takes a firm, experienced trainer to get them under control. Many owners are so upset by their dog's uncontrolled behavior and aggressiveness that they decide to give him away. Unfortunately, what they do not realize is that the next person does not want a problem dog either. So take my advice and control your puppy while he is young and trainable.

Teach him to be gentle by offering him tidbits in your hand. If he snatches the tidbit say, "No. Ow." If he continues to grab for it, give him a tap on the nose with your fingers, and then offer him the tidbit again saying, "Easy," in a soft voice. If he takes it gently, praise him. Repeat this lesson over and over again. After a lesson or two you will note that if you say, "Easy," and pause for a second before giving the tidbit to him, he will be gentle. This is a valuable lesson that can be learned easily and retained.

A variation of this lesson will be very useful from time to time. For instance if when you are playing with a toy, the puppy gets excited and starts to bite, just say, "Easy," softly. If he has learned his tidbit lesson well, he will relax and play gently.

Teaching Your Puppy Not to Jump Up

Puppies and dogs that jump up on you are only looking for attention, and it is your duty to give it to them. If when you enter a room your puppy dashes over to greet you, bend over to pet him. If you simply stand where you are he will probably want more of a greeting from you, and speaking to him is not enough. Remember that this display of affection is one of the ways your puppy will show that he loves you, and your affectionate response will assure him of your devotion. Dogs are gregarious creatures, and enjoy your company. Don't be surprised if your dog greets you with the same abandon with which he greeted you only a few minutes ago; it is a compliment.

If your puppy jumps on your friends or strangers when they come to visit you, another method must be employed. Since you could hardly expect anyone else to use the knee method to prevent the puppy from jumping on them, it is up to you. Have the puppy on a leash when a caller comes to the door, and as the puppy starts to jump up on him, jerk him back. Ask your friend to reach down and pet him. As you jerk the puppy back off balance, say, "No. Easy," to him. It is best to have a choke collar on your puppy at this time. The collar should not be heavy and it should fit properly.

If you wish to teach your dog later on to stand up against you, try this. Encourage him to stand against you by saying, "Up," and patting your chest. If the dog jumps and leans on you too heavily, hit him in the chest with your knee. Encourage him to try again, and when he leans against you lightly, praise him with your voice, and pet him. Here is another opportunity to use the word "Easy."

Tones of Voice

Your puppy can learn many things at a very early age by the different tones of voice you use and by the different inflections you give your words. He may not understand your new word commands until you have repeated them over and over, but he will instantly recognize your different tones of voice.

He will soon learn to recognize words when they are used in the form of a question. This is especially true when an act is performed each time a question is asked. Here are a few examples:

Do you want to go out? (As you go to the door.)

Do you want your dinner? (As you pick up the puppy's dish.)

Do you want a drink? (As you turn on the faucet.)

Do you want a cookie? (As you take the cover off the cookie jar.)

Do you want to go for a ride? (As you walk toward the car.)

Do you want to go to bed? (As you pat the dog's bed.)

Do you want to go for a walk? (As you pick up the leash.)

If you repeat these questions and go through the motions a great number of times, your dog will soon learn to understand all the words. At first upon hearing a question, he will look at you expectantly, and may wag his tail with anticipation. Later he may speak, and still later he may bring you his dish or leash. When your dog's training is completed, you can sit in your living room and ask any of these questions, and your dog will reply by acting out the answers. So, at first when you ask your dog questions, use a pleasantly excited tone of voice and emphasize the last word of the question.

When you use the word "No" to correct your dog, lower your voice, making it sound authoritative and firm.

When reprimanding your dog, lower your voice and draw out the words. "S-h-a-m-e. Ba-a-a-d d-o-g."

The tone of voice that is most important in training is the one you use when you praise your dog. Make it gay and full of good spirits. Include a laugh here and there, and be sincere, for a dog can spot insincerity easily. Put on a little act for his benefit, for this is his real reward for being obedient. Put your heart in your voice, and watch your dog respond.

If you give commands to your dog in actual training, use a moderately pitched, pleasant voice that is both firm and authoritative.

There is absolutely no reason to shout at your dog if he is working near you. A dog's hearing is at least sixteen times better than that of a human being. With such acute and sensitive hearing there is no excuse for you to speak to your dog above a moderate tone. If you wish to attract his attention, clap your hands, say, "Sssst," or call him by name. Even at a distance raise your voice just enough to be heard above the crowd.

If you find yourself continually shouting at him, it would be better to turn your dog over to another member of your family for training, since you are probably temperamentally unsuited for the job. If you find yourself confronted with a problem, and the dog seems to be getting stubborn, and you find yourself shouting at him, stop. Repeat a simple exercise the dog knows and understands, praise him, then stop for the day. Always end the day's training on a pleasant note. Next day you will accomplish more when you are both rested.

You may have attended Obedience Trials and have noticed that some of the handlers were shouting at their dogs. This is generally most noticeable on the Long Sit and Long Down exercises, but with many handlers it continues through every exercise. It certainly puts Obedience in a bad light when the noise erupting from the Obedience rings carries all over the show grounds. Obedience handlers should set a good example at all times and not invite ridicule. The type of handling where shouting is used is a form of intimidation. Instead of appealing to the dog's finer instincts and using various quiet tones of voice to control him, the loud voice is intended to bully him into obeying. By yelling at the dog in this rude manner some handlers expect to COMMAND the dog's attention, but in so doing they eventually lose the dog's respect. Only the most placid breeds will meekly tolerate this type of training. It is an insult to a dog's intelligence to expect him to respond to this crude method. Contrast this type of handler with one who asks his dog to heel in a pleasant, quiet tone of voice. The quiet handler in setting a standard of perfection would by contrast alone expose the loud handler's imperfections.

To quote from the American Kennel Club Obedience Regulations, "Commands which in the judge's opinion are excessively loud will be penalized." When handling your dog be gentle, make a companion of him, talk to him as you would to a friend, conversationally. You won't spoil him by doing this, but will gain your dog's respect. Your dog will be your best friend if you will just consider his feelings at all times. If you train him with patience, and establish a mutual feeling of companionship, he will be eager to work just to please you. A well-trained dog will execute any command perfectly, even if the order is given in a whisper. Gentleness and smoothness of handling can be acquired only through constant practice.

I know of one judge who bellows his commands to the handlers in a loud, rough voice. One sensitive dog that I was showing was so horrified by the judge's shouts that he sat crooked in order to keep an eye on him. To the dog's mind, anyone with so rude a voice bore watching. It is permissible for the handler to ask the judge to lower his voice if it interferes with the dog's work. Fortunately most judges have been handlers themselves and are very understanding.

Teaching Your Dog to Lie Down

One of the first things to teach your puppy is to lie down upon command or signal. If you can teach him to do this at an early age, life will be much easier for both of you. There will be many times during the course of the day when this simple exercise will prove its worth.

Have a nylon choke collar on your puppy or grown dog and attach a leash to it. Have your puppy sit, and stand directly in front of him. With the leash in your left hand hold it short and taut in back of his head. As you give him the verbal command "Down" also give him the Down signal by raising your right hand where he can see it, and pull him down with the leash. Quickly stroke him on the withers with your right hand as you murmur approvingly, "Down, good, down, good." If it is necessary, hold him down with the hand that is stroking him. The verbal command should be given in a very calm, quiet tone of voice. A loud intimidating tone of voice would only frighten or rattle him.

In the beginning it will be necessary to bend over a little as you give the signal. Later when he knows the exercise you can stand up straight and give the signal. When you pull the puppy down you should pull the leash either straight down, or slightly back away from you. If you pull the leash down toward you, the puppy will move forward and you do not want him to do this or he will crawl between your feet. He should go down exactly where he is sitting without moving forward.

This should be repeated several times until the puppy will go down on the signal and the verbal command. He will learn this very quickly if you will give him five or six very brief lessons during the day. At this point you should teach him to go down quickly when you give him just the Down signal.

To be effective the Down signal should be given by raising the right hand up and away from your body. Do not give a downward stroke or point to the ground. When you raise your hand quickly let your dog see the palm of your right hand, and if necessary repeat this signal. Many handlers confuse their dogs by giving them a very poor signal, then they wonder why the dogs do not learn the exercise quickly. Once the signal is given the hand should be dropped quickly. It is better to repeat the upraised hand signal than to hold the hand in the air. If after a week he isn't going down immediately when you give him the signal, you should try this.

Grown dogs and the occasional stubborn puppy can be taught to lie down immediately when you teach them this way. Have your dog sit nice and straight, step directly in front of him and give him the Down signal. If your dog does not drop immediately, lower your right hand,

Give your dog the down signal where he can see it, as you say "Down"

which gave the signal, and give him a tap on his nose. Whether the tap is light or sharp depends upon the size of the dog. It should be adequate, and if you have to tap the dog more than three times it is not a sharp enough tap. It is very, very important to immediately stroke the dog on his withers as you say, "Down, good, down, good." Praise him in a pleasant tone of voice. It is of the utmost importance that you show your dog that you are teaching him an exercise and are not punishing him. He will understand this if after the tap you follow through with the praise and the hand stroking.

Try this several times or until the dog has dropped on signal a few times without being tapped. If you do the exercise correctly, your dog should drop quickly after the second or third tap. With many dogs just one tap will suffice. Remember to praise your dog happily each time he drops on your signal. Once your dog has dropped on signal, move him a few steps away each time you try it so that he will learn to drop in a different place.

When your dog is consistent about going down each time you give him a signal gradually increase the distance between you so that eventually

Praise the dog when he goes down as you stroke him on the withers saying "Down, good, down, good."

he will drop on signal across the room from you. Even a four-month-old puppy should be able to drop on a hand signal given twenty feet away from him.

The German Shepherds we raise are very sensitive and they all learn to drop this way. Because of the manner in which it is taught they learn to drop in one lesson and become willing, happy workers while they are youngsters. This fast method of teaching a dog to lie down is simple and direct, and it prepares the dog for many advanced exercises. If the dog doesn't drop after two lessons, you are probably making one or more of the following mistakes:

Giving the wrong type of signal, holding the signal behind your dog's head where he can't see it, or pointing to the ground.

Pulling the dog toward you which might prevent him from going down.

Shouting "Down" at your dog. When a dog becomes rattled because of his handler's impatience, or lack of control, the dog stops listening.

Forgetting to press down on your dog's withers as you praise and pet him.

Not tapping him hard enough, and/or not praising him as soon as he responds.

This method works for every dog regardless of his size or breed. At first the small breed owner might be somewhat timid about tapping his dog, although it would only take one or two fingers to make him obedient. After a demonstration this person realizes how easily his dog learns to drop in one short lesson and that nothing else is comparable to it.

Teaching Your Dog to Ride in a Car

If you take your puppy home with you in your car, he will feel much happier if he can cuddle up next to you on the seat. It will give him a sense of security and make his first ride a pleasant experience. Have an old blanket or towel handy in case he drools or is sick. Hundreds of puppies take to riding the first time they are in a car and are never sick, but many others get used to riding only by countless short trips. As they get accustomed to the car's motion, the excursions can be gradually lengthened. Keep your windows open so that the puppy will have plenty of fresh air.

It is a good idea to teach the puppy to sit quietly in the car right from the beginning. Dogs that dash from one window to the other, or that jump from the front to the back seat, or those that are allowed to bark soon become a nuisance and a driving hazard. If you want your puppy to ride in the car, it is up to you to make him behave. Have someone other than the driver in the car, and every time the puppy stands up say, "No, sit," and make him sit by pushing his rear down. When he sits, praise him quietly. This will probably have to be repeated dozens of times but it is worth it to have a well-mannered dog.

In teaching an older dog to ride in a car follow the same routine unless you have a dog that is actually afraid of cars. In this case you must gain his confidence. First, you should put him on leash and give him the idea that something special is going to happen by asking in a pleasantly excited tone of voice, "Do you want to go for a ride?" Take him into the car with you and have him sit on the seat with you for ten minutes, talking to him and petting him. Repeat this the second day, and on the third day try it with the engine running.

Keep this up for a week, and then try it while you back the car out of the garage; park it in the yard for ten minutes, and then drive back in the garage. Be sure to keep talking to your dog, reassuring him and praising him. This slow method is the easiest, and brings the best results. When you have worked up to a two-mile ride around the block, you can gradually increase the ride to ten miles. If you plan to drive more than fifteen miles, it is a good idea to give your dog some carsickness pills an hour or so before starting. It will probably be many weeks before he is actually a good rider, but it will be worth the effort to have the pleasure and protection of his company.

Teach your dog to sit by the car and wait for your command to get in. Also, after a ride, have him sit patiently inside while you step out and until you have given him the command to get out. Everyone appreciates a well-mannered dog, and a few minutes' practice each time he goes for a ride assures you of owning one.

If you take your dog on a long trip, be sure to carry his water dish along. Dogs get thirsty more quickly than human beings. Keep a leash in your car at all times. You never know when you may need it on a trip. If you should have to stop to exercise your dog, always put him on a leash.

If you have a dog that barks madly when he is in the car, it is fairly easy to stop him. Purchase a water pistol, and squirt the dog in the face with it whenever he barks, saying, "No, stop."

Teaching Your Dog to Stay at Home or in the Car

Once your puppy is housebroken and is trusted enough to be allowed the freedom of the house, it is time to train him to stay alone.

Begin by leaving him in a familiar room that can be shut off from the rest of the house. Be sure to leave his toys in the room. Leave him for only a few minutes the first time, and gradually increase the time as he behaves.

If he scratches the door, open it quickly and slap him with your hand, saying, "No, shame." Repeat this as often as necessary.

To correct a puppy that has been getting into mischief by chewing things, set a trap and come upon him in the act as if by surprise. After you have scolded him a few times he will behave. If you do not want your puppy to get up on furniture, refuse to allow him to get up from the first day. To prevent him from climbing up on furniture when you are away, set mousetraps on the chairs and sofa.

It is easy to teach a dog to stay in a car, since he loves the car so much that he is perfectly happy to sit in it. Leave a window partly down on each side so that he will have plenty of fresh air. If he starts to bark, go back quickly and reprimand him with your voice, or if this is not sufficient use the water pistol on him.

Teaching Your Dog to Walk on a Leash

I put a thick round nylon choke collar on a puppy when he is about three months old, and this is the only type of collar that he ever wears. To form a collar, just slip the cord through one of the rings, and draw it all the way through to the other ring. If you do not wish to use the collar as a choker, you may attach your leash to the stationary or dead ring. If fitted properly, this is a very comfortable collar for a dog to wear, as it is never rigid but is strong and lightweight.

Dogs that are permitted to run free should wear a leather or heavy tape collar. The dog's license and rabies tag should be attached to it. A dog running in the woods, or jumping against a picket fence could catch his choke collar and hang himself. In the case of my German shepherds, all of them have thick ruffs, and the choke collars are hidden in the fur. A loose, ill-fitting choke collar is dangerous, and many dogs bite at a collar that hangs too low on their necks. It can get caught in the dog's mouth, and no amount of pawing or headshaking will free it. If any length of time passes before his predicament is discovered, the dog's gums may start bleeding and he will have a sore, tender mouth.

When walking on a leash for the first time, a puppy may pick up the leash and carry it along. This makes it much more fun for him, so don't correct him. Hold the leash in your left hand, and try to keep the puppy by your left side. If he moves over to the right side, guide him back gently and pet him with your left hand.

By reaching down and petting him occasionally as you walk along, and by calling him back to you when he runs out to the end of the leash, you will be able to keep him near you. The first few times the puppy is on leash, limit him to five minutes.

It is fairly easy to control a puppy on leash, but do not be tempted to train him seriously until he is at least four months old. Some of the larger breeds of dogs such as German Shepherds can get quite boisterous, and need to be brought under control at a slightly younger age. If this is necessary, start the training two weeks earlier, but the lessons should not last more than ten minutes.

Teaching Your Dog to Swim

All dogs do not know how to swim but it is easy enough to teach them how to do so. I have seen several older dogs jump into a swimming pool and immediately sink to the bottom. Someone had to jump in the water to pull them out.

When Hussan, Topper, and Arry were alive I lived in New England on one of the lovely lakes and I taught each of them lifesaving in the water. After a long lapse of time I am now able to continue training dogs to work in the water. Last year we built a two-acre pond on our property and now we teach all our puppies how to swim. Once they learn how

At first when teaching a puppy to jump in the water, the leash should be taut enough to keep the puppy's head from going under the water. Later, he won't mind dunking himself.

to swim, they learn to dive off our dock, retrieve articles from the water, and learn how to bring a supposedly drowning person safely to shore from the middle of the pond.

Ross built a narrow platform, one step down from the dock, at the end of the fifty-five-foot pier. Stairs lead up to this platform so that the swimmers can climb onto the dock without going in to shore. It is at the end of this platform that I lower a puppy into the water on leash, being careful to keep his head above water. The puppy is encouraged to swim toward the shore and I hold the leash taut enough to keep his head above water. The experience is a pleasant one and after it has been repeated twice the puppy will swim to shore on a very loose leash. Then the puppy is placed on the platform and told to "Jump in," as he is guided forward with the leash. He soon gets the idea and is jumping in off leash on the verbal command.

The next step is to have him jump to a person who is standing in the water and learn to swim nearby without scratching or climbing on him.

There are many things to teach a dog in the water and it comes under the word FUN. We teach them to jump off the dock, swim out to the raft in the middle of the pond, climb the raft ladder that is vertical, climb the vertical ladder to the upper platform that is ten feet from the water, and dive from it upon command. We also teach our dogs how to ride quietly in a canoe so that we can enjoy their company, and they can enjoy the ride.

Many of the dogs who attend our summer clinics are taught how to swim by their owners. It is a relaxing way to take a break between class sessions.

Swimming is the best form of exercise and once a dog has learned to swim he loves every minute of it.

Above: Wynthea's Victor, UD, climbing ladder. *Right:* Reaching platform.

Above: Diving into pond. *Below:* Summer fun! Wynthea's Elsie, CDX; Wynthea's Big Foot (5½ mo.); Ch. Wynthea's Julie, CDX; Wynthea's Elissa, CDX; Wynthea's Jasper, UD; Can. Grand Victrix Ch. Fara v.d. Erika-klause, CDX; and the author.

9

Practical Tricks

At first glance these tricks may not seem to be worth your attention. However, if you will read this chapter you will discover that I have a definite reason for suggesting you include them in your dog's training program.

Each one will be of great value to you as the training progresses. By this I do not mean that it is necessary to teach your dog tricks in order to train him to be obedient or prepare him for the Obedience Trials. He can earn his Obedience degrees without any preliminary training, but it will take longer.

I look at it this way. The more exercises you give your dog that will help him to develop mentally and physically, the better off he will be. Compare the English student who studies only what is required of him with the student who not only keeps abreast of the required work, but crams extra hours of reading into his daily schedule because he has a thirst for knowledge. Obviously the latter will soon be mentally superior.

This is equally true of dogs. If you want to give them the extra time it takes to teach them practical tricks or small chores, they will develop faster and become more responsive and alert to commands. They will gain coordination and agility, and the exercise will be good for them.

You should teach your puppy these tricks before he is ready for Formal Training. This is an ideal way to introduce new commands and signals to him that will be utilized later many times.

I taught my first German Shepherd these simple tricks back in 1941 before she was seven months old. I realized later that they had helped her to master the advanced work much more quickly. I have followed the same procedure with all my dogs, and I advise others to do the same.

Dogs that are alert mentally do not become bored. A wise trainer will prevent boredom by introducing a change of pace in his dog's exercises. Some dogs that are shown in Obedience become mechanical workers because their handlers have never taught them anything else. Dogs, like people, learn that variety is the spice of life. These Practical Tricks are the elementary steps in teaching a puppy the useful and practical exercises to come later.

When teaching your puppy some of these tricks, it is wise to offer him food as an inducement. Puppies are very fond of tidbits, and if they are rewarded with a dog cookie or a piece of meat, they will be eager to try something new. This applies to puppies only, since they become bored and restless very quickly; the food will maintain their interest until they have learned the trick. Later, when your puppy is older, he will be happy to do the tricks for praise alone.

Shaking Hands

Shaking Hands is the prelude to the Stand for Examination exercise. It teaches the dog to accept the attention of strangers at an early age. It is essential for shy dogs.

It is a very simple trick and can be learned in one or two lessons. Start by having your dog sit in a corner; he is less likely to walk away. As you offer your hand to your dog say, "Shake hands," and touch his right foreleg. If the dog doesn't raise his paw, lift it yourself. Repeat this until the dog understands you. To make it easy, as you offer your right hand, gently shift the dog's weight over onto his left foot by pushing his shoulder gently with your left hand. As soon as the dog lifts his paw, praise him and give him a dog biscuit.

Have your friends shake hands with your dog so that he will learn to do it for anyone. This trick is especially good for dogs that are shy of people. If the shy dog does not respond to the command, lift his paw yourself and ask your friend to take it. A shy dog will back away; put your left foot behind him to prevent this. Once a shy dog will permit strangers to shake hands, he will soon allow them to pet him.

Rolling Over

Rolling Over is excellent therapy for tense, nervous dogs. If they can be persuaded to relax by this exercise, formal training will be much easier.

Begin by having your dog sit, then have him lie down, and next push him over on his side. When the dog is lying flat on his side, say, "Roll over," making a circular motion with your right hand. At the same time grasp the dog's paw in your left hand and help him to roll over. Once he has rolled over, say, "Roll back," and help him to do so as before.

Once the dog has mastered this you can vary the trick by saying, "Roll over and over and over," and then, "Roll back and over and over." Eventually you can give the dog the verbal command and the hand signal without helping him at all. Many dogs are afraid to roll over on their backs themselves because this places them in a rather helpless position. This will teach them to have faith in you and to overcome their natural reluctance to get in this vulnerable position. Be sure to praise your dog each time he performs correctly.

Sitting Up

Sitting Up teaches a dog to sit squarely on its haunches, and the dog that can Sit Up is less likely to sit crooked later on. In the Obedience ring your dog will be penalized for crooked Sits.

This will be fairly easy to teach your dog, provided you always try it on a rug or a floor that is not slippery. Start by having your dog sit in a corner and persuade him to sit up by holding a choice morsel of food just above his nose. He will learn to maintain his balance if, at first you let him lean a paw on your left hand. When your dog sits up, give him the food, and then praise him. Soon he will be doing this the moment you say, "Sit up," and hold your right hand above his nose.

Once he sits up in the corner, bring him out into the middle of the room. Go through the same procedure. Remember that dogs with long tails should always have them straight out behind them to help maintain their balance. Dogs that are fully trained will do these tricks without food as a reward.

Saying His Prayers

This trick follows the last, and is easily learned. Once a dog has learned to sit up, he will naturally come over to you if you are eating something and beg for a piece. If you are sitting down, he will sit up and place his paws against you. This is the position he should be in to learn this trick.

Say, "Stay," to the dog, and gently push his head between his paws. Hold it there for a minute until you say, "Amen." Then praise the dog, and give him a biscuit. The dog will learn by repetition. Small dogs can do this trick by sitting on a chair and placing their paws on the back.

My first shepherd always enjoyed this, and would say her prayers repeatedly, without being told, if anyone was eating peanuts. She had a passion for peanuts and realized she would always get some with this trick, for no one could resist her plea.

There is a very useful side to this exercise. A dog does not like to hide his eyes; he prefers to see what is going on. "Saying his prayers" teaches him to be obedient and gives you more control over him.

Catching a Ball

Dogs do not have good eyesight. My firm belief is that if you teach your dog to catch a ball, he will watch for it so intently that the exercise will be beneficial for his eyes. One of my German Shepherds became so adept at catching a ball, that anything else in the air fascinated him. He would sit in the yard and watch a hawk circling in the sky, a plane passing overhead, or birds flying by. These innocent periods of watchfulness gave his eyes much-needed exercise. One of the prescribed exercises for near-sightedness is to look at an object close to you and then at one at a

Left: "Speak." *Right:* "Say Your Prayers." Topper of Wynthea, UD.

"Sit Up." Can. Ch. and O.T. Ch. Joll vom Summerland, UD.

distance. Since dogs are notoriously nearsighted, this trick is an excellent method to improve your dog's eyesight.

It will be easier to start in the house, since the dog will not be so apt to run away with the ball. I must caution you first not to use a ball that is too small for your particular dog; he may swallow it or get it caught in his throat. The exercise is perfectly safe, provided the ball is small enough to be caught and large enough not to be swallowed.

To begin, have the dog Sit. Get him interested by pretending to throw the ball. Do this several times. Then throw it directly at the dog's mouth saying, "Catch." The dog will make a grab for the ball, and if he catches it, praise him. Take the ball away immediately and try again. Remember to have him Sit each time. If you make this fun, the dog will soon be catching the ball and bringing it back to you each time for another try.

Once the dog has learned the trick in the house, move the game outdoors. This is a very good way to exercise the dog with very little work for you. A dog that will retrieve a ball in your yard will generally retrieve a ball floating in the water. The first time you try it, be sure to throw it near shore where the dog simply has to wade in to reach it. As he gets used to retrieving from the water, you can gradually throw the ball farther out. Swimming is excellent exercise for dogs, and retrieving makes it fun.

Many busy people who do not have time to walk their dogs find that retrieving a ball gives them sufficient exercise.

Backing Up

This exercise is especially beneficial to the dog that will someday learn Utility. The dog will learn to Sit upon command at a reasonable distance from you. Even though your dog will Sit at Heel it doesn't follow that he will Sit at a distance from you on command. By teaching your puppy this trick, he will learn to Sit anywhere. If you teach him to Back Up he will have no difficulty going away from you on the send-out portion of the Directed Jumping exercise. If he doesn't go out far enough, you simply tell him to "Go back." He will back up until you tell him to sit. Next time he will go out farther of his own accord.

Once your puppy has learned to catch a ball, he can learn this trick. If you have made it a point to have your dog sit and wait for you to throw, he now understands the word, "Sit." When your dog brings the ball to you, wave him back with your right hand saying, "Go back," and after he takes several steps back say, "Sit." When he sits, throw the ball. If your dog does not understand immediately, walk into him and push your knees against his chest, gently forcing him to step back. If you have a small dog you can push him back gently with your foot, but give him the hand signal at the same time so that he will get used to it. After he has backed up several paces, say, "Sit. Stay," return to your original position, and throw the ball. Always praise the dog. Repeat the routine until the dog understands.

My Topper picked up this trick practically by himself. After I got tired of throwing the ball for him I would sit down and read. He would come over and place the ball in my lap, back away, and sit, waiting expectantly for me to throw it. We would play a little game. Sometimes I would pretend not to see the ball, and after a minute he would come over, pick it up, and drop it in my lap again. Then he would back up with quite a flourish and speak softly. This version of playing ball was so intriguing that I taught it to my other dogs.

One day while playing with a large beach ball, I threw it to my German Shepherd, Jerry. She bounced it back to me with her nose, and a new trick was born. After that she would keep the beach ball going back and forth by stopping it in the air and bouncing it back to me with her nose. She never tried to catch it in her mouth or to bite it, figuring in her own mind that it was too big. She was so eager to retrieve balls that she would dive under the water and retrieve those that wouldn't float. This was up in New England where the water was very clear. At times she would even dive in after a fish that she could see swimming by. She never was able to catch a fish, but she did corner a turtle against the ledge that bordered the shore, and brought it to the surface. She played with the turtle the whole day as if it was her most prized possession. That night when we left camp I put it back in the water and it swam away, none the worse for its experience.

One day I looked up from my desk and noticed my Shepherd, Topper (named after my first Topper), sitting in the yard outside my window, looking up intently at the house. Just then someone threw a ball to him from the window upstairs. He caught it, and ran over to my window with it. As I was about to say something, a basket was suddenly lowered on a string from the window upstairs and passed by my window to the ground below. As I stood up to watch, Topper put the ball in the basket, and as it was pulled up to the second floor, backed up excitedly across the yard. Upon investigation, I found that my daughter was playing ball with him in this way.

Rather than run downstairs each time to get the ball, she had devised the idea of lowering the basket. Topper knew instinctively what to do, and though at first there had been a miss or two when the ball didn't land in the basket, he would pick it up and try again until he was successful. After a while he became very proficient. This little game is a good example of a dog's intelligence, for he was completely controlled at a distance. Topper was ten months old at the time, and by learning to play ball he had begun to think for himself.

Jumping

There is no reason why your dog should not learn to jump when he is a puppy. Once he understands the word "Hup," it can be used to advantage on countless occasions.

This trick is best suited for medium- or large-sized dogs, but many of

"Hup."

the small breeds love to show off their versatility by jumping gaily. Large dogs should not jump the full height required in shows until they are at least eleven months old. When you are teaching him, do not ask your dog to jump more than two feet. If your dog is small, begin by setting the jump at one half the height required in shows.

For a large or medium-sized dog, set the bar jump at twelve inches, and keep the dog on leash. Run up to the jump, say, "Hup," and jump over it with the dog. He will learn faster if you jump with him the first few times. If your dog balks at the jump, lift him over with the leash the next time you run up. Soon he will be jumping by himself as soon as you run up to the jump and say, "Hup." Next, teach the puppy to jump by himself. Have him sit about six feet from the jump, and tell him to stay while you take a position behind the jump. Say, "Come. Hup," and clap your hands over the jump, beckoning him toward you. Try always to keep his attention focused on a point higher than the jump so that he will clear it.

Once the puppy has learned to jump by himself, take off the bar and hold it in your hands. If he refuses, put him on leash and encourage him to jump. From this you can progress to a short bar or a hoop, or have him jump over your arm.

My three dogs, Topper, Hussan, and Arry, learned to play leapfrog after they learned to jump. Arry would sit while Topper and Hussan would stand in position about twenty feet apart. Arry would jump over the other two, and then take a standing position while Topper would jump over Arry and Hussan. They became very proficient, and would enter into the spirit of the game with much gaiety, producing gales of laughter from the gallery.

10

Dog Shows

There are hundreds of licensed dog shows held throughout the country each year, so you should have no difficulty in finding one close enough to you in which to compete.

These shows are licensed by the American Kennel Club, and are permitted to give championship points in the Conformation Classes and legs toward an Obedience title in the Obedience Classes. It is possible in one day at an all-breed show that holds classes both in Obedience and in Breed to gain points toward a Breed championship and a qualifying score toward an Obedience title.

Dog shows are put on for the individual dog clubs by licensed superintendents. A list of the coming shows is published in the dog magazines. The American Kennel Club compiles this list, and publishes it in their official magazine *Pure-bred Dogs, The American Kennel Gazette.* You will find the date of the show, the judges, the name of the club, the superintendent, and one of the officers and his address. Occasionally a dog club puts on its own show, and in this case you should write to their secretary for the premium list.

If you write to any of the superintendents listed below and ask them to put your name and address on their mailing list, they will be glad to send you Premium Lists for the coming shows.

Mrs. Bernice Behrendt, 470 38th Ave., San Francisco 21, Calif. 94121
Bow Dog Show Org., 9999 Broad St., Detroit 4, Mich. 48204
Mr. and Mrs. Jack Bradshaw, 727 W. Venice Blvd., Los Angeles 15, Calif. 90015

Roy J. Jones, P.O. Box 307, Garrett, Ind. 46738
Foley Dog Show Org., 2009 Ranstead St., Philadelphia 3, 19103
Jack Onofrio, P.O. Box 25764, Oklahoma City, Okla. 73125
Moss Dog Shows, P.O. Box 20205, Greensboro, No. Carolina 27420
Jack Thomsen, Box 521, Littleton, Col. 80120
Webb Dog Shows, 500 W. North St., P.O. Box 546, Auburn, Ind. 46706

The premium lists will give you all the pertinent information about the shows such as the location, date, judges, prizes, closing date, classes, et cetera. You then fill out the form included in the premium list that asks for your dog's name, breed, registration number, birthday, sire, dam, breeder, class, your name and address, and send it back to the show superintendent with the stipulated fee. This varies slightly from show to show but is generally ten dollars for each class. The closing date is three weeks prior to the show, so you must plan to mail your entry a few days earlier to get there in time. A week before the show you will receive an entry slip which is your admission ticket. A schedule will also be included that will tell you at what time the various Conformation and Obedience classes will be judged, your dog's number, and the number of entries in each class. If the show is benched, your entry slip will give your bench number. (Shows licensed by the American Kennel Club are for purebred dogs only.)

Point shows are held indoors and outdoors, and are benched or unbenched. When they are benched it is necessary to keep your dog in a stall except when he is being shown or exercised. Dogs of the same breed are benched together in adjoining stalls which are separated by partitions. Take a rug four feet by twenty-six inches for your dog to lie on; he will be more comfortable. You will find a metal ring in the back of the stall and you may secure your dog to it by means of a bench chain. These chains are sold at all benched shows, and come in different lengths. Dogs must be kept on leash except when being shown.

Match shows are put on by the individual clubs, and can be entered the same day as the show. There are no championship points or Obedience credits given, as these shows are for practice purposes only. They are always unbenched, and you may leave when you wish. There are two kinds of match shows. Plan A is given by the club that is trying to get permission to hold a point show. The club publishes a premium list, and conducts the show like a Point show. No points are given. Plan B is purely for fun, and the atmosphere is one of informality. You will find nonregular classes in Obedience at these shows such as Sub-Novice (all the work is done on leash), Graduate Novice (a drop is included in the Recall exercise), and the Long Sit and Long Down are the same as in the open exercises. The Graduate Open and Graduate Utility classes are for the dogs that have their degrees. Novice handlers should try competing in Match shows before going into Point shows. The experience gained at Matches will be of great value to them later.

If you want to know when and where there will be a Match show, ask someone who is participating in dog shows. They will be able to supply this information. In the Northeast area a Match Show Bulletin is sent out each month that gives the Matches for the next two months. This handy bit of information is sent out by Mrs. Grace Sachs, Box 214, Massapequa, N.Y. 11758.

In the Breed Classes a dog is judged against the standard of his particular breed, and the judge determines which of the dogs present are the best representatives of this breed in type and temperament. The judge examines the dogs for soundness while they are gaiting and posing.

There are five regular classes in Breed—Puppy, Novice, American-Bred, Bred-by-Exhibitor, and Open, and the dogs and the bitches are judged separately. If your dog wins his class he will then compete against the winners of the other classes for Winners Dog. It is the winner of this class that will win points toward his breed championship. The bitch classes are then judged and the Winners Bitch is chosen. If there is a special entered (a dog that already has won enough points to gain his or her championship), he or she will now compete against the Winners Dog and Winners Bitch for Best of Breed and Best of Opposite Sex. When this is decided the Winners Dog and Winners Bitch will compete against each other for Best of Winners. If the Winners Bitch has earned more points than the Winners Dog, he automatically gains the same number of points by defeating her.

If he wins Best of Breed he is now eligible to compete in his Variety Group. There are six Variety Groups and a miscellaneous classification for rare breeds. For instance, if you were the owner of a German Shepherd, he would be in the Working Group. If by some good fortune you were to win this group, you could then show him with the winners of the other groups for the top honor, namely Best in Show. During this competition if your dog were to win over another dog that had picked up more points that day, this would entitle your dog to the same number of points. The largest number of points that can be acquired at one show is five, and if you have a popular breed of dog this means that a large number of dogs will be competing against one another. A dog needs to gain fifteen points in order to become a Champion but he must have won two major shows worth three points apiece under two different judges.

The Conformation Classes have nothing whatever to do with Obedience, and a dog can become a Champion without displaying any signs of intelligence. The Obedience Classes have a definite purpose, since each exercise clearly shows the dog's ability to work and obey under difficult conditions. If you have a purebred dog, it does not matter if he has a fault that would disqualify him in the Conformation Classes; in Obedience it is the dog's working ability that counts. Spayed or castrated dogs can be shown in Obedience. It is a pleasure to live with an Obedience-trained dog when his good behavior is a way of life.

Obedience Trials are held in conjunction with most all-breed shows. There are also Obedience Trials held separately and sponsored by Training Clubs. The latter cater to the Obedience exhibitors and feature such niceties as large rings, close-cropped grass at outdoor shows, efficient stewarding and an impressive trophy list.

There are three regular classes at an Obedience Trial: Novice, Open, and Utility. The degrees that correspond with these classes are CD (Companion Dog), CDX (Companion Dog Excellent), and UD (Utility Dog). A perfect score in each of these classes is 200 points, and in order to gain a qualifying score your dog must earn 170 or more points and more than 50 per cent of each exercise. When you have received three qualifying scores in the Novice Class under three different judges, the American Kennel Club will send you a Companion Dog Certificate with the name of your dog and the title CD after his name. This makes it official, and you may now compete in the Open Class whenever you are ready. You need the same number of qualifying scores to earn a Companion Dog Excellent and a Utility Dog certificate. Once you have the CDX title you may compete in the Open B Class as often as you wish, and you may go ahead and try your dog in the Utility Class. Later when he has his UD title you may wish to compete in both the Open B and Utility Classes just for the fun of it.

Use the titles CD, CDX, and UD after your dogs name as soon as he earns them. They represent a great deal of work and are a badge of distinction. A very small percentage of the dogs in this country have earned the right to use them.

11

Equipment

In the Novice Classes your dog will need a choke collar and a leash. If you take him to a benched show he will need a bench chain. This is a chain with a clip at both ends, and the length of it is determined by the size of your dog.

When you compete in the Open Classes your dog will need a dumbbell, similar to that shown in the illustration. He will retrieve this on the flat, which means he will get it in an open area where there are no jumps. Then he will retrieve it over a high jump. This is a solid jump made up of boards, and the correct height is determined by the size of your dog. Next he will jump over a broad jump which consists of a maximum of four eight-inch boards laid flat and raised off the ground and telescoped in size from one to six inches. Again the number of boards and the length of the jump are determined by your dog's size.

In the Utility Class as in the Open Class, all the work is done off leash. You will need three white work gloves, a set of Scent Discrimination articles, a high jump which you will also use in the Open work, and a bar jump. The bar jump consists of two uprights which hold a wooden black and white bar. The high jump and the bar jump will be set at the same height, determined by the size of your dog.

When you buy a choke collar for your dog, be sure that it is the correct size. When it is pulled snug around the dog's neck there should be no more than three and one-half inches left, including the ring. The chain links should be small for the small breeds, medium-sized for the large breeds. Don't make the mistake of getting a heavy collar with large links because you have a large or aggressive dog. The medium-sized links are strong enough, and when the leash is jerked the collar will tighten and then release itself immediately. The collars with large links are too heavy on the dog's neck, and often fail to release when jerked. The collar is designed so that when it is jerked it will tighten quickly and then release itself. This throws the dog off balance, and reminds him to behave. The rest of the time when the dog is wearing a choke collar it should be comfortably loose. If your collar is too long, it will be useless and possibly dangerous, so take the trouble to get the right size.

I prefer to start all dogs, regardless of age or size with thick, round nylon choke collars that are the right size. The only exception would be a large, wild, rambunctious dog.

There is a proper way to put on the collar so that it will be most effective. The ring that can be drawn down from the stationary ring should point toward the dog's right shoulder. When the collar is worn in this manner (as shown in the illustration), it can be jerked more easily and will release itself instantly. The collar can be made of leather, fabric, or chain, and nothing may hang from it.

Some Obedience clubs and individuals recommend and use collars with clips on one end so that the dog is fitted with a tight collar, that is kept

EQUIPMENT: Five-foot leash, grab leash, nylon choke collar, chain choke collar, dumbbell, three white work gloves, Scent Discrimination articles, tracking harness, tracking leash, two tracking flags, five tracking poles, and a bench chain.

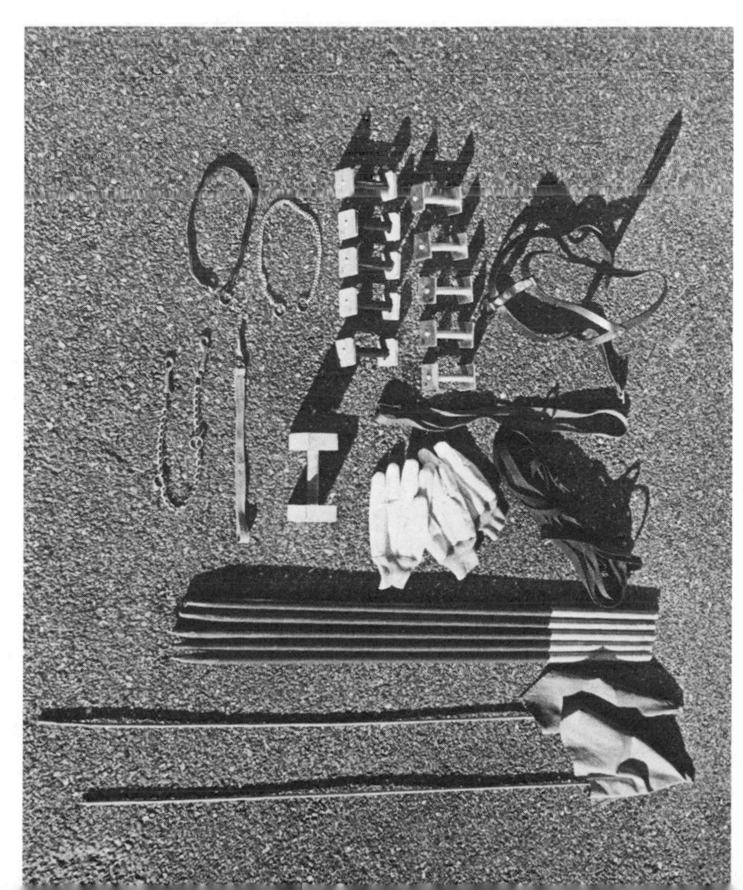

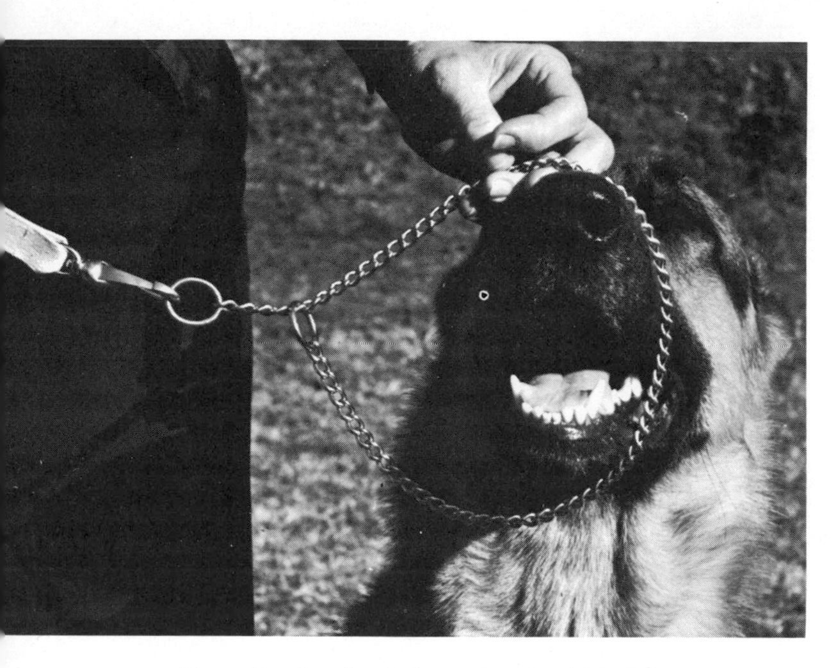

Above: Putting the choke collar on the dog correctly. Notice the spring slip that is used. *Right:* Pass the chain through one of the rings to form a collar.

high on his neck. Dogs are not permitted to compete in AKC Trials with these collars, spike, or pinch collars. These collars are unnecessary. With the right training methods intelligent and humane trainers do not need them to train dogs.

The leash that I prefer myself and always recommend is made of cotton webbing three-fourths of an inch wide and five feet long. Any leash more than five feet in length is just a nuisance. The clip is a spring clip as shown in the illustration. This leash is very soft and pliable but strong and durable. It is easy on your hands, and will fit in your pocket. It is so light that your dog will be unaware that it is attached to his collar. Later, when this type of leash is removed for training off leash, it will make little difference to your dog, since he has not experienced any pressure from a heavy leash. This is a subtle method I suggest you use to prepare your dog to Heel off Leash. If the dog begins his training with a light leash, it gives him the impression that he is free and on his own. By the time you advance to a point where you remove the leash, he will accept this next step without running away from you. There is no great change to attract his attention such as removing a heavy leather lead which has been weighing him down. I started making my own leashes when I discovered I could not buy what I wanted. I wanted a five-foot lead, lightweight, soft, but strong, and in a variety of colors to match whatever dress I was wearing. My second choice is a five-foot leash of soft leather with the same type of clip. Saddle soap will make leather more pliable. If you have arthritis in your hands, it will be easier to handle the leash if you put two or three knots in it.

Chain leashes are worthless for Obedience Training. First, they are too heavy on a dog's neck, regardless of his size. Second, they can cut or blister the handler's hands when he tries to jerk the dog. And third, all corrections, to be most effective, should be made swiftly with the element of surprise in them. This is not possible with a chain leash, since the slightest motion makes them rattle, and alerts the dog.

You will also need a tracking leash made of the same webbing about thirty feet in length.

For tracking you will also need a harness, which can be obtained at any pet supply store. It is difficult to obtain harnesses for large dogs, but your local harness maker will make one to fit.

You will need a dumbbell for the Open work, the small size for small dogs, the medium size for medium to large dogs. Great Danes and other breeds of their size will need the large size. Be sure that the centerpiece is high enough off the floor so that your dog can grasp it easily with his teeth. In picking up a dumbbell the dog thrusts his lower jaw under the centerpiece or uses one canine fang to lift it. The centerpiece should be wide enough for your dog to grasp comfortably. The ends should be square so that it stops quickly when it lands. Paint the dumbbell white so that your dog can see it easily. Many dogs fail to retrieve an unpainted dumbbell because the color blends in with the ground.

You will need three white work gloves for the Directed Retrieve exercise. You might as well buy three pairs so that you will always have a clean set.

You will need a set of Scent Discrimination articles, five of leather and five of metal. If you are handy at making things, it is a simple matter to make the set yourself. Make five rectangular blocks of wood one by four inches for large dogs, or one half by two inches for small dogs and cover them completely with leather, using small upholstery tacks or a stapler. For your metal articles, get some aluminum tubing and cut it to the right size. Each set—leather and metal—should be numbered from one to five so that they can be easily identified. If you make your own set, make one extra article of each kind so that you can practice with them. Matched sets can be purchased at most shows holding Obedience Trials. The ready-made sets are available for any size dog, and come with twelve articles. Be sure to leave your two practice articles at home when you compete in a show.

The instructions and illustrations for making the high jump, broad jump, bar jump, and portable jumps are at the end of the book. My husband, Ross, has designed an ingenious set of portable jumps that are an absolute joy to use. All three hurdles, the solid, bar, and broad jumps, fit together in a very light-weight and neat package. It is imperative when training dogs for advanced work to practice in various locations with different distractions. These jumps make this training much less tedious. They stand upright on cement, and will not blow over when set up on grass even on the windiest day.

Try to assemble all your equipment before you begin formal training; you will need everything within a few months in any case. For instance, if your jumps are there when you need them, you can begin teaching your dog to jump whenever you feel he is ready. If they are not, you may lose two or three months' time waiting to have them built and painted.

My red tracking flags slip down snugly over steel rods. The other ends of the rods are pointed so that they can easily be pushed into the ground.

My tracking poles are the same in size as broom handles, rounded on one end and pointed on the other. They are painted green except for the rounded end; this is red, and is painted with fluorescent paint to make it visible to the tracklayer at a distance. Your poles should be numbered consecutively so that upon removing them the tracklayer will pick them up in the correct sequence.

12

Formal Training

This and the following chapters will deal with all aspects of Formal Training (competitive training of a more serious nature), as a prelude to handling your dog in American Kennel Club licensed Obedience Trials.

Formal training may begin any time after your puppy is four months old. It is both impractical and unwise to delay training until he is older. The longer you put off training him, the more bad habits he will acquire, and you will waste hours of training time trying to correct them. The Novice exercises are so simple that any puppy can learn them quite easily. Therefore, regardless of his temperament, start your Formal Training early while your puppy is young and tractable.

If you have followed my suggestions in the chapter on Preliminary Training and Practical Tricks, your puppy will be quite advanced.

Although it is best to start training early, dogs can learn these Obedience exercises at any age. I trained Champion Questor Maximian von Grossland, UDT, when he was six years old. He earned his Companion Dog Excellent, and Utility Dog degrees with very high scores, and passed Tracking with perfect form. This fine German Shepherd Dog was always very young at heart.

My German import, Canadian Grand Victrix and Am. Ch. Fara von der Erikaklause, CDX, began her training when she was six years old. She earned her CD and CDX in three and a half months with four Firsts, one Second and one Fourth, including a Highest Score in Show. She did this between having two litters. It is much more difficult training an older dog, particularly one who has lived with someone else, and been abused by them.

A dog eight years of age should not be trained to jump. By the time he reaches eight he is beyond his prime, and jumping will do him more harm than good. He lacks the coordination, timing, and vigor of younger dogs, and cannot take the rigorous practice necessary to learn the advanced work. At eight, a dog has earned the right to take life easy. Small dogs who are light on their feet are the exception to this. Many of these are still going strong when they are ten years old.

I never asked my dogs to jump after they were eight years old, but they still spent many happy hours doing simple errands, and being generally useful. This satisfies their intrinsic need to be included in all family activities.

My method of training is to teach the dog advanced exercises as soon as he is ready to learn them. Novice work becomes very dull to a dog if it is repeated in a monotonous fashion week after week. One of the main reasons why handlers drop out of shows after obtaining their Novice degrees is because they have become bored and discouraged with the length of time it took them to master the basic work. For the same reason a high percentage of handlers drop out of Obedience Training Classes. If you follow the training program I have outlined at the end of this chapter, you will advance too rapidly for either you or your dog to get tired or discouraged.

Whether you are training to obtain titles for your dog, to enrich your life, or just for the fun of it, you can count on getting your CD, CDX, and UD titles within a year's time. It will be more interesting to give yourself a goal to shoot at, and an incentive is conducive to consistent practice. Any handler with a sound dog of any breed can accomplish this. In fact, you might do it in less than this. It is also possible to earn your Tracking title within the year if you enjoy working outdoors.

Once you have earned your Utility title you can continue to compete in shows by entering the Open B and the Utility Classes. In all probability you will need no urging to continue; long before this you will have become an enthusiast.

This book has been written with the desire to show you how you can obtain high scores with precision handling and have fun doing it. A dog loves and respects a handler more for insisting upon perfection than for training him halfheartedly. Dogs have an enormous amount of pride, and can appreciate a job well done as much as you can. It will require no more effort on your part to train your dog correctly from the beginning. By doing this you will avoid most of the pitfalls the casual trainer encounters. If you are shooting for the top, remember that no error is too small to correct. Dogs learn by correction.

I would suggest that you read each chapter through several times before going out to train your dog. The small details that will seem unimportant to you at first will make you an expert handler. When all these details are fitted together like a jigsaw puzzle, the result becomes training magic to the uninitiated.

The one question that I have been asked repeatedly over the years is, "How do you handle dogs so smoothly?" The answer is found in my training method which is an accumulation of a great number of training tips that I have perfected.

With this method your dog's spirit will improve. In fact you must continually strive to instill a feeling of fun in your training to keep your dog enthusiastic. In the normal process of training dogs I often improve their personalities, and make gay, eager workers out of dullards. Improving a dog's character is the most difficult phase of training, but definitely the most rewarding.

When I started training Margelen's Chieftain, UDT (Topper), I found that praise was as necessary to him as breathing. Throughout the years I have used praise as an incentive, and as a reward in personally training hundreds of dogs. Knowing when and how to give praise is extremely important, and an integral part of my training method. I have stressed the use of praise in my Obedience classes, clinics, lectures, and magazine articles and am glad to note that other trainers have gradually come to recognize its importance. It is gratifying to know that many thousands of dogs who are being trained in various parts of the country are now praised for their efforts because of my belief that this is a vital factor in training dogs.

Regardless of your dog's temperament, you should praise him for all good work and for every gallant effort; and praise should be used as an inducement to encourage better work. Do not be embarrassed if someone overhears you praising your dog. Be proud of it. You are setting a good example for him to follow.

Remember this while training. You are striving to perfect your dog's work every second you train; you want straight sits, precision turns, immediate response to commands, and you should always be watching to see that you get them. When your dog sits straight, turns, or heels with precision, don't just make a mental note of it—tell him about it; praise him. You do not have to stop the work. If a turn is good, keep right on Heeling, but say to your dog. "That was good! Good boy!" Always watch for each opportunity, however small, to praise your dog for his efforts.

Another important phase of training is learning to correct your dog promptly. I have seen so many handlers look at their dogs as if they were stunned when a mistake was made, instead of applying correction immediately. Timing is important, and corrections and praise should be given instantly; always try to remember this important fact. A handler should never reprimand his dog more than once, or prolong the punishment just because he feels like letting off steam. The punishment should always be administered firmly and quickly, and the lesson continued at once, so that the dog can be induced to do the next step correctly.

Study your dog carefully, and never punish him if he is confused. It is far better to repeat the exercise and show him exactly what you want.

Once the formal training has begun do *not* give your dog food as a reward for working. This is a crude approach to training and will only work with dogs that think more of their stomachs than of their owners. This is not at all the same thing as giving a young puppy a tidbit as an incentive to do tricks. When puppies are young, food is of prime importance to them, but as they grow older, you should appeal to their minds. You must always appeal to a dog's finer instincts if you wish to get the best out of him. A dog that is attuned to training should refuse food if offered to him during a lesson. His refusal proves that he is more eager to work than eat. Keep your training on a high level, and you will never need to bribe your dog with food. Your aim is to establish a bond between you that nothing can dissolve.

The member of the family who is with the dog the most and who has the time to train him consistently should be his handler. When two people train the same dog, they do not handle him in exactly the same way, and the results are never as satisfactory. Generally, when a dog is trained by more than one person, it becomes confused with the erratic handling. It is better to have one person train him completely; then he will work for anyone in the family.

I would suggest that you train your dog at least five days a week. When you start the Novice Training, half an hour will be sufficient; but as you add additional Open and Utility exercises, your training period should be increased to an hour or more a day.

It is entirely possible and practical for you to train your dog yourself without the help of a second person. I have done so repeatedly with success. In the Stand for Examination exercise, where a second person is involved, a member of your family or a friend can participate with excellent results.

If you train your dog yourself, it is advisable to attend a few sanction matches to get his reaction to working under strange conditions. Unless your dog has a very steady disposition and is already acquainted with the world, he is apt to forget what he has learned, momentarily, until he becomes accustomed to the many distractions of show competition. Puppies especially need the experience of working among other dogs and people. Sanction matches offer a good opportunity to get this experience.

A sanction match can be entered on the day of the show; no points are given toward a dog's championship in Breed, or legs toward its Obedience title. It is simply a practice run to get you and your dog used to show conditions. Additional information concerning shows will be found under the AKC Obedience Regulations reprinted in this book.

Obedience Training Classes will not always afford the answer to Formal Training. Many classes are overcrowded, and advancement is pathetically slow. The result is that it takes many months to accomplish what you could have done at home in a few weeks. However, if you have a shy dog or one that is easily distracted, Obedience Classes can offer the proper atmosphere to correct these problems.

I am wholeheartedly in favor of Obedience Training Classes, provided the type of training outlined in this book is maintained. If the classes are limited to twenty, and show conditions are duplicated or exaggerated, the dogs will become very reliable. Many owners work better in groups, and are not so easily discouraged when they see that other people have the same training problems. Group training can be fun if everyone is congenial. It is almost as enjoyable to see your friends make progress with their dogs as it is for you to progress with your own.

If you decide to join an Obedience Class, be sure that the instructor is qualified to teach. So often today when a handler gets one or two degrees with his dog, he decides he knows it all, and proceeds to pose as an experienced trainer. The inexperienced handler will use a hit-or-miss training method that creates more confusion than control.

Think twice before joining an Obedience class that condones the use of spoke or pinch collars. These collars are cruel and are absolutely unnecessary. Avoid trainers who throw heavy chains at the dogs in their classes to frighten them into submission. And shun like the plague the trainer who advises the handlers to shout at their dogs. This method shows no consideration at all for the dog's feelings.

So, as you start your Formal Training, resolve to train your dog sensibly by using a formula of praise, patience, firmness, and understanding. Never use a spike collar, loud voice, tight lead, nagging voice, or food. Never hit your dog with anything but the fingers of your hand, and then if necessary, only once for each correction. If you follow this method it will work like magic.

I have in writing this book stressed the best way to train and handle your dog so that your work will at all times be close to perfection. You will automatically become a good handler if you follow the instructions carefully.

Every July and August we give a five-day Obedience Training Clinic at our home for handlers and instructors. Every phase of Obedience training is covered thoroughly, and in great detail, for most people want to learn my method so that they can teach or practice it back home. Hundreds of people have attended from this country and Canada who wanted to share their vacation with their dogs, and have the enjoyment of working with them in a congenial atmosphere.

13

Training Program

First and Second Weeks	Heeling on Leash—including turns and automatic sits Figure 8 on Leash—including automatic sits Recall on Leash—including automatic sit Stay Command Long Sit on Leash Long Down on Leash
Third and Fourth	Above, plus Finish on Leash
Fifth	Heeling on Leash Figure 8 on Leash Stand for Examination on Leash Recall off Leash (Short) Finish on Leash Heeling off Leash (Short period)—including turns and automatic sits Long Sit off Leash Long Down off Leash
Sixth and Seventh	Long Recalls off Leash Long Period of Heeling off Leash Figure 8 off Leash Finish off Leash

	Distance of at Least Forty Feet on Long Sit and Long Down Exercises
Eighth and Ninth	Add to above, Jumping Exercises on Leash Start Dumbbell Retrieving on Leash—Getting, Holding, Reaching for It.
Tenth	Jumping off Leash Carrying a Dumbbell Picking up Dumbbell from Ground
Eleventh	Retrieve Dumbbell from Short Distance Do Broad Jump Try Novice Work in Strange Surroundings Stand for Examination off Leash
Twelfth	Retrieve over High Jump (one-half required height) Longer Retrieves on Flat off Leash Try to Perfect Novice Work

Time to Try Your Dog in Sanction Matches

Fourth Month	Concentrate on perfecting the above work If your dog is ready for Point Shows it will have done well at the Sanction Matches A week prior to entering any Point Show, concentrate on the particular class you intend to enter
Fifth	Retrieve over Jump, full height off leash If you have your CD degree, start practicing the Drop on Recall, and add it to rest of Open work Signal Exercise Long Sit and Down, out of Sight
Sixth	Directed Retrieve
Seventh	Scent Discrimination Directed Jumping Group Examination

Try Your Open Work at Sanction Matches

Eighth	Compete in Open for your CDX degree
Ninth and Tenth	Concentrate on Utility but Practice Open

Try Your Utility Work at Sanction Matches

or

Eleventh and Twelfth	Enter Point Shows whenever confident

14

Regulations for Obedience Trials

When you have started your Formal Training, it is time to sit down and read the American Kennel Club Obedience Regulations. This material has been reprinted at the back of the book for your convenience and information.

These Regulations are printed in booklet form by the American Kennel Club, and the latest edition can be obtained without charge by writing for it. I have always passed copies of them out to my students, as it is imperative that these rules be studied thoroughly before you enter an Obedience Trial.

You cannot become a good handler, trainer, or judge unless you thoroughly understand the Regulations. Reread them occasionally: there may be minor points that you have overlooked. An expert handler should be as familiar with the Regulations as the judge.

Here are some typical questions that you may have in mind, that are answered clearly and simply in the Obedience Regulations booklet.

Can a bitch in season be entered in an Obedience Trial? No.

How old must a dog be before it can compete in Obedience Trials? Six months old.

May a dog that has its CDX title continue to compete in the Open Classes? Yes, in the Open B Class.

Could an exhibitor enter more than one dog in the Novice A Class? No, only one dog for each exhibitor, and the dog should be owned by the exhibitor or a member of his family.

May an exhibitor enter more than one dog in the Novice B Class? Yes, provided each dog has a separate handler for the Long Sit and the Long Down exercises.

Is there a specific number of dogs that must compete in the various classes in order to gain an Obedience title? Yes, six or more dogs must compete in the combined Novice A and Novice B Classes, six or more dogs in the combined Open A and Open B Classes, and three or more dogs must compete in the Utility Classes.

If a dog failed an exercise, could the handler decide not to show him any further? No, the dog must compete in all the exercises in his class.

Could a handler get to the show early and practice working his dog in the Obedience rings? No, this is strictly forbidden.

Can the handler praise his dog at will? No, praise is permitted only between exercises.

Is it permissible to jerk a dog in the ring if he isn't paying attention to his handler? No, such action should be penalized by the judge, even between exercises, since the handler is disciplining his dog.

Is it permissible to shout at a dog in order to intimidate him into obeying? No, this is another form of disciplining a dog by the handler, and will be penalized.

Could a handler give a dog extra hand signals while heeling in order to keep the dog up with him? No, any extra signals should be penalized by the judge. If the handler can't keep his hand in one position while he is heeling, he should be penalized for furtive signals.

May a handler jump his dog lower than the required height for his breed because he feels the dog is unable to clear the jump? No, the same rule applies to all handlers and their dogs. If there is any question about height, the dog should be measured in the ring. The judge should watch this point carefully in the advanced classes.

Should a handler walk slowly so that his dog will be sure to keep up with him? No, the rules specifically state that the handler should always walk briskly. Any handler that deliberately adapts a slow pace should be penalized.

If a dog is lagging, is it better for the handler to hop up and down on the fast instead of running? No, this should be penalized by the judge. Every breed of dog can run fast; it is up to the handler to train the dog to stay with him before he goes to a show.

It will be to your advantage to understand the Regulations thoroughly. If you do, you may show your dog anywhere in the country with complete confidence.

15

The Novice Exercises

Heeling on Leash (40 points)

The Novice exercises consist of Heeling on Leash, Figure 8 on Leash, Stand for Examination off Leash, Heeling Free, Recall off Leash, Long Sit for One Minute, and Long Down for Three Minutes. To obtain your CD (Companion Dog) title you must earn some 170 points out of a possible 200 to qualify; and in doing so, you must earn more than half the points for each specific exercise. You will need to earn a qualifying score at three different shows under three different judges to gain your CD. This degree is equivalent to an elementary school diploma.

Heeling for your dog is your most important exercise; it will occur in Novice, Open, and Utility work. Heeling is not merely a routine where the dog walks at the handler's left side. It calls for perfect coordination between the handler and the dog, and the changes of pace, turns, and frequent halts must be so smoothly executed as to seem effortless. The perfect rhythm and complete harmony between a well-trained dog and an expert handler are beautiful to behold but, unfortunately, a rare sight. The dog must show his zest for the work by the rapt expression on his face and the proud manner in which he moves. After "Exercise finished," he should happily wag his tail. Many people think that because a dog wags his tail continuously he is an exceptionally happy worker. Actually this is often a nervous trait and not always a true indication of a dog's well-being. An expertly trained, intelligent dog knows as well as his trainer when he has done a good job; his eyes fairly sparkle with joy. The word of praise and the hand caress are nevertheless essential so that complete harmony exists between dog and handler.

You should practice in an area at least forty feet square, fairly smooth, with no trees or posts on it. You will progress faster and both you and your dog will concentrate better if you start your training in a quiet secluded area. A fenced-in area is ideal. When you have completed about eight weeks of training, start taking your dog to different surroundings to practice. At first it will be beginning all over again, but gradually your dog will become accustomed to working anywhere.

I have described the equipment you need, so assuming that you have the choke collar on your dog correctly and the leash attached, let us begin. Always start your practice sessions with your dog sitting at your left side, perfectly straight, as in the illustration. By "perfectly straight" that is just what I mean. It does not mean to have your dog's left foot ahead of the other or vice versa. Nor does it mean that the dog may slouch into a lazy sit. Any dog of any breed can be taught to sit straight if watched carefully and corrected. Nor may the dog lean his weight against you as many of the large breeds are prone to do. It is up to you to watch your dog constantly from the very beginning to see that all his sits pass inspection.

When I refer to Heel position I will mean that your dog is sitting by your left side and his right shoulder is in line with your left knee. I am currently training a Pug, a Standard Poodle, and a Great Dane. At Heel position the Pug's shoulder is just above my left ankle, the Poodle's shoulder is at my left knee, and the Great Dane's shoulder is above my left knee. They are all being taught to sit straight at Heel position and Heel with precision.

The Pug has a small head and short neck, and when he is in Heel position his toes are not quite even with mine; however, when the Poodle and Dane sit, their toes are even with mine. If the Pug's head was to be ahead of my left foot when he was Heeling it would mean that he was forging, but if his head was in line with my left ankle instead of his shoulder the difference would be so slight that few, if any, judges would notice. This is one instance where the handlers of small dogs have a decided edge over the larger breeds.

If the Great Dane was Heeling correctly—with his shoulder in line with my left knee—his head would have to be ahead of me. By teaching him to watch me all the time he will learn to keep very close, even on turns, without actually touching or crowding me. His shoulder should be in line with my left hip continuously. Now if, during the fast pace or an about turn, his head was in line with my hip and his shoulder was behind me, this would mean that he was lagging and not Heeling with precision. Since this type of Heeling is far from perfect he would be penalized.

Very few people realize what precision Heeling means. It does not mean that one minute the dog's nose is in line with your left knee and the next minute his shoulder is there. It is considerably more difficult to train a dog to Heel with precision 100 per cent of the time, but it can be accomplished with any dog that is started correctly in the beginning. The right method plus perseverance equals precision Heeling.

Your dog is sitting at your left side in the Heel position. If you are under five feet five inches tall, and you have a medium or large-sized dog, take the end of the leash and make a single loop, and hold this loop with both hands as illustrated. If you are over five feet five inches, hold the leash in your left hand. Keep both hands in front of you close to your waist. One common error beginners make is holding the leash away from the body and over the dog. This is wrong. *Never* Heel with a tight leash; your dog must never be aware of any pressure on his collar from a tight leash. Remember this point. It is very important. If the clip on the leash is hanging down, your leash is loose enough for practice work. Later, when your dog will Heel, you can concentrate on your foot work.

Many people make a fetish about starting off on their left or right foot until you get the impression that their dogs cannot Heel without this assistance. Don't think about it or purposely practice it. Concentrate on teaching your dog to Heel regardless of which foot you lead off with. Dogs that have to watch for knee signals keep their heads down and lack animation.

Dogs taught to Heel using my method will be watching your face. Just as you would watch another person's face if you were conversing with him, so will your dog watch yours when you converse with him. This is one of the examples of appealing to a dog's finer instincts.

Give your dog the command, "Hussan, heel," and start walking forward on the Heel portion of the command. Always speak your dog's name first to get his attention, and give the command in a firm well-modulated voice; *never* use a loud voice. Remember—a dog's hearing is acute, and high-pitched feminine shrieks are as unpleasant to him as domineering masculine bellows. Learn to control the tone of your voice so that it sounds both pleasant and firm. Your voice is an important part of training, and it must carry authority.

Your dog will probably attempt to stride out ahead of you; quickly jerk him back, and command him to "Heel," then walk along briskly in the direction you choose. Now, in executing this order you will encounter a problem. Let me explain what I mean. By a quick jerk I mean that you should exert just enough force by jerking on the leash to throw the dog

Left: At the beginning hold the leash in both hands for medium or large dogs. The leash should be tight enough for you to control the dog, but loose enough so there is no pressure on his neck.

Right: If you have a small dog, hold the leash in your left hand as illustrated and control the dog with a wrist motion.

off balance and bring him back to your side. When the dog is jerked correctly the choke collar will tighten for an instant and then immediately release itself. With large dogs you need both hands on the leash to aid you in doing this quickly and with dispatch. With small dogs use your left hand and exert just enough force to make them lose their balance and bring them back to your left side. If the choke collar becomes slack immediately, you will know that you have used the right amount of force. Remember to watch the collar tighten and then release. *Never* have your leash tight; it should be slack at all times except for the brief moment when you jerk your dog. I cannot emphasize this strongly enough. A handler who keeps a tight lead on a dog and pulls him back while Heeling and making turns is just wasting his time and making the dog miserable. A dog does not mind being jerked back, but he highly resents the humiliation of being dragged around on a tight leash. The pressure from

Correct: The dog should Heel with his shoulder in line with your left knee. Although this looks smooth and perfectly natural, it is precision Heeling. Expert handling should always appear to be simple and effortless.

a tight lead is extremely uncomfortable and ruins a dog's spirit. The loose lead makes him feel gay, carefree, and trusted, and the quick jerk keeps him under control.

Small dogs can be controlled very easily, and taught to heel with precision if the handler will gather his leash in his left hand and hold it down by his left side. The leash should be short enough so that a dog who is forging ahead can be jerked back, or the dog who is heeling too wide can be jerked close to his handler's side. The jerking should always be done with a wrist action. The leash should be loose enough so that there is no pressure on the dog's neck. With this method I can teach a small dog to heel with precision on leash in a few days. The size of the jerk depends upon the size of the dog. Exert just enough force to make him lose his balance and bring him back by your side.

It takes a Novice handler quite a while to learn how to make this movement correctly because he must first overcome a feeling of guilt at the thought of handling his dog in such a rough manner. Actually you are not being rough—you are simply using the choke collar in the manner for which it was designed. Once you have mastered this phase of training and practiced it for a week, you will find that very little jerking will be necessary. A dog that is trained properly learns fast. Keep an eye on your leash; if it is tight you are doing it wrong.

Regardless of the size of your dog, your pace should be brisk so that the dog will not lose interest. This is the natural walking pace for most people including myself, and the normal trotting pace for dogs. It is also the most invigorating. Be certain to walk in the direction you choose, and do not let your dog take you where he wants to go. Remember during Formal Training that you are the trainer, and you make all the decisions.

Walk along briskly and *jerk the dog back to you as often as is necessary to keep him by your side*; and as you walk, keep talking to him. When you jerk him back, tell him to "Heel"; and when he is by your side again, say, "That's it," "Good boy," or something similar. Encourage him occasionally by reaching down to pet him while Heeling. He may try to jump up on you when you pet him, so just say "No," and continue walking without breaking your pace.

After walking about twenty feet in one direction, make an about turn by pivoting to the right slowly on the soles of both feet and reverse your direction. As you make the about turn, say "Hussan, heel," and if your dog is not with you, give him a jerk, and then praise him when he is again by your side. Later, when you have mastered the turn, do not slow down but pivot and reverse at the same speed so the whole movement is smooth. By pivoting you are giving your dog the time he needs to walk around you so that at the first step you take from the about turn you will be together. The dog's shoulder should be on a line with your knee.

Make several right-angle turns, jerking the dog if he is not up with you and praising him when he is. To execute a right-angle turn, keep both your feet together and take a quarter-turn pivot on the shoes of your feet to the right. Don't rise on your toes. This looks unnatural. Make your turns to both the right and left. If you catch your dog with your knee as you are making the left turn, he will soon learn not to bump into you or to get in your way. If you have a small dog, check him on left turns by lifting your foot to block his path. He will then watch for these turns and will hesitate long enough so that you can turn together. Novice handlers quickly learn to negotiate the turns with ease if they use this method. Later, when they have become so proficient at turning that they do not think about it, they will automatically substitute shorter steps for the actual pivot, as I do. Be consistent about jerking your dog when he is not with you on a turn, and, what is equally important, be ready with a word of praise.

Always watch your dog carefully, and if he is not paying strict attention, make a turn and jerk the leash. When you begin to train a dog, keep one eye glued on him so that you can correct him the second he makes a mistake. If you find that your dog is Heeling wide or lagging behind, slap your left leg and encourage him with your voice to Heel closely. When he moves up by your side, praise him. If your dog is Heeling very close, this is excellent, for as you progress, the dog will naturally move over slightly so that you will be Heeling in perfect precision. A dog who does this is anxious to please, and as he becomes more confident of his work he will realize it is not necessary to crowd you. In extreme cases where a dog persists in crowding you after several weeks of training, you can correct him by doing the goose step. The dog will be bumped and thus discouraged from leaning against you.

From the very first week when you are teaching your dog to Heel, you should practice a change of pace. There is the normal pace which is a natural brisk walk. There is the slow pace where you move along slowly but not so slowly that your dog expects you to stop. Jerk your dog back

Left: Incorrect: Poor handling, leash held too tight. *Below:* Incorrect: Poor handling. Note unnatural position of leash in right hand.

if he doesn't change to the slow pace, saying, "Heel, easy." If he does change pace with you, praise him.

If you are changing from the slow pace to the normal pace, jerk your dog, saying, "Hussan, heel." Praise him when he responds. To change from the normal pace to the fast pace is a little more difficult. Your dog will not be alert enough at first to keep up with you. To execute a fast pace you must run forward briskly. This does not mean to run fast. Neither does it mean a fast walk or a pantomime where you go up and down and not forward. It is simply a natural running pace. Small dogs can run just as fast as you can, so insist that your dog keep up with you. If you make a game of it, your dog will be eager to stay at Heel. By making a game of it I mean to touch your dog playfully, clap your hands, laugh a little, or encourage him with your voice so that it is fun for him to stay up with you. Be sure to keep control of your dog. If he should start jumping when you start to run, say, "No, heel," in a matter-of-fact tone of voice, but if he persists, give him a quick jerk.

When first practicing a change of pace give your dog a warning by telling him to Heel. If the dog is lagging, say something to get him excited enough so that he will want to stay up with you. Dogs that lag need a great deal of encouragement before they will eventually stay by your side.

Incorrect: Poor handling. Note unnatural position of left arm.

Occasionally a jerk will help, but it is the talking that will do the most good.

For changes of pace, try these variations. Slow-normal-halt. Slow-fast-halt. Normal-fast-halt-normal-slow-halt. Normal-fast-normal-slow-about-turn-halt. Normal-halt-normal-right-turn-normal-left-turn-slow-normal-about-turn-normal-right-turn-normal-fast-halt. You will have fun making your own patterns. Try having someone in your family call the paces and turns for you. Every time your dog executes the correct change of pace or turn, praise him.

In a show the judge will tell you what to do, and you must keep moving at the pace he calls until he orders you to do otherwise.

By observing your dog very closely and by refusing to allow his attention to be diverted elsewhere, you can teach him to Heel with quite reliable precision in about twelve weeks.

When your dog is under control and will Heel reasonably well it is time to concentrate on your own precision. Each time you start to Heel with your dog take the first step with your left foot. I recommend this because it looks smarter and more precise. It will not make any difference to the expertly trained dog, because he will heel with precision even though you start off with your right foot.

This also applies to about turns and right turns. On either turn take just enough small steps to negotiate the turn but immediately thereafter step out with your left foot. Don't bow, stop, nod your head, duck your shoulders, take one step backwards, or leave one foot way in back of you on the turns, but do practice turns until you can execute them very smoothly and naturally.

Remember to talk to your dog so that he will look up at your face. The dog who is trained to look at the handler's legs will generally work like a robot. He may acquire a certain amount of mechanical precision but his performance will be dull and uninteresting.

As soon as your dog is Heeling by your side satisfactorily and without your having to jerk him back too often, carry your leash in the advanced manner as in the illustration. Hold the leash in your left hand, and keep it in front of you near your waist. Swing your right hand as you normally would when walking.

In training a dog, try to be as natural as possible. Avoid any exaggerated signals or poses that look ridiculous. It is great fun to compete in shows, but do it naturally. The primary purpose of this training is to teach the dog to be obedient under any conditions. If you are taking your dog for a walk on leash, the most natural and most simple way is to hold the leash in your left hand and swing your right. This is the properly balanced method. Your right hand is free to open doors, shake hands

The advanced way to hold the leash when your dog is heeling nicely.

with friends you meet, or do a dozen other normal things. If you are carrying bundles with your right arm, your dog is completely under control close to your left side with the leash in its most unobtrusive position. This is natural, and it looks and feels good. Later when you take your leash off to Heel Free, your dog is ready, because he is now used to Heeling without being aware of the leash.

According to the AKC Regulations you may hold the leash in either hand or both, but I think holding the leash in the right hand looks awkward and unnatural. It is always in the way, and the dog is subjected to countless unnecessary disheartening tugs on his collar or a constant pull.

In an Obedience Trial praise and patting are permitted only between exercises, but the dog must be under control at this time. Two weeks before entering a trial, practice each exercise without giving him praise except where permitted to see how your dog responds.

Sitting at Heel is to be incorporated into the Heeling routine from the very first lesson, so the following instructions should be studied before you are ready to start teaching your dog to Heel.

Teaching Your Dog to Sit at Heel

This is comparatively simple, and should be started with the first Heeling lesson. You should start the Heeling lesson by having your dog Sit straight by your left side. Have the dog Heel a short distance, and then halt. When you halt, grasp the leash about a foot from the dog's collar with your right hand holding him steady by your *left side*, as illustrated, and very quickly reach down and give the dog a sharp tap on his croup with your left hand. Do not move your feet out of position. *Immediately* pet the dog with your left hand, and praise him. This should all be done with such speed that it will be almost one action. Repeat this until the dog sits automatically.

At first, each time you halt and tap the dog, tell him to Sit. If you notice the dog about to Sit do not tap him but quickly praise him in a very pleased tone of voice. If your dog is not sitting automatically after a week, then you are not tapping him properly. A Novice handler is hesitant about tapping his dog sharply, and compromises by pushing him down with his left hand. If you do this, it will take you months to teach the dog to Sit automatically; and in the meantime the dog will lose his respect for you as a trainer. When you tap your dog and praise him instantly, the dog's mind is on the praise. A dog respects authority when it is administered pleasantly. A correct tap is done with the fingers only, and you may practice on yourself by tapping your right hand with the fingers of your left hand. Think of the tap as a reminder. If you are right-handed, that fact will not lessen your ability to correct your dog with your left hand. After a day or so you will be able to use both hands with equal ease.

At first your dog may sit wide; and if this is the case, it may be because he is heeling wide. Make the dog Heel in close, and his Sits will be straighter. When the dog stands straight in the Heel position, the tap should be on his croup just above his tail. Never step over to your dog as you stop in order to make him look good. You are fooling no one but yourself. Your dog must be taught to Sit straight wherever and whenever you stop, and he should be immediately corrected if he fails to do so.

If your dog is in close but swings his hindquarters wide to your left, tap him quickly on his left thigh as you halt. This will make him Sit quickly; at the same time it brings him in close and straight.

Do not strike your dog repeatedly to make him Sit. This sort of treatment is unnecessary. Your dog should be tapped just once, but it should be a sharp enough tap to make him Sit, and the praise should follow instantly. A dog will learn to Sit automatically in a few days if this method is used correctly.

Tap your dog to make him sit.

Immediately pet and praise your dog.

If your dog forges ahead of you when you halt, this can be easily corrected. As you stop, grasp the leash about a foot from his collar with your right hand but *hold the leash steady by your left side*. This will prevent him from bolting ahead, and you can then easily tap his croup for a quick Sit. You must learn to be very fast on these corrections if you wish to get results. As soon as the dog sits, *be sure the leash is slack*, and praise him. The dog should not be aware of the leash at all. As the dog begins to sit automatically, you should gradually release all pressure on the leash until it is completely slack.

The common error that most beginners make is to permit the dog to walk out ahead of them when they stop. The dog is then out of reach, and they cannot control the Sit. You must hold the leash taut by your left side, as you tap the dog to make him Sit quickly, and then praise him. Do not pull up or jerk on the leash to make the dog Sit. This will eventually cause him to back up a step or two to avoid the correction. It creates a bad habit.

If the dog leans against you when he Sits, step aside quickly so that he will fall over. Then ask him to Sit again, making sure that he Sits straight; and praise him. Sometimes if you give a slight nudge with your left knee, you can make him sit straight.

To correct a dog that Sits with his hindquarters in back of your left foot, push him over into a straight Sit with the side of your right foot. If the dog has made this mistake once, you know it will happen again; so be prepared. Try to catch the dog just as he is Sitting, as it is easier to direct the Sit with your foot. Another correction to try for this type of Sit or for the dog that Sits straight but a little too far back is to hold the fingers of the left hand out beyond the dog's nose and motion him to come up to your fingers. When he comes up by your side and Sits again, praise him.

If, when the dog Sits, he slouches over slightly on his hind leg, reach down and pull the offending leg out where it belongs. Or, if it is a very bad Sit, ask the dog to sit over again.

Use the verbal command, "Sit," each time you halt until you are sure that dog understands what it means. If, during the second week of training, your dog stands when he is supposed to Sit, command him to "Sit" in a quiet tone of voice. If he Sits, then he understands the Sit at Heel. He probably would not sit anywhere else for you but at Heel Position unless you have started his training with the tricks I explained at the beginning of the book.

Right: Straight Sit.

Wrong: Sloppy Sit

Right: Straight Sit.

Wrong: Great Dane is not sitting up straight.

The Figure 8

In a show your dog will be asked to Heel in a Figure 8 pattern around two stewards acting as posts. You yourself will face the judge on the opposite side, in the center, in line but not between the stewards.

When beginning this exercise at home, use the posts from your bar jump. Place them about eight feet apart. Give your dog the command to Heel, and go through the center and around the post to your left, then again through the center and around the post to your right. Then halt. This is the Figure 8. Practice starting off to the left, and then changing to the right to keep your dog alert.

Make this a game with your dog, talking to him, and coaxing him to stay up with you. If he lags at any point, you may need to jerk him at that spot the next time around. If he crowds against you on the inside turn, bump into him with your knee. You should always keep close to both posts and encourage your dog to do the same. Practice your halts in various places around the Figure 8.

When practicing always walk at a very brisk pace. Do not slow down to accommodate your dog on turns. If he lags, quicken your pace and encourage him to keep up with you. In shows maintain a steady normal pace. Do not be discouraged if your dog lags on this exercise. It takes many hours of practice and many words of encouragement to do it perfectly.

When you compete in the Novice Class in a show you will do this exercise on leash. However, when you start Heeling off Leash, practice the Figure 8 each day both on and off leash. The Figure 8 off leash is one of the exercises in the Open work and you may just as well learn it early.

In keeping with my theory that Obedience should be a part of daily life, I teach my dogs to do the Figure 8 around other dogs as well as people. I want my dogs to get along together, because I keep several dogs loose in the house. This teaches them to be friendly, to ignore other dogs, and to keep their minds on their work.

I have never had a dogfight in my home, although I have introduced dozens of dogs into the family circle over the years. The other male dogs

The author and her dog stand opposite the judge as they prepare to do the Figure 8 around two German Shepherds who are acting as stewards.

accept the newcomer with friendly interest, and their attitude sets the behavior pattern for the new arrival.

The Figure 8 exercise has a very practical purpose. If your dog is Heeling with you in a crowded area, you want him to stay close by your side as you pass people along the way. An untrained dog will very likely go to the left to avoid a pedestrian as you go to the right, and this tends to create an embarrassing entanglement. This is the reason why you should train your dog to stay close to the posts. Handlers who take a wide circle around the posts in the Figure 8 exercise have missed the point entirely. What good will this type of training be on a busy city street? If the handler tries to make a wide circle around every person he meets, he will be bumping into every other one. A dog that is expertly trained should be able to Heel on a busy street quite unobtrusively. He should unconsciously stick close by your side as you pass people, lampposts, or any other objects.

The Shy, Nervous Dog

In teaching the high-strung dog to Heel and Sit you must never aggravate his temperament. Your manner must be one of assurance, your tone should be quiet and authoritative, and you should remember that this type of dog is very sensitive.

A shy dog will learn to Sit after two or three taps, and can be encouraged to work by your voice. If he should Sit behind you, do not push him with your foot. Encourage him to Sit straight by your side by holding your fingers in front of his nose and asking him to step up into a straight Sit. Do not jerk him to make him Sit.

The shy dog is apt to lag behind because of his timidity. You must talk him up by your side continually, and slap your left leg occasionally to encourage him. Reach down and pet him gently as you heel so that he will be happy to be close to you. Don't be surprised if he ducks away from your hand as you reach to pet him, for he will be suspicious of everything. If necessary, hold him by the ruff while you pet him until he gets used to it.

The shy dog may be afraid of people, noises, strange places, storms, other dogs, or anything flapping in the wind. Whatever he fears must be overcome by working him in that environment.

You should always be calm and assured. A nervous dog is easily panicked. It takes the utmost patience and many hours of work to succeed, for you must first heal his mind before you can get through to him to train him. The dog must trust you completely, and if you make one harsh correction you may ruin your earlier work or add many more weeks of additional training before you regain his confidence.

Even when this type of dog is expertly trained he may someday be frightened into disobedience by an unexpected incident or an overwrought mind.

Praise, patience, understanding, and firmness compose the formula you will need.

I trained three dogs of this type (not Topper, Hussan, and Arry), and they each became top workers and won many firsts with very high scores. The judges and spectators admired their spirit and gaiety, and never realized their true temperaments. It was a long grueling process reshaping their personalities and giving them courage and fortitude. But I proved to myself that it could be done, and that satisfaction was reward enough.

However, there are shy, nervous dogs that never entirely overcome their fears. Despite the fact that they have been trained with kindness, praise, and understanding, there will be instances when they appear to be cowed. While the over-all improvement is about 95 per cent, the true character of the dog will be evident when it shrinks away from being petted or approaches the handler timidly. To a judge this may look as if the dog has been harshly trained or overtrained. Nothing could be farther from the truth. A firm "No" given in a moderate tone of voice is all the punishment necessary for this type of dog. The balance of the training is spent trying to encourage the dog to work through patience and kindness.

The owner of a timid, neurotic dog is generally eager to have him trained because he feels sorry for him and wants to help him. If the owner loves his dog, this type of training is worth all the time and effort spent on him.

Some time ago I was asked to train a timid dog that was very neurotic. The dog liked people, yet would always shrink from being petted and would cower on the ground as if he had been struck. This was an inherited trait and a difficult problem to overcome. The dog didn't know how to play, and wouldn't touch a ball or squeaky toy. He refused to lie down flat on the floor, and would become rigid if I tried to roll him over. Eventually I taught him to Roll Over, and this helped him to relax. I went ahead and taught him the Novice, Open, and Utility routines, and when he was ready showed him in Obedience Trials. He got his CD, CDX, and UD in exactly five months with an average of 195. He learned to work fast, and seemed to enjoy it. The most difficult thing for him to learn was the simple feat of coming to me and Sitting straight. His natural impulse was to shrink back and Sit crooked to avoid looking me in the eye. He would lower his head and show the whites of his eyes. When he was concentrating on his work he would Sit straight but in a strange place he would forget, and this inherited trait would govern his actions.

He was an intelligent dog but one of the most difficult I have ever trained. The only punishment he ever received was a verbal reprimand "No," or "You are a bad dog." The latter was used if he was being very stubborn, and on hearing this he would crawl around on his stomach and cry as if he were in pain. I rarely said this to him: he became too upset. The training he received was good for him, but no amount of training could completely control his imaginary fears.

The Rough, Aggressive Dog

This dog, though rough and wild at first, can be a lot of fun once he starts to grasp his training. The method outlined below of bringing a very rough or tough dog under control is not to be tried on any other type. You must realize that what is good for one dog is entirely wrong for another of a different temperament.

If you have a large, strong dog, over a year old, that is very difficult to control, try this: have the dog sit in the Heel Position. Take hold of his ruff in your left hand. If you grasp the skin below the dog's left ear you can hold him steady while your right hand slides the choke collar under his chin and just in back of his ears. Next Heel with the collar in this position and jerk the dog if he tries to bolt. In just one or two lessons the roughest dog can be brought under control with the choke collar up high. After this, leave the collar down in its normal position: the dog can now be trained like any other. If the dog should become obstreperous occasionally, move the collar up, and the dog will very likely quiet down without being jerked.

Once you have shown the roughneck who is master, he will respond quickly if you give your commands in a quiet tone of voice. This type of dog craves praise, and can often be turned into a top worker by lavish praise when he is good and quick punishment when he is bad. By punishment I mean a high jerk or a disapproving tone of voice.

The dog will not learn to respect you if you yell at him or speak sharply when you start to lose your temper. You must speak calmly, quietly, and with authority. It is amazing what you can do with these dogs with your voice alone. After a couple of weeks I have been able to take the leash off this type of dog and control him with my voice alone. Although I could tell from the dog's expression that he wanted to bolt, I could stop him from doing so by saying quite calmly, and in a matter-of-fact tone of voice, "No, heel." The dog would meekly Heel along and I would praise him quietly. If the dog on an about turn would stand and look at me boldly, I would simply continue to Heel, beckon the dog with my left arm, slap my leg, and quietly tell him to Heel. This is appealing to the dog's finer instincts, and it works in 99 cases out of 100. If I had raised my voice or seemed the slightest bit unsure of myself, the dog would have bolted.

These dogs are so excitable that they keep jumping up once they have sat at Heel position. If the dog is beginning to get out of control, grasp his ruff and give him a sharp tap on the nose saying, "No, sit, stay," then hold him quietly for a second saying, "Easy," then praise him.

Dogs that are biters through lack of earlier discipline can be cured effectively. An older dog that has been allowed to run wild is going to resent any attempt to control him. If such a dog should try to bite you, quickly give him a sharp tap on the nose. If he snaps at you, give him a sharp tap under his chin. Don't do this slowly, or miss, or you may get bitten. This type of dog does not bite out of meanness, but only because he is fresh. You must tell him quickly that he is a bad dog and should be ashamed of himself. You should make it very clear to him that you are boss. Look him in the eye when you reprimand him. Be sure to praise him when he deserves it.

Friendly dogs that are somewhat rough, and jump up biting the handler's hand while Heeling, should also receive a sharp tap on the nose. There is no excuse for such behavior, and it should be stopped. A habit of this kind can only go from bad to worse. Two or three corrections, properly administered, will correct this.

Vicious Dogs

There are some dogs that come under the above category, and no amount of training will make them trustworthy. You may teach them to go through the motions but beneath the surface lies an evil disposition. If a dog bites without justification you can tell by his expression whether he is mentally ill. Such a dog should never be bred, for he will pass his bad disposition along to his offspring. The wisest course is to have the dog put away before he injures an innocent human being or kills another dog.

The Recall Exercise (30 points)

(You may start teaching your dog this exercise on the same day that you start teaching him to Heel.)

To start the Recall exercise have your dog on leash in the Heel position. Now, with your leash taut in your left hand and held in back of your dog's head, step directly in front of him and face him. Continue to hold the leash taut in back of his head as you say "Stay" and give him the Stay signal with your right hand. Show your dog the palm of your right hand and have your fingers pointing down toward the ground. Hold pressure on the leash as you step back, and if your dog tries to follow you, hold the leash steady so that he can't move toward you, and say "No, stay." If the dog steps out of position before you can control him, say "No, stay," and quickly put him back where he was originally. Put your right hand under his chin and push him into a sitting position. Next time try to caution him to Stay before he actually gets up.

After the third or fourth attempt you should be able to step back two or three steps. If he stays a few seconds, quickly call him to you giving his name first and the word "Come." Don't worry about the leash at this point but concentrate upon gently putting your left hand under his chin

Hold the leash taut in back of your dog's head as you give him the stay signal and the verbal command "Stay."

Encourage your puppy to come in to your hands on a loose leash. Never pull your puppy in to you on a tight leash as if you were hauling in a fish.

to lift his head up when he comes to you, tapping him quickly on the croup with your right hand as you say "Sit," then petting him immediately with your right hand. Your left hand at this time should be scratching him under the chin. This should all be done very quickly and smoothly on your part and after you have practiced it a few times it will become automatic.

When you have your part down pat leave him again, give him the verbal command "Stay" and the Stay signal, and try to step back to the end of the leash. Do this gradually and when you feel that there is no pressure on the leash from the dog trying to surge forward call him. If he starts toward you praise him, and repeat the aforementioned procedure. If he doesn't move when you call him give him a jerk toward you with the leash, then when he responds praise him and let the leash go slack. You should practice recalls like this until you can do it smoothly and correctly each time. If you do it right, your dog will be sitting automatically in one or two lessons.

Be prepared to take your dog back to his original position many times before he really learns to Stay. It takes patience and persistence to teach a dog to Stay. When you have progressed to the point where the dog will do this nicely, you may go on to the next step.

Never give your dog's name when you order him to Stay.

If you have already taught your dog the preliminary training as outlined at the beginning of this book, he will be so accustomed to responding to your commands that he will come to you willingly when he is called. If not, try this.

Put the tracking leash on your dog, give him the Sit-Stay command, and leave him. Walk away about twenty feet, then turn around and face him. Call him to you, and use the leash only if you find it necessary to guide him just as you did on the short leash. As your dog starts toward you, clap your hands and praise him. Try to get him to come in to your hands. As the dog learns to come in to your hands you can eventually place them down by your sides quietly. Talk to the dog as he sits so that he will look up at your face. If the dog wanders, jerk the leash, order him to "Come," and praise him when he responds. Be sure he sits straight. Repeat this until he responds nicely on the full length of the tracking leash. A straight Sit is often the difference between first and second place in a show. Insist upon straight Sits at all times.

The simplest way to teach a dog to Sit straight in front is this. If the dog swings his hindquarters out to your right, quickly push the side of your right foot against his hindquarter. It is easier to accomplish this if

Insist that your dog sit perfectly straight in front of you each time he comes to you. Your hands must be placed down by your sides whenever the dog returns to you.

you catch the dog just as he is Sitting. You can push him into a straight Sit. The same can be tried with the left foot. Do *not* kick the dog. Exert just enough pressure to make him Sit straight. If you push him too hard, you may make him Sit off center. This method will save you from bending over every time to correct a crooked Sit. However, if you are training a shy dog, you will have to bend over and straighten him with your hand. A shy dog will become frightened if you use your foot. The temperament of your dog must be considered when giving corrections.

It is very important that you remember to be gentle with your dog when he comes to you. When you grasp his ruff, or hold him under the chin, do so very gently, just enough to hold him steady. The tap to make him Sit must be sharp if necessary, but the praise should follow so quickly that the dog has not time enough to be aware of the tap.

A dog may develop a mental block about coming in to his handler because of some earlier unpleasant experience he has had. It may be that the handler tried to straighten his dog's Sit by jerking his collar, grabbing his fur, or slapping him for racing in too fast. Any of these unjust corrections would make a dog shy away from his handler.

One thing to avoid when teaching the Recall is not to keep calling him to you. If the dog does not respond to the first call, jerk him toward you. As he starts toward you, praise him. Do not pull your dog in to you on a tight leash as if you were hauling in a fish. Keep the leash slack except for the brief moment when you jerk him, then release it again.

The tone of your voice is very important at this time. When you call your dog, raise your voice just loud enough for him to hear you, and make it pleasant but firm. Do not yell at your dog in a domineering tone or a high-pitched shriek, or he will want to go in the opposite direction. And do not say "Stay" in the form of a question. You are not asking him to Stay; you are ordering him to do so.

When your dog has mastered the Recall on the long tracking leash you may go back to the short leash. Those of you who have done the preliminary training, or are training puppies, may find that this is your next step. Have your dog sit at Heel position, give him the verbal command and the signal to stay, leave him and go to the end of the leash. Always precede the verbal command Come with your dog's name. Besides the fact that your dog should learn his own name, this will get his attention. Unless you have your dog's undivided attention you are not going to be successful in training him. Call your dog, and when he is coming to you run backwards, throw the leash off to your left side, clap your hands, and encourage him to come directly in front of you by bringing your hands in close to your body. Gently guide him into a straight sit. If he doesn't sit automatically tap him on his croup, then praise and pet him.

The next step is to try the Recalls off leash. When you leave your dog stand about ten feet from him at first, and be sure to praise him in a happy tone of voice when he responds to your call. As he is coming to you, the praise should be distinctive, such as "Good boy," or words of your own choosing. "C'mon, c'mon" is not praise, and many people say this repeatedly even though their dogs are completely disinterested. Praise should not be given continually or your dog will stop listening. It should be earned, or used to encourage better work. Next try fifteen and twenty-foot recalls, and when your dog is coming to you, run backwards to get him to move briskly.

If your dog is doing twenty-foot Recalls off leash, it is time to try the next step. When you call your dog at twenty feet do not run backwards when he is coming toward you. It is time that he learned that you are going to stand still and he will have to sit straight or be corrected. When you command your dog to "Come" the dog should be taught that this means to come and sit straight in front of you. No other command should be used. Repeat "Come" if it is necessary.

Do not step over to your dog if he is coming in crooked. Stay where you are, and make him come to you. Then, straighten his sit before he sits. You should notice if your dog is standing at an angle when he is in front of you; if so, quickly tap him on the hindquarter with your hand or push him over with the side of your foot, so that he will sit straight. With experience you will become adept at using the exact amount of pressure to teach him to sit straight. If he comes in too fast, tell him to sit when he is about two yards away from you. This will slow him down so that he will sit directly in front of you. If he comes in too slowly, make it more fun; call to him encouragingly and clap your hands. Sound very gay and cheerful, and laugh a little. If he continues to move slowly go up to him, put his collar high on his neck, give him a good jerk as you say "Come," and run backwards. One or two such corrections will teach him to move quickly.

So remember to remain in place without moving your feet whenever your dog is returning to you, unless he is returning slowly. This is the only exception, and the aforementioned correction should be used throughout the Novice and advanced exercises whenever necessary. It is an excellent way to teach a dog to move faster. I have found that if this method is used correctly, it will speed up any dog's work.

Up to now the different steps in teaching a dog the Recall have taken about three weeks. Any handler with a new dog who is following my method in its entirety can accomplish this very easily. However, if you have a dog who is being retrained, an older dog who has acquired bad habits through lack of training, a hardheaded dog who has inherited the inclination to be stubborn, a bright dog who has outwitted his inept handler who neither understood nor controlled him, or a dog who has been force trained with a cruel method, it will take about twice as long to train these because one must first gain the respect and trust of the dog, and through the correct training method build a sound foundation for intelligent communication.

The same method should be employed to teach one of these dogs the Recall but the handler must be very firm and insist that the dog obey the first command. If the dog is told to Stay and he disobeys the command the handler should walk toward the dog, give him a sharp tap on his nose as he calmly, but firmly, says, "No, shame," and puts him back where he was. The correction should be given at the point where the handler meets the dog. The exercise should be repeated immediately. If the dog doesn't come the first time he is called, he should receive a sharp jerk toward his handler.

The dog who is extremely headstrong, stubborn, or stupid should receive a more severe correction if this does not work. When you approach him after he has been willfully disobedient, put his collar as high as it will go on his neck and jerk him sharply two or three times. Keep your voice low and calm as you say, "Bad dog, I told you to stay." By remaining in control of the situation you can accomplish miracles. It is never necessary to string a dog up to train it. Such cruel practices should be outlawed and certainly never condoned by intelligent dog owners. Despite the fact that the dog must learn to obey the first command, or receive a quick correction, he should always be praised and petted when he does something correctly. Consistency is a key word in dog training.

Sooner or later the dog that you are training will run away from you. I always like this to happen in the early stage of training so that the dog can get this normal phase out of his system and get back to the business of learning. In the very beginning if your dog runs away from you but returns after you have called him two or three times you should praise him. Later if he runs away and refuses to come after you have called him once you should go after him. Follow him until you corner him, clip the leash on his collar, say, "Come," jerk him toward you as you run backwards a few steps, and repeat this four or five times. Then do a Recall and praise him if he responds. If he runs away more than once, keep your leash out of sight when you go after him, or he will associate the leash with the correction. Seeing the leash might make him hesitate about coming to you. If you kneel down when you call your runaway dog it is more likely that he will come to you. The dog assumes that you are friendly if you are in this position.

About the second week of training your dog to do Recalls try a

Finish every third Recall. Watch the dog very carefully, and insist upon a straight Sit in front and at Heel position.

Do not let your dog bump into you when he comes in. If he nudges you in a show he will be penalized. This method of gently holding his head up with your hand when he comes to you will teach him where he should sit. Dogs are not permitted to sit between their handlers' feet as small dogs are prone to do. Your dog must sit close to you, in front of your feet, without touching you, and you should be able to reach his head easily. If he sits straight in front of you but so far away that you cannot reach out and touch him without moving a foot or stretching forward, he would fail the exercise.

Now try thirty-foot Recalls and as your dog improves increase the distance to forty or fifty feet. By this time you should incorporate the Come signal with the verbal command. As you stand with your arms down by your sides, raise your right arm out shoulder high and then sweep your right hand in to your chest. Then drop your arm to its original position. Once your dog has learned this signal, which you will use later in Utility, return to the verbal command. Use the signal often enough to make sure the dog retains it.

It is about the sixth week in your training schedule and you should be concentrating upon your dog's precision in coming and sitting in front of you. It is possible that he doesn't know what Come means, and just trots toward you when called without realizing that he must sit very straight in front of you. To help him learn where he should sit you should now practice angle Recalls with him. After you leave him take a position that is not directly opposite him, but at a slight angle. When you call him to you motion him into position with your hands and repeat the command "Come" so that he will associate the word with the straight sit. Try this repeatedly at different angles and from different directions so that he will become proficient at coming to you and positioning himself for a straight sit in front of you. When he will straighten his Sit in front of you when you say "Come," or motion to him with your hand, then you know he understands what is expected of him. An expertly trained dog will execute the Recall even though his handler has his back to him. This dog will prove that he understands the command, and is not merely ring trained. When you have reached the point in your training where you can control your dog with your voice, or a slight motion, you will experience the thrill of working together as a team.

Each time you call your dog remember to place your hands down by your sides. The rules require that you hold your hands in this position whenever your dog is returning to you. If you use my method of training to teach your dog the Recalls, you will find that your dog will be looking up at your face and he will center himself in front of you as he does so. If your dog tries to nudge your hand as he is going to Heel position, just press your hand flat against your leg and he will gradually stop this.

Practice your Recalls in various locations until you feel that your dog will obey you anywhere. If you do not trust him at first in a strange place, use the tracking leash, then let him drag the short leash, and finally try him off leash. Use both the signal and the verbal commands until the dog is responding with precision.

Left: Try angle recalls. Stand facing away from your dog. Hold your hands out to guide the dog to you as you say "Come."

Above: When he is close guide him into a straight sit with your hands, as he looks up at your face, and you encourage him with your voice as you say, "Good, come."

Try the same thing without using your hands. Control him with your voice.

Keep his attention on you as you talk to him.

And praise him.

Teaching Your Dog to Go to the Heel Position

Once you have learned the following exercise, you will be able to use it to good advantage if your dog sits crooked when Heeling. The Finish exercise will be used many times throughout the Novice, Open, and Utility Classes. In every exercise where the dog comes and sits in front of you he will be asked to Finish (go to Heel). He should learn to do so smartly and with precision.

To begin this exercise, step directly in front of your dog and face him. Hold the leash in your left hand, palm down, about a foot from the dog's collar, as illustrated. Keep the right foot stationary while you take one step back with the left foot. As you step back, put most of your weight on your left foot, give the dog a sharp jerk, and say, "Hussan, heel." The jerk should propel the dog past your left side, at which point you give him another jerk, which makes him turn to his left toward you and brings him into the Heel position. Switch the leash to your right hand, but hold

Above: Hold the leash taut in your left hand about a foot from your dog's collar.

Left: When you say, "Joll, Heel," jerk him back past your left side as you step back with your left foot.

He should turn in toward you, and, as he does, bring your left foot back in line with your right. The leash should be slack at this point.

Tap your dog to make him Sit.

He Sits.

Immediately pet and praise your dog.

it taut by your left side. If the dog refuses to Sit, give him a quick tap on his croup with your left hand, and then pet him with your left hand and praise him. He should now be Sitting straight by your left side. If the dog Sits with his hindquarters out to the left, tap him on his left thigh; this will bring him in close.

The important point to remember in teaching your dog this exercise is to give him a quick jerk past your left side. Do not pull him around on a tight leash or he will learn to hate the exercise. If you pull him or drag him around, he will balk and probably refuse to move. If you do get him to move, he will get into the habit of moving slowly and halfheartedly. The jerk will teach him to move fast, and get him back far enough so that he has room to turn, take three steps, and Sit next to you. Do not let your dog anticipate the finish by moving when you speak his name; he must wait for the "Heel" portion of the command.

When the above exercise is performed correctly it takes about three seconds. Most dogs learn this exercise after six or seven attempts. When your dog begins to understand, you will find that he doesn't need the second jerk, for he will walk right into the Heel Position. You must praise him extravagantly when he Sits so that he will enjoy the exercise.

After the sixth attempt, see if your dog will do the exercise without being jerked. Try guiding him past your left side with the leash held in your left hand, help him turn toward you and walk up by your side, then have him Sit, and praise him. If he stops before he is completely past your left side, quickly jerk him all the way back telling him to "Heel." When a dog goes halfway back and makes a shallow turn, he sits with his hindquarters out to the left. Only the toy breeds can turn in a small space. The larger breeds must, of necessity, go past your left side in order to have room to turn completely around toward you, reversing their direction and taking the two or three steps that will bring them in line for a straight Sit at Heel Position. If you insist upon the dog going far enough back each time you try the exercise he will soon get the idea.

You will find that soon you will only have to jerk his collar occasionally. As he becomes proficient, do not step back, but be sure that the dog goes past your left side or he will turn too quickly and Sit crooked. Insist upon a straight Sit every time.

Teach your dog to respond to the verbal command or a signal. The signal is a quick sweep back with your left arm. Since the dog is already used to the downward sweep when you jerk him back on leash, he will readily understand what you mean. This is one of the signals you will use in the Utility work. Keep your right arm folded in front of you out of the way. If your right arm is hanging down by your side it will attract the dog's attention, and he may start to the right.

There are other methods of teaching a dog to go into the Heel Position which are accepted in shows, but this is my preference and it is the most natural. With the idea in mind that your dog will be your companion, this method is the most practical. If, for instance, you were shopping and had your arms full of bundles, and the dog stepped out ahead, you could tell him to go to Heel and he would do so very simply and smoothly. If, on the other hand, the dog was trained to go to your right to get to the Heel Position, he would get you entangled in the leash.

If you wish to retrain a dog who has been taught to go past his handler's right side to Finish, use the same method but keep your right arm folded in front of you until the dog is doing the exercise correctly. The dog will follow your hand signal. A dog can be retrained to do the left Finish in one lesson. However, it may take the handler several weeks to break his own habits.

Beginners will have difficulty with this exercise if they pull their dog back instead of jerking him. The leash should be slack as soon as the dog is jerked, but the jerk must land the dog past your left side. Then the dog will turn and walk up into Heel Position and Sit. The dog should be praised the very instant he Sits. The important point to remember in teaching a dog to Finish is that it requires speed. The Jerk Back, the Turn, the few steps to reach Heel Position, the Quick Sit, and the praise should all be accomplished with such alacrity that it is almost one motion.

Once the dog is trained, have him Finish from different positions. Have him sit at Heel Position and suddenly take a ninety-degree turn to the right as you tell him to Heel. Don't step out to do this, just move your feet in the same spot. Now try a ninety-degree turn to the left and stay in the same spot by pivoting on your right foot and stepping back slightly with your left. In both instances make the dog move swiftly. He will have to get up and go to Heel all over again. If you practice this now your dog will be partially trained for the Directed Retrieve exercise in the Utility Class.

This exercise should not be practiced for too long a period of time, as it makes the dog start anticipating. Dogs that are trained to Finish every time they are called will anticipate the Finish, and fail to sit in front of the handler. This error can be avoided by doing three or four Recalls to every Finish at first. Later, when your dog is trained you won't have this problem.

At Obedience Trials I always notice dogs who sit slowly throughout the various exercises. This is caused by the handler who has inadvertently taught his dog to Sit slowly by pushing his rear end down. The dog forms the habit of sitting slowly, and later the handler places the blame on the dog when, in reality, it is his own fault for training his dog incorrectly.

If you want your dog to sit quickly, my method of switching hands on the leash, sharply tapping the dog's croup, and immediately petting him, will give you a fast-moving dog. This method is particularly effective when the dog is heeling, or finishing.

Stand for Examination (30 points)

(As soon as your dog will Sit automatically at Heel, and Stay upon command, he is ready to learn this exercise.)

The Stand for Examination exercise teaches your dog to accept the attention of strangers in a quiet, friendly manner. It is also of great benefit to the dog that is shown in the Conformation Classes. A well-behaved dog that will hold his pose is much more likely to attract the attention of the judge. Many people who show dogs in the Conformation Classes have objected to Obedience Training on the grounds that the dog automatically Sits when the handler stops. This may be true in some cases, but when the following method is used, there is no danger of that. You simply give your dog the Stand-Stay signal and walk him into the pose suitable for his particular breed. Now, your dog is set up for the judge to admire, and it has all been done very smoothly.

When I show my dogs in the Conformation Classes I find this training gives them a decided advantage over the untrained dogs. My dogs will not only walk into a Stand, but will hold the pose indefinitely.

To teach the dog to Stand, start Heeling at a normal pace, and then take two slow steps. At this point quickly bring your right hand down in front of the dog's nose with the fingers outstretched and pointing down, and tell the dog to "Stand, Stay" in a firm tone of voice. As you do this, quickly move out to the end of the leash which you are holding in your left hand. Stay there for a few seconds. Then, as you move back to the Heel Position, give the dog both the verbal and signal commands to Stay. Extend your left arm, and hold the leash on the dog's right side as you walk around his left side, then in back of him and so into Heel Position. Stay there a few seconds, praise him, and then ask the dog to Heel a few steps. With some dogs, it may be necessary, at first, to hold the leash taut in the left hand to prevent them from moving forward. This should be done as you give the hand signal to Stay. Be careful not to jerk up on the leash or you will make the dog sit.

From the moment you tell your dog to Stay he is not to move his legs or body out of position. If he should move at first, which is normal, tell him to "Stay." If he tries to move say "No," firmly.

Left: "Stay." Can. Ch. and O.T. Ch. Joll vom Summerland, UD.

Right: If you have a small dog, hold the leash taut in your left hand and place your left foot under your dog's stomach to prevent him from sitting as you give him the signal and verbal command "Stay." At first bend over this far to give him the signal. Later, when he is trained, it will not be necessary to bend over to give him the signal.

If your dog sits as you leave him, you may be too slow in giving the hand signal and stepping away. This must be done quickly. If he still continues to sit, try this: reach down with your left hand if he is a large dog and hold his right hind leg as you tell him to "Stand, Stay." Then repeat the Stay command and move away. With a small dog, just place your foot under his stomach to prop him up. Do not kick him; hold your foot there while you command him to "Stand, Stay" again. Your dog may try to turn in a circle as you return to him. If he does, bend over and hold his right hind leg with your left hand as you quickly walk back around him. If you hold your dog's hind leg it will prevent him from walking or sitting.

If your dog should sit when you return to the Heel Position, make him stand again and walk in circles around him until he remains standing. If, when returning to your dog you will stand there for a few seconds, he will soon realize that he is not to move until you give him the command to Heel. Caution him to "Stay" if he tries to move.

If you are training a small dog it is completely unnecessary to bend over to give him the Stay signal. Teach your dog to look up at you in the early stages of his training, and later when you start his advance work it will be much easier. Give the signal as illustrated and if your dog ignores it quickly correct him. You may have to correct him several times in the beginning but it will be worth it to gain his attention. When a handler bends way down to give his dog a signal it is a sign that the dog is not paying attention and an indication of inferior training and handling.

The shy dog must learn to accept the attention of strangers while he is sitting before he can go on to the aforementioned routine.

Left: As you walk forward slowly, quickly hold the leash taut and give your dog the Stay signal and the verbal command "Stay."

Right: At first, when you return to your dog, hold your dog's right hind leg so that he won't move or circle.

When your dog has reached the point where he will Stay in position until you return and tell him to Heel, you may go on to the next step. Now, when you go to the end of the leash, drop it on the ground and wait there a few seconds. Next, step up to your dog, and as you tell him to Stay, run your hand over his head, shoulders, back, and croup. Circle around the dog and go back to the leash and pick it up. Then return to the dog, as in the illustration. If the dog moves one leg at any time, say, "No, stay," and place his leg back in its original position.

When the dog has mastered this phase of the exercise, it is time for you to ask someone strange to him to go over him as would an Obedience judge while you hold the leash. When the stranger has finished examining your dog, return to him by holding the leash in your left hand and walking around and in back of your dog's forelegs. If you return and stand ahead of your dog he may feel he should step forward to be with you. Stand there for five seconds before you tell your dog to "Heel." Praise him as you move forward. In a show you are not supposed to move forward until the judge says, "Exercise finished," which is approximately five seconds. If the dog were to move when you returned to Heel Position he would be penalized. If your dog growls or shies away from a stranger the correction should be given immediately to be effective. The dog that growls should receive a sharp tap on his nose as you say, "No, shame." The dog that shies away should be put back in position quickly and cautioned, "No, stay." You will probably have to repeat this exercise many, many times before the dog will stand quietly and let a stranger examine him, but he will gradually reach the point of perfection.

When your dog is very steady on leash and will stand quietly every time a stranger examines him, you may remove the leash. This exercise will be performed off leash at shows. Give your dog the command, "Heel," and walk forward a few steps. Notice when he puts his weight on his right front foot, for his left foreleg will be raised off the ground at this time. Quickly give him the Stay signal and say, "Stay," and he will place his left foot in line with his right. Practice this until you both do it smoothly. After you have told him to Stay, walk out at least six feet from him and turn and face him. The judge will examine your dog and then ask you to return; you will do so by walking around and in back of your dog and into Heel Position. After the Judge says, "Exercise finished," you may praise and pat your dog.

It is permissible to pose your dog by hand, but I think this encourages poor handling. Why fuss over your dog, adjusting each leg, etc., when you can walk him into a Stand very smoothly and expertly? You will be way ahead of the game if you teach your dog to Stand this way. Beside the fact that this method of handling is far superior to any other, it is also the quickest and most practical. By teaching your dog the Novice Stand

Give the Stay signal as your dog is bringing his left foot up in line with his right. This method looks smoother than any other. It is perfect teamwork and expert handling.

this way you have also taught him the Stand-Stay signal you will use later in the Utility exercises. This is another instance where expert training improves your handling.

In the Novice Class the judge is expected to touch only the dog's head, body, and hindquarters. In the Utility Class the judge is directed to examine the dog as in the Conformation Classes. This means he will approach the dog from the front and go over him with his hands. He is not supposed to examine his teeth or testicles.

If you plan to show your dog in the Conformation Classes, I believe you should teach your dog to stand quietly while you examine his teeth, and you can learn to do so without putting your fingers in his mouth. Wait until your dog can perform the Stand for Examination very well; then when you start to go over him, open his mouth to examine his teeth. Place your right hand over your dog's nose, lift his lip up on one side with your fingers, and on the other with your thumb to expose the teeth. Then draw the lips back to show the front teeth and bite. This should all be done quietly and gently as you talk calmly to the dog. If the lips are drawn back correctly you will find you do not have to put your fingers in the dog's mouth to examine his teeth.

Heel Free (40 points)

If you have been precise about following my instructions for the Heeling on Leash, this phase of Heeling will develop quite smoothly.

You are ready to try Heeling off Leash when your dog is doing very nicely on leash, which should be about the fourth week. At this time he should Heel quite close to you and take turns and changes of pace reasonably well. The Sits at this point should be automatic.

First, do the Heeling on Leash, the Figure 8, the Stand for Examination, and the Recall exercise. If you are somewhat uncertain of your ability to keep your dog under control off leash, try the following method first. Tuck the end of the leash in your belt, or throw it over your shoulder and try Heeling by controlling the dog with your voice and hands. Use the leash if the dog tries to bolt. On turns, clap your hands to alert your dog and remind him to Heel. If he is not paying attention, call his name. If he lags behind, tap your left leg and tell him to Heel in a pleasant voice. Correct poor Sits by commanding him to "Heel," both verbally and by signal. If he Sits slightly back, signal him to come up by your side by motioning to him with your fingers. If he goes wide, slap your leg, and motion him to Heel close to you. If he does not respond to your voice or signal when he forges ahead or goes wide, jerk him back with the leash. Praise the dog sensibly, that is, for everything he does well. Train him to move forward on the Heel portion of the command and not on his name.

When you are confident that you can control your dog quietly, remove the leash and fold it in half. Hold the fold in your left hand, and let the ends dangle. The dog seeing the leash will think he is still attached to it. Continue to Heel as above. Do not panic if the dog runs out from you. Simply command him to "Heel" in a calm tone of voice as you continue to walk forward. Praise the dog if he starts to respond.

You should give your dog the impression that you trust him. Be very calm and assured, and your dog will sense this and be calm himself. Many times a handler feels sure that if he takes his dog off leash he will run away; and when he summons up enough courage to try it, he handles the dog in an entirely different manner. He keeps looking at his dog nervously, and his handling becomes jumpy and erratic. If the dog forges ahead or goes wide the handler panics; he raises his voice to give commands and wildly waves his arms in exaggerated signals. The dog confronted with this peculiar handling takes advantage of the situation and runs away.

If you have used a loose leash consistently, its removal will make little difference to your dog. Holding the unattached leash in your left hand will give you a feeling of security, and you will be able to control the dog in a normal manner. Once you realize that the dog will stay with you, you will be confident enough to try the next step.

Do not Heel Free too long the first time. Make the occasion a pleasant one. Try to avoid any errors by outguessing your dog. At this point you know your dog's weak points, so be prepared to meet them smoothly. One place to watch is when you go from normal pace to fast. The dog may spurt ahead of you. If this happens, gradually assume a normal pace as you say matter-of-factly, "No, heel," and slap your leg to get the dog back by your side. If you treat this capriciousness lightly, the dog will resume Heeling. If you make a wild grab for your dog, you will panic him and he will dash away. To control a dog off leash you must let him think that you trust him; if you don't, he will outwit you.

If you think that your dog is going wide too often, reach out quietly as you are Heeling, grasp the choke collar, and jerk him toward you saying, "Heel," in a firm tone of voice. Then continue Heeling, and if the dog is with you reach down, pet him, and praise him. If the dog sits slowly, be sure to tap him for a quick Sit but be ready to hold him by the ruff in case he moves.

If you have started the training with a mature, obstreperous dog, you should start the Heeling off Leash by using a tracking leash for a few days to get the dog's reaction. A light line such as a Venetian blind cord is

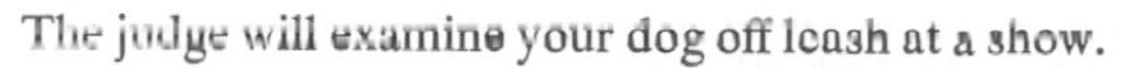
The judge will examine your dog off leash at a show.

Heeling off leash. Incorrect: This is unnatural. Hold your left arm folded in front of you, out of your dog's way, and swing your right arm down by your side in a natural manner.

ideal for small dogs. If the dog dashes off after you have corrected him several times, your only recourse is to go up to him by walking on the leash and jerk him toward you a couple of times, saying, "No, Heel." Some dogs are below average in intelligence, and only respect and understand this form of correction. When the dog begins to respond, use the short leash in the same way, and then continue as mentioned in the beginning. Whenever this type of dog acts up, put him back on the tracking leash for some practice work where you can reach him quickly to correct every error.

While you are practicing the Heeling off Leash, do the Figure 8. Keep your dog close by talking to him, and clap your hands or speak his name to get his attention. Make this fun, and watch your dog carefully so that you can correct him the instant he makes a mistake. Be careful about Sits, and insist that each one is perfect. I have found that the most common error incurred in the Figure 8 exercise is that the dog will lag. An occasional jerk will help correct this, but talking to your dog and making the whole exercise seem like fun will make him eager to keep up with you.

If he should crowd you on the inside turn, bump into him with your knee. When he steps back into Heel Position speak to him in an encouraging tone of voice as you continue Heeling. I have observed in shows that the majority of dogs lag on the outside turn, so practice this exercise until you can do it perfectly. Encourage your dog repeatedly with your voice to keep him from lagging. Be careful to Heel fairly close to the posts.

When your dog is Heeling off Leash nicely, add a Heeling signal to your routine. As you say, "Hussan, heel," remembering to alert your dog by calling him first by name, give him the signal to Heel. This signal, which is a forward scooping motion with your left hand and arm, should be given in front of the dog's head where he can see it. You do not need to bend down to give the signal to small dogs. They will notice the same signal given with your left arm held down lower. This signal will be used in the Utility work, and it is practical to teach it at this time. As soon as your dog understands the signal, go back to using the verbal command only.

The Long Sit—Novice (30 points)

The Long Sit in the Novice Class is for a duration of one minute; but when you practice each day, gradually increase the time to three minutes.

You may start this exercise the first week of Formal Training, and practice it with your dog every single day that you train.

To start this exercise, have your dog sit in the Heel position on leash. Give him the verbal command to "Sit, stay," and the hand signal; then walk out to the end of the leash and drop it on the ground as you turn and face your dog. I would suggest that you assume the same position each time that you leave your dog on a Long Sit or Long Down. I think you will find the most comfortable position to maintain is to fold your arms across your chest. If you hold them down by your sides, it will become tiresome; and if you change your position, the steward in a show, or your dog, may interpret it as a signal.

If your dog moves toward you, say "No, stay," and take him back to the exact spot where you left him. Again say "Sit, stay," and leave him. Repeat this until the dog will remain in position. When the one minute is up, pick up the leash and return to the Heel Position by walking around the dog's left side and in back of him. Stand by your dog for a few seconds quietly, and then praise him. You may have to caution him to Stay as you return to him. He is not supposed to move until you speak to him.

When the dog is doing well, gradually increase the distance between you to forty feet.

Some dogs will bolt and take the leash with them. If your dog should

Dogs taught to sit this closely in class will become very reliable in a show.

do this, quietly tie the leash to a post or fence, and the next time he tries to run he will jerk himself back. One or two experiences of this kind will convince him that he should Stay.

If your dog will Stay on a three-minute Sit on Leash at a distance of forty feet, it is safe to remove the leash entirely and try it. At this time it is not necessary to give the dog the Stay signal. When you remove your leash, place it on the ground about two feet behind the dog. In a show you would tuck the leash into your armband, making sure that the judge can see the number on the band. The judge enlists the help of his stewards to watch the dogs and handlers for the duration of the Long Sit and the Long Down exercises. If the dogs move, or if the handlers signal to their dogs, such action will be noted on the individual's score sheet, and points will be deducted.

When you give your dog the command to "Stay," your tone of voice should be low but firm. Do not raise your voice. Nothing sounds more crude than the handler who yells at the dog sitting by his side. If you have attended Obedience Trials, you have probably noted that many handlers are guilty of this offense, especially on the Long Sit and the Long Down exercises. They are trying to intimidate their dogs into submission by shouting at them. They have evidently never tried the gentle approach.

If you are training a dog that simply refuses to Stay after you have repeatedly taken him back to his Sit-Stay position, try this. When the dog follows you, turn around and grasp him by the ruff and give him one sharp tap on his nose saying, "Shame, bad dog." Put him back in position, look him in the eye and say, "Sit, stay." The dog will quickly decide it is wiser to Stay if you use this correction. There is no point in being squeam-

ish about this; a dog has no respect for someone he suspects of being weak. Sometimes a dog will lie down when he has been told to Sit. The quickest way to correct this is to jerk him into a sitting position, command him to "Sit," and leave him without further comment.

The Long Sit—Open (30 points)

The Long Sit out of sight in the Open Class is for three minutes, but in practicing, gradually increase your time to five minutes. It is time to try this exercise when the dog has done the Long Sit with you in sight consistently, even in different locations.

Leave your dog as before, but this time disappear out of sight around the corner of a building. Watch your dog without showing yourself to be sure he is Staying. By doing so you can catch him the second that he either moves out of position or lies down. If this happens, quickly walk back and correct him. Do not try to correct him from a distance, but go right back to him every time. Gradually build the time up to five minutes, and try a variety of locations.

Sometimes a handler will have a problem he cannot solve. I have never yet come across a training problem I could not solve, so I have been able to help many people with theirs. Several people have had dogs that would do the Long Sit everywhere but at a show, and there the dog would eventually leave the ring to look for his handler, or lie down.

You cannot correct the dog in the ring, but you can correct him before you go in the ring. Tell your dog to "Sit, stay," and have a friend sit nearby to watch him, but do not let the dog be aware of this. Since a dog at a show must be on leash at all times except when he is working in the ring, spread your leash on the ground quietly near your friend so that he may grab it instantly if the dog breaks. It is easy to fool a dog this way if you use a lightweight leash. As you spread it on the ground with one hand, pet the dog with the other, and talk to him to distract his attention. If the dog breaks, your friend should hold the dog until you return. Walk away from your dog and hide. Keep an eye on your dog so that you can return the instant he breaks. When he does, return quickly, hold him by the choke collar with the left hand, take him back, and make him Sit exactly where you left him. Continue to hold the collar in your left hand, and shake your right finger in the dog's face saying, "Shame, bad dog. I told you to Stay. Shame on you." Then leave him again, pointing your finger at him and looking him in the eye and saying, "Now you sit, stay." By this time the dog will feel humiliated from the scolding and the finger wagging, and he will stay.

The Long Down—Novice (30 points)

The Long Down in the Novice Class is for a period of three minutes; but when you practice each day, gradually increase the time to five minutes.

Practice this exercise directly after you have done the Long Sit each time you train your dog.

You would think that a dog would be glad to perform this exercise after he has been practicing, but a novice can be quite contrary about it.

If you have followed my directions for Preliminary Training, your dog will already know how to lie down by voice or signal. If not, go back and reread the chapter "Teaching Your Dog to Lie Down."

Many Novice handlers experience difficulty in making their dogs drop because they do not tap the dog on the nose properly. They tap the dog's nose as if they were brushing away a speck of dust. You must give the dog a sharp tap very quickly, and follow through immediately with praise. Don't abuse your dog by tapping him more than once, or by swinging at him and missing several times. Do it correctly each time you want him to drop.

This is the signal you will use in the Open and Utility work, so insist upon a quick drop without allowing the dog to move out of position. If he tries to crawl aside, hold him and tell him to Stay. Next time you give the signal, hold the leash in your left hand about a foot from the dog's collar. If the dog tries to crawl, hold him back with the leash as you command him to "Stay."

Do not permit the dog to roll over on his back or lie flat on his side.

Give your dog the Down signal without bending over. Teach him to watch you

Correct him immediately if he does this by pushing him into a relaxed Down position.

If the dog becomes playful and refuses to lie down quietly, jerk him into a sitting position, again give him the Down signal, and leave him immediately. As soon as you leave him the dog will lie down properly. If you stay near him, fussing over him, he will only become more excited. Be calm and firm with a playful dog. If you laugh at him or fuss over him you will get nowhere. If you experience any difficulty, reread the instructions to be sure you are following them correctly.

When you have reached the point where the dog will drop on command and signal, which will be the first lesson, you may leave him and take your stance at the end of the leash. If the dog gets up, take him back to his original position, and put him down again. Gradually increase the time to three minutes, don't pick up your leash, return to the Heel position as in the Long Sit, and praise your dog. At first you may have to caution him to Stay. He is not supposed to move in a show until the judge says, "Exercise finished," or until, in practice, you speak to him.

Handlers should stand about twenty feet from their dogs. Later the distance be increased to forty feet.

Do not get into the habit of asking your dog to Sit as soon as you return, or he may anticipate this and do it without command. Stand beside him for ten seconds before you reach down and before you praise him. You may then have him sit.

Proceed to teach him to Stay Down using the same method described for the Long Sit.

When your dog fully understands the Down signal and verbal command, start practicing the Long Down the inconspicuous way you will do it in a show. Have your dog sit at Heel position and give him the Down signal and verbal command, "Down," without bending over. Just use your right hand and arm for the signal and if he doesn't drop immediately reach down and tap him. If he did drop be sure to praise him.

In shows a handler is permitted to bend as far as necessary to bring his hand on a level with the dog's eyes in giving a signal, but I believe this encourages both poor training and poor handling. If you train your dog expertly from the beginning, these excessive body signals will never be necessary and your handling will be smooth and natural.

In a show you will wait for the judge to tell you to Down your dogs before you do so. The handler that touches his dog or his dog's collar to make him go down will be penalized.

The Long Down—Open (30 points)

In the Open work, the Long Down out of sight is for a period of five minutes, but in your practice sessions increase it to seven minutes.

When you leave your dog on a Long Down and disappear from sight, he will be anxious to see where you are going, and may sit up to do so. Watch him constantly from a hiding place so that you can hurry back to put him down if he moves. If he sniffs the area near him or if he creeps forward, go back immediately and correct him, saying, "No, stay." Be firm with him from the beginning and insist that he obey your command to stay down. If you can make your dog realize that you will not tolerate any nonsense from him, even though he cannot see you, he will decide to be good. You can control a dog at a distance or out of sight if you are quick with corrections, and impress upon the dog that you are watching him every second.

Be sure that your voice is low and firm when you tell him to Stay. Later, you may wish to put your dog Down by quietly giving him just the voice command. This is an excellent way to do it.

The dog that whines or barks during the Long Sit or Long Down exercises should be corrected early in his training before this becomes a serious problem. This is easy to correct in the beginning with either a tap under the chin, a jerk of his collar, or by quickly holding his jaws shut as you say, "Stop that," in a very serious, firm, low tone of voice.

These corrections may not work on the dog who is spoiled. The dog who is genuinely upset because he thinks his handler is leaving him can be taught to Stay quietly if the handler will just teach him the exercise gradually. Remain in sight of the dog and gradually increase the distance between you, if he stays quietly, until you are fifty or sixty feet from him. If a correction is necessary because your dog has moved, whined, or barked, administer it swiftly.

When you are ready to try a Long Sit or Long Down out of sight, leave your dog and walk about fifty feet from him and hide behind a tree or corner of a building. Be sure to let the dog see you peeking at him. If he knows you are just around a corner or bush, he will feel secure and gradually accept your disappearance as just another lesson. The exercises should be practiced once or twice a day in different locations.

If your dog tries to follow, you should return and correct him where you meet him. If he moves a little, sits, or stands when he should lie down, lies down or stands when he should sit, you should return to him quickly and correct him. Later, when your dog is obedient about staying but makes an occasional mistake, you can correct him at a distance with a verbal command or signal. However, don't correct your dog this way in the beginning, or make a habit of correcting him at a distance. It is better to go right back to the dog and give the necessary correction.

Handlers who have permitted their dogs to develop bad habits such as whining, should try this method of leaving their dogs. If the dog will stay but persists in whining, an assistant should be employed. The dog should be on a fifteen-foot leash and it should be spread out directly in back of him. The assistant, who is stationed at the end of the leash, should quietly jerk the dog out of position when he whines, then his handler should run back quickly and correct the dog. The timing should be perfect and the exercise should be repeated until the dog has learned to stay quietly. If the dog becomes suspicious of a person sitting a few yards in back of him, the leash should be placed under, or behind, a tree or object so that the dog cannot see the assistant. Later the same method should be employed in a practice class where several dogs are lined up for the Long Sit and Long Down exercises.

A dog should be able to learn the Long Sit and Long Down exercises out of sight in about a week. However, the exercises should be practiced every time the rest of the Open exercises are taught. This daily practice will make your dog steady and eliminate any costly failures when you are in show competition.

The basic training you give your dog is the most important training he will ever receive. In this chapter I have stressed the correct way to teach your dog to heel with precision. This means your dog should keep his shoulder by your left leg regardless of the pace you adapt, or the type of turns you make. He should heel by your side without crowding, going wide, forging ahead, or lagging behind.

When you leave your dog he should stay on one command. When you call him he should respond willingly and immediately, and his attitude should reflect the kind of training he is receiving. Your dog should be trained to sit straight in front of you, and at heel position. He should thoroughly understand the word Come.

Every dog who is destined to become a top working dog will have to master these fundamentals. The formula for success is contained in this chapter and any breed of dog can be an Obedience Champion if this method is applied correctly.

Once your dog has mastered the basic work the Open and Utility exercises are relatively simple. The dogs who repeatedly fail the advanced exercises are doing so because they have never actually learned to be obedient. The handlers in Utility have a rude awakening when they find their dogs are failing not because of a new exercise, but because they are basically disobedient and lack even elementary precision.

I suggest that you continue to strive for perfection as you start your Open training. You will not experience any failures tomorrow if you give your dog a sound foundation today.

16

Handling

Handling is an art that can be acquired only through experience. It is not anything you will pick up in several months. It is the culmination of all the knowledge that you have attained through different sources such as: reading, studying the different breeds of dogs, digesting the Obedience Regulations, frequent practice sessions, observing top handlers in competition, and developing your own style for Obedience competition. Of course the first requisite is a genuine love for dogs, and if you have that it should follow that you will have the patience and understanding to cope with them. The second requisite is perseverance, for without it you will not get very far; and last but not least you must have a sense of humor for in obedience trial competition anything can happen.

The following is a true incident that happened when I was showing Joll. He is a dog that thinks and acts more like a human being than any dog I have owned. I generally take him everywhere with me, for he is extremely well behaved and very good company. He is an American and Canadian Utility Dog and in gaining these titles had many near perfect scores as well as perfect scores. He is a dog that is expertly trained and can work with flawless precision; however, after he won his Utility titles he decided it was all too boring at shows and he would add a little spice to his routine. He had done a commendable job one day in the Open exercises and we were doing the Long Sit and Long Down out of sight. He did the Long Sit exercise perfectly. The handlers left their dogs on the Long Down and we filed out of the ring and went walking off and disappeared out of sight behind a tent. As soon as I was out of sight Joll got up and stood for a while, then he crossed the ring and stood quietly, minding his own business, and just looked around at the large crowd watching at ringside. The judge didn't touch him, for he wasn't disturbing anyone. When the five-minute period was nearly up he walked back to his original position and lay down exactly as I had left him. It was just as if he was thinking, and I'm sure he was, "I'd better go back before Wynne gets back." I filed back into the ring with the other handlers and noticed the smiles and chuckles at ringside but didn't realize Joll was the cause of all the hilarity. He looked so angelic that I praised him for being a good boy, and then the judge came over and explained what he had done. Joll at this point was sitting there smugly, thinking he had pulled a fast one, so I turned to him and said, "Oh, you were a bad dog, were you?" A guilty look swept over his face as he realized I knew. He has never done this since. I think it is very funny, as did the people who witnessed it.

It has long been my contention that if you want to learn something you should go to the person who is most qualified to teach it. By qualified I mean he is at the top of his profession because of what he has accomplished personally. The teacher who has made a fine record himself in Obedience is the one who can help you. There are hundreds of Obedience trainers in the country, but most are passing on bits of training advice they have picked up willy-nilly. With coaching like this you can expect very little consistency and much confusion.

I feel qualified to teach you how to train and handle your dog, because my record shows that all the dogs that I have trained and handled myself over the past twenty-five years have been in the ribbons 99 per cent of the time. The training advice that I give you in this book will help you to become a top handler; and the observations I make on handling in this chapter and throughout the book will acquaint you with the proper techniques.

The first thing you will notice when you watch a top handler is the relaxed, easy manner in which he controls his dog, and the rapport that is evident between the two. The dog will be attentive and responsive to the handler's firm but soft-spoken commands, the signals will be given with just one hand and arm, and the exercises will be performed very smoothly and skillfully. The first time you witness this type of handling you will be more impressed with how easy it looks than by anything else. If you haven't started training you will be quite certain that you could do it yourself—it looked so easy.

The first step to becoming a good handler is to train your dog correctly. Good handling is synonymous with expert training. Your voice is important—give the commands in a firm, well-modulated tone and praise your dog in a very pleased tone that rings with sincerity. When the dog is close to you teach him to respond to commands that are given to him softly. When working away from you teach him to execute the commands that are given crisply but just loud enough for him to hear. Don't keep repeating commands, rather correct him for not paying attention. I do not believe in giving a command twice—I haven't got that much time to waste. If the dog doesn't respond to the first command I immediately show him what I expect him to do. This teaches the dog to be attentive. Remember, you can't teach a dog anything if you don't have his attention.

Signals should be given with one hand and arm only. In the early stages you may exaggerate the signals to gain the dog's attention, but in the final analysis all signals must be given smoothly and swiftly without any excess body motion. The size of your dog is not a factor here, for you can train any dog to pay attention, and if he is paying attention to you he will see your signals. The people who would disagree with this theory are those who have yet to learn how to make their dogs pay attention to them. You will have to watch yourself very carefully to avoid giving unintentional body signals to your dog. It is natural for a beginner to nod his head, lean forward, or move his hands when he calls his dog. He is so intent in watching his dog that he is unaware of his own actions. Have someone watch you so that he can tell you when he notices you doing this.

Be consistent, never scold a dog for a misdemeanor one day and praise him the next for the same act. You cannot expect your dog to understand an exercise if you keep changing your training methods each time you try it. Dogs learn the basic work by repetition, and the entire training program should proceed smoothly and consistently. For instance, the techniques that you will use in the Novice training will be repeated in the advanced exercises and your handling will be just the same.

You should study your dog so that you can foresee his reaction to any situation. You should become attuned to your dog's sensitivities. If you have a gentle, quiet dog, do not antagonize him by rough treatment. He will become very alert and responsive if you train him in a calm and gentle manner with consideration for his feelings. Aggressive or overly playful dogs need a more forceful approach. While your voice should remain moderate in tone, your correction should be fast and to the point. Dogs of this type should always be aware that you are the master. If you neglect to be firm, the dog will try to take advantage of you. You will have to learn to outguess him throughout the whole training period. Dogs, like people, have different temperaments and personalities. Your training methods must vary according to the temperament of the dog. As you become adept at handling, this fact will become very apparent to you.

Be careful of your turns, for many points are lost on these deceivingly simple moves. On the left turn your dog should turn precisely when you do without touching you. Small dogs are afraid of being stepped on, so they will watch out for you. Be ready to jerk a small dog closer to you after a turn for they have a tendency to veer off to the left. The larger dogs can be taught to take a left turn with precision if you lift your left knee and bump them or tap them over lightly with your right hand.

On the right turn and about turn don't stop to wait for your dog. Teach him to keep his shoulder in line with your left knee at all times. Keep your feet close together on the turns by taking short steps, and get your dog in the habit of moving fast. If you make a military about turn and leave one foot out behind you, your poor dog will have to walk all the way around it in order to make the turn; he will lag and you will be penalized for a poor turn. Any bending over, nodding your head, wiggling your fingers, or any overt motion made with your arm or body will be construed as an extra signal to your dog and will be penalized.

When the judge orders you to Halt, take one or two steps to bring your feet in line, no more. Do not keep turning around to look at your dog when Heeling, and do not turn to look at him when he is going to Heel position. Keep your shoulders straight, your head up high, your left arm tucked in close to your waist, and your left eye on your dog. Your attention should be focused on the judge so that you can follow his commands swiftly, and you should proceed in a straight line when Heeling until ordered to do otherwise.

When your dog is Heeling he should do so with precision. Besides keeping up with you he should remain an equal distance from your side at all times. He should not weave in and out as you are walking. This precision can only be acquired by practicing with him consistently and in different environments. If you keep your left eye riveted on your dog while you are practicing, you can correct him the second he gets careless.

Your commands should be given crisply. The command should not be drawn out until it is as lengthy as a sentence. For instance, if you use the verbal command to drop, it should be "Down," not "Dow-w-w-w-w-w-wn-n-n-n." The verbal command to jump should be "Hup," or "Over," not "O-o-o-o-o-o-o-ver-r-r-r-r-r." Of course, shouting commands at your dog is another indication of poor handling, for it shows that he has been improperly trained and you neither trust nor control him.

Talking to your dog, snapping your fingers, clapping your hands, swinging your arms too fast to create the illusion that you are going fast, adapting your pace to that of your dog in an attempt to hide his faults will all be penalized by the competent judge.

I say "competent," because not all judges are capable of judging good work or recognizing good handling. Generally speaking, judges have trained one or more dogs before they decide to try their hand at judging.

If they have not been very successful at training their own dogs it is unlikely that they will appreciate the finer points of handling when they see them. It will take considerable judging experience for them to develop an "eye" for good work. Some judges are considered "tough" because they deduct more points than others for a specific error, such as a poor Sit. Yet they haven't the ability to distinguish top handling from that that is mediocre.

Although some judges are competent in scoring the dogs in their classes they completely lack the correct ring procedure. They follow the handler and his dog so closely, even running next to and bending over to watch the handler and his dog on the fast pace, that they actually interfere with the dog's work. When they give the halt command they run around the handler and his dog to observe the dog's sit from all angles. This sort of freakish behavior makes both the handler and his dog wonder about his capabilities. A judge should be able to observe the handler and his dog when he is ten or more feet from them and see every possible error that they can make.

Some judges do well in every respect but forget to keep an eye on their stewards or their rings. Children might be playing on the ropes that form the ring, spectators and their dogs might be crowding too close, or under the ropes, and trash might be blowing inside the ring. Stewards might be standing gossiping, unaware that they are in the dog's way when he is retrieving, or finishing an exercise. Some stewards even walk directly in a dog's path when he is about to jump the broad jump or some other exercise. The judge is blissfully unaware of anything that goes on in his ring and penalizes the handler for infractions caused by his own incompetence.

Do not pick your dog up and carry him in an Obedience ring. In the Novice Classes you will be permitted to guide your dog gently by the collar between exercises, but this will not be allowed in the Open and Utility exercises.

Everyone competing in Obedience likes to get high scores, but I believe they should be earned fairly. Both handlers and judges alike should understand what constitutes good work. Both should carry a mental picture of the theoretically perfect performance, and score the dog against this standard of perfection. A novice handler is happy at first to get a leg toward his title, but after he has been in a few shows he wants more than that—he wants to place in the ribbons. This is natural. It is the American way—to want to excel in what you are doing, and in my book it denotes character. You can do well if you are particular with your handling. I don't believe in taking the "easy way out" or the "path of least resistance" in training a dog or handling one. It is just as easy to train and handle your dog properly from the first lesson and the first show as it is to train him halfheartedly and then try to cover the dog's errors in the ring by cheating. It is certainly more fun for you and the dog when he is trained so well that you can enter the ring with confidence, knowing that, whatever transpires, your handling was above reproach. A well-trained dog may one day goof a particular exercise, but it should not disturb you. Remember that you are working with an animal, not a machine. I expect a dog to fault once in a while. This is perfectly normal even for the most brilliantly trained dog, but the balance of the work should be nearly perfect. What I cannot condone is sloppy handling or poor basic work, for this shows that the handler is unfamiliar with the regulations, has not trained his dog properly, and is too complacent to care. A good handler who has trained his dog expertly doesn't have to resort to various and sundry cover-up maneuvers to win: he relies solely upon his knowledge of the Obedience Regulations and his faith in his dog's ability to remember his training.

My training method produces consistently high scores and superior handling; by following it carefully, with close attention to details, you will automatically become a good handler. Dogs trained with this type of handling become happy, alert workers. It gives the handler a great sense of achievement when he can handle his dog faultlessly.

"If something is worth doing, it is worth doing well."

17

The Open Exercises

Heel Free (Figure 8) (40 points)

The Open exercises consist of Heel Free, Figure 8 off Leash, Drop on Recall, Retrieve on the Flat, Retrieve over a High Jump, Jump over a Broad Jump, a Long Sit out of sight for three minutes, and a Long Down out of sight for five minutes.

By qualifying in these exercises in three shows, under three different judges, you may earn your CDX (Companion Dog Excellent) degree. This is equivalent to a high school diploma.

The Heel Free exercise has already been described in the Novice chapter, so at this point all you will require is practice to keep your dog perfect. The Figure 8 is done off leash, and has also been described, so that we do not need to discuss these exercises further.

Drop on Recall (30 points)

There is a preliminary exercise you should teach your dog before you try the Drop on Recall exercise. Stand in front of your dog and give him the Down signal. If he doesn't drop immediately follow the instructions in the chapter, "Preliminary Training," Teaching Your Dog to Lie Down. If you give your dog the Down signal and he lies down immediately without moving forward or sideways, it is called a fast drop. When your dog does this it is time to try dropping him at a distance. Since a dog can be taught to drop fast in just one lesson you should be ready for the next step in just two or three lessons.

Have your dog sit and stay and try the Down signal at five feet. If he drops go back to him and pet and praise him. If he doesn't drop go up and tap him on the nose as you quietly say, "Down." Then as you continue to practice the Down signal increase the distance between you five feet at a time. Always insist upon a very fast drop. It is important to praise him exuberantly when he does it correctly, and equally important to tap him if he tries to ignore your signal.

Once your dog has mastered the Down signal at a distance of forty feet, and responds quickly and consistently, you are ready for the next step. I have found that dogs who learn the Down signal this way have no trouble when given the signal during a recall. At this point they understand the signal and there is no doubt in their minds what it means. Your dog may be surprised the very first time you give him the Down signal when he is coming to you but he will drop. You should quickly say "Stay, good," and go to him and praise and pet him.

The first time that you try a Drop on Recall with your dog try to have the right attitude. If you have a negative attitude your dog will sense it, and you will probably show it when you give him the signal. I always expect my dog, no matter which one I am training, to do the work correctly. As I train each individual dog I learn to read him so that I can determine what his reactions will be to a given situation. For instance: a very sensitive dog will probably drop fast the first time you give him the Down signal on a recall, but he will turn so that he faces away from you. By giving this dog quick praise in a happy tone of voice you will soon have him dropping fast and looking at you. By communicating with your dog you will have a fast, happy, reliable, accurate worker.

The handler who doesn't teach his dog this preliminary exercise before he trains his dog to drop, either verbally or by signal, has to correct his dog dozens and dozens of times when he is responding to his call. This has a crushing effect on the dog, and his recalls become slower and slower as he halfheartedly responds to his handler's call, and anticipates being corrected on his way in.

I prefer to use a signal for the Drop because it teaches the dog to be more alert and attentive, and it is one more signal that the dog will use in the Utility work. The majority of people who shout "Down" at their dogs do so in a very loud, unpleasant tone of voice. If you decide to use your voice, make it firm but pleasant and just loud enough for the dog to hear you. A loud, intimidating tone of voice is as much an error as a hand signal held too long.

When your dog has mastered the first step have him sit at heel, and give him the command to stay. Go back about forty feet, turn and face your dog, wait a few seconds, then call your dog to you saying, "Hussan, come." Remember to use your dog's name first in giving all commands except the stay command. When he has covered two-thirds of the distance, give him the Drop signal and say "Down." The dog will drop. Command him to stay while you go up to him and praise him in a very pleased tone of voice. Again tell him to Stay, and leave him; go back to your first position, wait a few seconds, then call him in to you and have him sit. Praise him, and then have him go to the Heel position and praise him again. If you do not intend to drop him with the verbal command just use the signal.

If the dog does not drop, take a heavy step toward him and repeat the signal. Quickly walk up to him and pet and praise him if he drops. A dog who stubbornly ignored the signal should be tapped on the nose sharply. He should be left in a down position and the handler should go back forty feet, call his dog and drop him when he is halfway in. If the dog drops the handler should quickly pet and praise him. This routine should be practiced by doing three or four straight recalls, then practice a drop on recall. When your dog becomes proficient at dropping fast, a word of praise should be given instead of going up to the dog each time and petting and praising him. Even when he is fully trained, a word of praise for a good Drop will let your dog know that you appreciate his good work.

When you give the Down signal your right hand and arm should be raised quickly. Show your dog the palm of your right hand, with your arm just about shoulder high. Many handlers give their dogs poor signals and wonder why their dogs fail to respond. Don't bend your wrist backwards over your shoulder as the dog will ignore this type of signal. Get your hand in plain view where your dog can see it.

Usually in the Open Class at a show the judge will instruct the handler to drop his dog opposite the jump or himself. This means that the dog will cover about half the distance before he is dropped. Very few dogs ever drop opposite the specified object. Study your dog thoroughly, and practice with him until you can drop him exactly where you want him. To get your dog to drop at a certain point you will have to run up to him quickly the second he takes that extra step. As he does, say, "No," and repeat the Down signal. If the dog ignores you he should receive a sharp tap on the nose. Although the regulations say the most important part of the exercise is the fast drop, it follows that if you can drop your dog at any specific point during a recall it proves that he is fast and accurate.

Your dog will learn this exercise very quickly, so be sure not to overdo

Left: Raise your right hand quickly for the Down signal as the dog is coming to you. *Right:* Place your hands down by your sides after the Down signal and when your dog is coming in to you.

it. If you practice it too frequently, he will start to slow down, anticipating the Drop. When this happens, call him in quickly without dropping him. Do not practice the exercise every day. Practice dropping your dog in different locations, and increase or decrease the distance between you to vary the routine. If after the drop the dog starts to walk in slowly in response to your call, go up to him, put your finger in the ring of his collar, give him a sharp jerk as you say "Come" and run backwards. You might have to repeat this two or three times, but it is a very effective way to get a dog to move fast.

Retrieve on Flat (20 points)

The Retrieve on Flat must be learned step by step.

First, you should teach your dog to take the dumbbell and hold it. Even though a handler has never tried this with his dog he should be able to accomplish it in one lesson. If you are training a dog who refused to retrieve when some other method was used, and he has become stubborn, or frightened, it might take two or three lessons. The length of time it takes will depend upon your skill in using your voice as you tighten his collar. Scores of handlers who have spent many, many futile months and tried various cruel methods on their dogs have taught them to retrieve quite willingly during one of our five-day clinics.

My method of teaching a dog to retrieve is one of persuasion, since your voice is your most important asset here. You must use your dog's name repeatedly before each command and do so in a most persuasive tone of voice. Your voice should be kept low, firm, and pleasant and you should talk to the dog continually as you urge him to take it. When the dog takes the dumbbell you should immediately sound very pleased and praise him happily and excitedly as you pet him. Never raise your voice in anger or impatience if the dog appears to be stubborn, never shove the dumbbell in your dog's mouth or against his gums, never jerk your dog's collar, and don't hit him over the head with the dumbbell. Be gentle but firm with him at all times.

Start your dog in a quiet corner and keep him on a leash for the first three steps. Stand by your dog's right side, or kneel down if you have a small dog, and hold one end of the dumbbell in your right hand. Always keep your fingers off the middle piece (the dowel). Place the dumbbell under, in front of, and close to, your dog's upper lip, and as you tell him to "Get it," put your third finger behind his canine tooth. This will open his mouth slightly and you can gently slide the dumbbell into his mouth. If you can't use your right hand to open his mouth use the index finger of your left hand. Quickly tell your dog to "Hold it," as you stroke his nose on top, in one direction away from his nose, with your right hand, as you stroke him under the chin with your left hand. By stroking him this way you will keep the dumbbell in his mouth. You should be praising him as you do this. Keep the dumbbell in your dog's mouth for two or three seconds at first so that he can get the feel of it.

"Get it." "Hold it."

"Get it," as you lift one end of the dumbbell.

Most dogs accept the dumbbell gracefully and hold it firmly the first time. This is especially true of puppies who will actually reach out to take it and hold it for you. However, some dogs will put up a struggle, and you will have to hold their jaws closed gently with both hands around their muzzles, as you command them firmly, but quietly, to "Hold it." Generally speaking the majority of dogs will hold the dumbbell if you are gentle with them and talk to them reassuringly. Be careful not to bang the dog's teeth with the dumbbell. Once in a great while you will find a dog who becomes hysterical if something is placed in his mouth. If gentle handling and verbal control doesn't work, a good slap on his nose will calm him down. This type of dog is not any fun to train, but he can learn the exercise.

After placing the dumbbell in your dog's mouth two or three times to get his reaction to it, now teach him to take it by himself. Slide your dog's medium link chain, or heavy nylon choke collar, up high on his neck, behind his ears and high under his chin, and hold it in your left hand. Your right hand will be holding the dumbbell. By pushing against the dead ring with your thumb you will be able to draw the collar into the palm of your hand very steadily and smoothly. Do not jerk the collar, just tighten it smoothly and quickly. When the dog takes the dumbbell you should let go of his collar immediately and praise him.

It is very important that you talk to your dog at the same time you are tightening his collar. Say, "Hussan, hold it," and keep repeating the command, your dog's name, and a few words of encouragement, until he takes the dumbbell. I find that most dogs will reach for the dumbbell the second time that I tighten the collar and encourage them in a very persuasive tone of voice to "Get it." It is not necessary to tighten the collar after this, but if it is kept high on your dog's neck it will act as a reminder. Be sure to let go of the collar when your dog takes the dumbbell, and praise and pet him. The type of verbal praise you give your dog after you take the dumbbell from him is very important; you must let your dog feel that he did something very special and wonderful.

If your dog doesn't reach out to grasp the dumbbell, it is because you either stopped tightening his collar, didn't tighten it smoothly and continually, or didn't notice that he wanted to take it and you failed to keep the dumbbell close to his mouth. Remember to keep the dumbbell directly in front and next to his upper lip all the time, even when he turns his head.

The second step is to teach your dog to reach out and take the dumbbell when he is standing, turn and carry it to you as you run backwards, and sit and hold the dumbbell in front of you. Your dog should be ready for this step the third or fourth day. Walk forward slowly, reach down to

"Get it," as you walk forward slowly and hand the dumbbell to your dog at his level.

the level of your dog's head, and hand the dumbbell to your dog with the command "Get it." When your dog reaches out and takes the dumbbell swing around quickly and as you turn backwards say, "Come." The dog will hold the dumbbell because he is coming to you briskly, but you should command him to sit as you place one hand under his chin to prevent him from dropping the dumbbell. Practice this, and the first step, for several days. Your dog should learn this step easily if you praise him excitedly as he is coming to you. It is normal for a dog to drop the dumbbell at first, either when he is coming in, or when he is sitting, so be forewarned and prevent this by placing your hand under his chin as you command him to "Hold it."

If your dog doesn't take the dumbbell, you might be making one of the following errors: You could be walking too fast. Stop, and give your dog a chance to take it. You are making the routine too dull. Sound excited when you encourage your dog to take it. You may be holding the dumbbell too high, too low, or too far away from his mouth. By positioning the dumbbell correctly your dog will be willing to take it.

The third step is to throw the dumbbell about six feet from you, and

When the dog takes the dumbbell quickly run backwards as you say, "Come, hold it."

as you give your dog the command "Get it," run out with him. There could be several different reactions at this point as not all dogs respond the same way. A young dog or a puppy will pick it up immediately and carry it to you. Praise this fellow vociferously. Another dog might run out with you and lower his head but refuse to pick it up. Wiggle the dumbbell and hold it a few inches off the ground. If you encourage him to take it, he will do so. If you run out fast and lift the dumbbell a little lower each time you practice, you can get this dog to take it. Very soon you will be able to run out with him and just place your hand over the end of the dumbbell. The dog will pick it up off the ground if your hand is there. Just be sure to run backwards quickly and make a fuss over him when he follows you, and sits. Then there is the dog who runs out with you and balks completely. Put the collar high on this dog's neck and as you hold his head over the dumbbell tighten his collar and command him to "Get it." If you do this when he gets stubborn, he will be willing to pick it up for you.

Throw the dumbbell six feet away, run up to it with your dog and encourage him to retrieve it as you say, "Good, get it."

Your dog can learn this third step very quickly if you will just time your praise correctly. In other words, just as the dog is reaching down for the dumbbell you should say "Good, that's it," and run backwards. By failing to praise the dog at the right time he could easily lose interest and refuse to cooperate.

Your dog should have been working on leash up to this point. If you find that he is coming along nicely and retrieving the dumbbell on leash it is time to practice the same work off leash.

In the beginning when you trained your dog to take the dumbbell from your hand, you taught him to hold it quietly until you took it from him. At this time you did this so that he would learn not to chew or mouth it. This point should be emphasized not only in the beginning, but every step you go through in teaching him to retrieve. When your dog carries the dumbbell to you and sits, you should watch him carefully and be ready to caution him to hold it if he tries to chew it. You can stop this from becoming a bad habit by either tapping the dog on the nose, or by gently holding his jaws closed over the dumbbell. When he is still on leash and retrieving the dumbbell from the ground be ready to correct him if he mouths or chews it. You should also watch him carefully through each step to be sure that he holds the dumbbell by the middle piece and never by the end. It is normal for a dog to try this occasionally but he should be corrected immediately. Either make him pick it up off the ground while you hold one end or hand it to him so that he must grab the middle piece. If necessary, take it out of his mouth and hand it to him so that he holds it correctly. As you progress from one step to the next, these are two of the errors you can avoid by anticipating them, and correcting the dog before either one of them becomes a bad habit.

The handler who has failed to correct the chewer or mouther will find either one a very difficult habit to break. Have your dog practice retrieving a dumbbell with a middle piece he will not want to chew, such as heavy metal, or studded metal. Save the solid wooden dumbbell for shows.

You are now ready for the fourth or last step.

The first few times you try the Retrieve off leash, run up with your dog, command him to "Get it," then run backwards as you say "Come," and have him sit. Take the dumbbell, praise him, and then have him finish.

Increase the distance that you throw the dumbbell as your dog responds. Then, as he starts to run after it, stop, and let him continue alone. If he stops halfway, run up and send him on again toward the dumbbell. You will have to repeat this until he is willing to go all the way alone.

Gradually drop the command "Hold it" as he progresses. However, if at any time he chews or mouths the dumbbell, caution him to "Hold it."

Now, when you take the dumbbell from him, tell him to go to heel. Check the finish each time to be sure that he sits straight. If he refuses to go out, take his collar and scoot or throw him out.

As soon as your dog starts retrieving the dumbbell at a distance of fifteen feet or more, precede the command with your dog's name. He should start forward on the command "Get it." Many dogs enjoy retrieving so much that they go dashing out after the dumbbell as soon as you throw it, and before they are ordered to do so. If your dog anticipates your command and retrieves the dumbbell before you have a chance to tell him or stop him, try this.

Put your left index finger in the ring of his collar, and as you do so scratch his neck so that he will not realize you are holding him, and give him the verbal command, "Stay." If he darts out before you command him to "Get it," jerk him back, saying, "No, stay." If you have a small breed attach a two-foot nylon cord to his collar; you can hold this in your left hand and let go of it when you say, "Get it." This short grab lead will save your back when you are training the smaller breeds. Make your dog sit there for ten seconds before you send him out after the dumbbell. Try this every time he anticipates, and he will soon be waiting for your command. It is a sign of superior handling if you can control your dog with a quiet verbal command, "Stay," and eliminate the signal. However, if you prefer to give your dog both a verbal command and a signal, do not give the signal with the hand that is holding the dumbbell.

Your dog should return the dumbbell to you without touching you, and he should be close enough so that you do not have to step forward or lean over to take it. This can be accomplished in training by holding him gently when he comes in, either by the ruff or under his chin. It is simply a matter of showing him where you want him to sit.

Encourage him to go out fast each time, to pick up the dumbbell without hesitating, and to return at a trot. Some dogs naturally run when they retrieve, but it is not necessary. The dog that trots back and forth at a brisk pace deserves as much credit, for he is using his natural gait. If your dog should anticipate any of your commands, call him back to you, repeat the exercise, and make sure that he waits the next time.

When your dog is retrieving consistently at a distance, the exercise should look like this. Your dog should sit straight in the Heel Position while you tell him to "Stay," and you throw the dumbbell. When you give the command, "Get it," he should move forward briskly and pick up the dumbbell and return it to you at a brisk trot. (If he runs, that is also correct.) He should then sit straight in front of you and hold the dumbbell in his mouth without chewing or mouthing it until you take it. Once you have taken the dumbbell, he must remain stationary until you tell him to "Heel," whereupon he will finish in a smart manner, and sit straight.

If it is a hot day when you are practicing retrieving, and the dog is panting, you will notice that the dumbbell will move up and down in the dog's mouth. This is neither chewing nor mouthing, and points should not be deducted from your score in a show for a similar incident. The dumbbell is merely moving in rhythm as the dog breathes hard or pants.

Teaching Your Dog to Jump

(As soon as your dog is Heeling off Leash, you may begin the following exercises.)

To quote in part from the American Kennel Club Obedience Regulations: "The High Jump shall be jumped clear and the jump shall be as nearly as possible one and one-half times the height of the dog at the withers, as determined by the judge, with a minimum height of 8 inches and a maximum height of 36 inches. This applies to all breeds with the following exceptions." (Check the Regulations at the back of the book for these.)

"The Broad Jump shall consist of four hurdles, built to telescope for convenience, made of boards about 8 inches wide, the largest measuring about five feet in length and six inches high at the highest point, all painted a flat white. When set up they shall be arranged in order of size and shall be evenly spaced so as to cover a distance equal to twice the height of the High Jump as set for the particular dog, with the low side of each hurdle and the lowest hurdle nearest the dog. The four hurdles shall be used for a jump of 52 inches to 72 inches, three for a jump of 32 inches to 48 inches, and two for a jump of 16 inches to 28 inches. The highest hurdles shall be removed first." (Check the Obedience Regulations in the back of this book for a more detailed explanation.)

Lift your dog with the leash as you run toward the high jump and take a detour around it at the last second.

Before your dog can learn to retrieve the dumbbell over the high or solid jump, he must first learn how to jump. Not all dogs are natural jumpers, and many of them must be taught to jump smoothly and with coordination. Two of the main problems are dogs who jump too close to the jump, almost from a standstill, and those who start too far back. Any dog can be taught to jump smoothly if he is started correctly and if he is physically sound. Even in cases where a dog is not sound physically you can make jumping much easier for him by teaching him to jump with rhythm and coordination.

If you have started with the preliminary training and tricks, you are well ahead at this point. Your dog will take to formal jumping with very little effort. A puppy that I am training as I write this book has learned to jump the three jumps at three-quarters of the desired height, and retrieve over the high jump—all within three days. This puppy has mastered all the tricks I have explained, and so has found formal jumping easy.

If you are just starting, I suggest that you follow this procedure. Set up the solid jump and the bar jump on opposite sides of a square about twenty-five feet apart, with the broad jump laid out on a third side. The solid and the bar jump should be set at about one-third the height that your dog will be required to jump in a show; the broad jump should be about one-half as long. Use three boards on the broad jump and turn two of them over on their edges. After your dog has jumped in this way two or three times, lay the boards of the broad jump flat.

Have your dog on leash at Heel Position in back of the solid jump. Run up to the jump; and as you say, "Hup," jump over it with your dog. (People with small dogs get a break here.) If your dog balks, encourage him; and as you near the jump, try to start him over by lifting him with the leash. Whether you help your dog or not, be sure to praise him lavishly each time he jumps. Keep repeating this until your dog jumps on a loose leash. Try the same routine with the bar jump and later with broad jump.

As soon as your dog realizes that he is to jump, walk around the jump instead of jumping with him. Keep close to the jump, even move toward it, but take a detour around it at the last second, holding the leash in your left hand over the jump so that your dog will continue straight on and over. (You will note as you advance with your training how natural and practical it is to hold the leash consistently in your left hand as you train your dog.)

When the dog will do all three jumps on a loose leash, combine the three by running around in a circle and having him jump each one as you come to it. Try not to stop, but have him jump the three jumps before you pause to pet him. Words of praise can be given on the way.

Watch your dog closely, and when he is in the most advantageous position for a smooth jump, command him to "Hup." Repeat this until your dog has acquired the rhythm on leash.

The next stage is to repeat this off leash, being careful that your dog jumps smoothly. An athlete with the correct rhythm and coordination will perform smoothly, and the same is true of a dog.

As the dog improves, increase the height of the bar and high jumps to three-quarters of the height he should jump. Increase the length of the broad jump by the same amount.

Large breeds of dogs, such as the German Shepherds, should not be asked to jump the full height until they are over eleven months old.

Further instructions on Jumping will follow in the ensuing chapters.

Retrieving over the High Jump (30 points)

When your dog has mastered the Retrieve over the High Jump, the exercise should go smoothly. Your dog is sitting attentively at Heel Position. You give the command, "Stay," in a quiet tone of voice and throw the

Call your dog to you as you place your hands just above the high jump.

When your dog retrieves the dumbbell and starts toward you, quickly raise your hands in the air to encourage him to jump as you say "Hup."

dumbbell. Then, with the command, "Get it," the dog runs forward, jumps gracefully, retrieves the dumbbell, jumps cleanly on his way back with the dumbbell, and Sits straight in front of you, holding the dumbbell patiently. You take it and tell him to "Heel." He goes to the Heel Position smartly and Sits straight. When the judge says, "Exercise finished," you praise your dog.

Now that your dog knows how to jump, you will find this exercise quite easy.

Adjust the jump so that the dog will jump one-half the required height.

Stand about fifteen feet from the jump with your dog in Heel position. Give him the command, "Stay," and throw the dumbbell, being careful to have it land about fifteen feet beyond the jump if you have a medium- or large-sized dog. If your dog is small, throw the dumbbell about ten feet beyond the jump. As you give your dog the command, "Get it," run up to the jump with him saying, "Hup." As soon as the dog jumps, again command him to "Get it," and point to the dumbbell. When the dog reaches

Tell your dog to "Stay."

Look at the spot where you want the dumbbell to land, then throw it.

for the dumbbell, praise him, saying, "Good. Come," and as the dog starts back say, "Hup. Hold it." If it is necessary, touch the top of the jump with your hands to direct your dog over. As the dog jumps, step back quickly and stand in your original position. Have your dog sit in front of you holding the dumbbell for a few seconds; then take it and praise him warmly. Next, command him to "Heel," and praise him again.

The AKC Obedience Regulations state that the handler must stand at least eight feet or any reasonable distance beyond eight feet, from the jump, but must remain in the same spot throughout the exercise. Good instruction should foster expert training and handling, and I believe that to do this in this instance it would mean that the handlers with large breeds should stand fifteen to twenty feet from the jump, and the handlers with toy breeds should stand at least ten feet from the jump. A distance any closer than this could hardly be called reasonable and would in fact encourage poor work.

If your dog starts to wander after he jumps, call him back, and make him pick up the dumbbell, jump again, and finish as I have described.

If your dog tries to come back around the jump, quickly block his path, take him back several feet, and insist that he jump. You will probably have

Your dog jumps when you tell him to get it.

He retrieves it.

to hold his collar as you run up to the jump with him and, if necessary, give him a lift to get him over.

Remember that this is new to the dog, and for this reason be patient. It is more difficult for him to jump with a dumbbell in his mouth. If he should drop it a few times at first, tell him to "Get it," again, and resume the lesson.

Eventually, if not at first, the dog will drop the dumbbell when he comes back to you. This is where the step-by-step method of retrieving will be of great value. When you tell your dog to "Get it," he will understand the command is to reach down and pick it up again. Do not move out of position yourself. When the dog picks it up, caution him to "Hold it." The next couple of times caution him to "Hold it" as he approaches you. This command will come in handy many times in the future when you want your dog to hold some object firmly. Never permit your dog to chew, mouth, or play with the dumbbell when he is retrieving.

If your dog is working too slowly, inspire him by running up to the jump with him, repeating the command, "Get it," in an excited tone of voice, and clapping your hands when you say "Hup." Praise will also work magic. It is up to you to convince your dog that retrieving is fun.

There is a knack to throwing the dumbbell that you can learn after practicing. If you take the trouble to become expert at throwing, you can always place it in the best position for your dog. Contrast this with the handler who, when he throws, hits the jump, lands the dumbbell too far away, or tosses it to the left or right, thereby making the retrieve unnecessarily difficult.

To throw the dumbbell correctly, grasp one end in your right hand and hold it down by your side. As you throw it, flip it up in the air, spinning it toward the spot where you wish it to land. The dumbbell should stop dead on landing.

Stand back far enough from the jump so that your dog can jump gracefully, and come up to you in just a few steps.

Increase the height of the jump until your dog is jumping the required height he will jump in a show. Be careful that he works smoothly. Whenever he veers from a graceful, coordinated jump, help him by calling "Hup" at the right moment.

I had my regulation-size jumps made for my first German Shepherd. She persisted in either climbing or touching the jump, so I installed four-

He returns over the high jump with the dumbbell.

Above: He sits straight in front of you holding the dumbbell patiently. Then you take it. *Left:* Your dog goes to Heel position and sits straight. You praise him.

inch brackets on both sides, one-inch below the top of the highest board. I had two bars made for the bar jump, and set these on the brackets, about four inches out from the top board. She quickly learned to jump clear to avoid hitting the bars. The bars can be moved in closer to the boards depending upon the specific jumping problem. I passed the idea on to other handlers having similar problems, and they found this method worked well.

In recent years I have used my four-foot practice jumps for training purposes. They are just plain jumps with no aids whatsoever. Made of plywood and very light in weight, they are narrower than the regulation jumps so that they fit in my car. I have been able to correct any type of jumping problem by calling "Hup" at the right moment.

Once you teach your dog the rhythm of jumping, he will retain it. To do this properly, you must study your dog while he is in the act of jumping to determine the correct distance from the hurdle that he should leap to jump clear. This varies with the size of the dog, or the way he jumps. If you are consistently correct in your judgment, your dog will trust you and jump at your command. When he has learned to coordinate his movements and has the rhythm down perfectly, it will not be necessary for you to cadence his jump.

Oversensitive dogs will sometimes develop a mental block about jumping if they had an unpleasant experience, like knocking the jump over accidentally. Even though they are physically able to jump, they become afraid of it. The only way to conquer this is to pace them carefully and call "Hup" at the precise moment. It will be necessary to start on leash with the jumps set low. As the dog improves you can gradually reach the required height.

If you force a dog to jump higher than he is able to, you may cause him to strain himself needlessly. A sensitive dog who strains to clear a jump will become afraid to jump. When asked to jump he will approach the jump and stand there, hesitating nervously. Then when he attempts to jump he will fling himself into the jump, striking the top. Do not ask your dog to jump more than the required height unless he is a natural jumper like a Doberman. Do not let him anticipate your command.

If your dog refuses to release the dumbbell when you reach for it, grasp the end of the dumbbell in your right hand, say "Out," and give him a quick tap under the chin with your left hand. The tap will surprise him into releasing his hold on it, and you can then take it from him. After he has been corrected in this manner once or twice he will be willing to release the dumbbell as soon as he sees you reaching for it. It should not be necessary to use the command "Out" after this.

Insist upon perfect Sits in front and at Heel Position.

You should practice the Retrieving and Jumping in different locations until the dog will work consistently anywhere.

The Broad Jump (20 points)

The Broad Jump consists of four flat boards or hurdles, so designed that they are raised from one to six inches off the ground to telescope for convenience. To execute this exercise the handler should have his dog sitting at Heel Position ten feet from the Broad Jump. He should command his dog to "Stay," and take a position two feet out from the sides of the jump opposite the space between the third and fourth hurdles. Upon the handler's command, "Hussan, hup," his dog should jump straight ahead and clear all the hurdles without touching them, turn, and sit straight in front of his handler. At the command, "Hussan, heel," the dog should go to Heel smartly.

If you have read the suggestions on Jumping you are ready for this chapter. Your dog will enjoy this exercise if you start it at the same time that you teach him to jump the high and the bar jumps. Dogs that learn the three jumps at one time rarely have difficulty with the broad jump.

To start, use three hurdles; the first and third should be lying upright

Lift your dog over the Board Jump with the leash as you run around it.

on their edges, and the middle hurdle should be flat in its normal position. The first few times, jump over the hurdles yourself with your dog as you say, "Hup." Then, with the dog still on leash, run up to the jump and as you say, "Hup," help him over with the leash as you swerve around the jump. Next, as you approach the jump, say, "Hup," and hold him on a loose leash. The leash, of course, is held in your left hand.

When your dog has mastered this exercise, lay the hurdles flat in their normal position, about eight inches apart, as shown in the illustration. If the dog steps on a hurdle, lay the fourth hurdle on its edge in front of him, run up to the jump with your dog on leash, and lift him over as you say, "Hup." Try this two or three times before you repeat the procedure on a loose leash. Then try it with all the hurdles laid flat in their normal position.

When this point has been reached successfully, try this. Have your dog sit in the center and face the broad jump six feet away. Tell him to "Stay," walk over to the first hurdle, and stand there. Call your dog's name; as he responds, say, "Hup," and assist him over the jump with your left arm

As you stand near the first hurdle, be prepared to lift your dog over as you say "Hup," and run alongside the Broad Jump.

Look at your dog to be sure he is sitting straight, tell him "Stay," and leave him.

and leash. Repeat this several times until he does it well. The next step is to stand in the same position and try this off leash. When you give the command, "Hup," wave your dog over the jump with your left arm. If you run alongside the hurdles as your dog approaches, it will give him the incentive to jump them. Be sure to praise him every time he clears the hurdles and also to pet him. If he steps on one of the hurdles or in between them, say, "No," and quickly put your left index finger in the ring of his collar, run up to the jump with him, and lift him over. As soon as he starts to jump, let go of the collar.

If you have a stubborn dog who persists in stepping on or in between the hurdles and this method does not work, try this. Have someone hold the bar, from the bar jump, down on the ground between the first and second hurdles. As you run up to the jump with your dog, the bar should be raised about four inches above the hurdles. Your dog will have to clear the hurdles or crash into the bar. If he does, he will soon learn to pick up his feet and jump clear. This should be tried on leash first.

Sooner or later your dog will run around the jump instead of jumping over the hurdles. When this happens say, "No," quickly take his collar, run him up to the jump, and assist him over it. Help him this way twice before you let him try it again by himself.

Above: Stand two feet from the Broad Jump, between the first and fourth hurdles, as you give your command "Hup." *Below:* When your dog is midair, pivot a quarter turn.

When your dog lands he should turn toward you.

The hurdles should be spaced so as to cover a distance equal to twice the height of the high jump. As the dog learns to jump on command, gradually lengthen the jump to the desired number of feet. When your dog stands in the Heel Position, you should be at least eight feet from the jump; and when you leave him, you should stand facing the right side of the jump two feet from it and between the first and last hurdles. I have found through experience that the ideal place to stand is between the last two hurdles.

Call your dog's name first, and then give the command, "Hup." He should move forward on the "Hup" portion of the command. When he is in mid-air over the jump, take a quarter turn to the right, in the same spot. You will then be facing your dog after he turns and comes in to you. If he goes too wide, it may be necessary to call him in to you after he jumps. As your dog lands tell him, "Come," and have him sit straight in front of you. Always make him return to you promptly, go smartly to Heel and Sit straight. Never permit him to anticipate your commands.

At this point in your training you should concentrate upon straight Sits in front of you. Almost any dog will come in to his handler and Sit straight if the handler is in a direct line with him. This is simple enough for him to learn, but it is not enough. A dog should come to his handler and Sit

Above: He should sit straight in front of you.
Below: And finish with a perfect sit.

straight in front of him even though the handler is facing away from his dog. Try calling your dog to you from various angles. Even turn your back on him and call him to you. Once he has mastered this he will come in for a straight Sit regardless of the direction in which he had to approach you. This will be of value to you in the broad jump exercise in case the dog takes a wide turn.

I am again emphasizing the point here that you can obtain top results in your training only if you strive for perfection. I have taught all my dogs to come in to me from any direction, and they have rewarded me with dozens of perfect scores or near-perfect performances.

The dog that I am training as I write is so delighted with his ability to Sit straight in front of me that he beams like a ray of sunshine each time he does it. I have made quite a fuss over him for his efforts, and he is very eager to do it correctly.

This is still not a guarantee that he will have a perfect Sit each time in a show, but it is the next thing to it.

If, when the jump is fully extended, your dog should absent-mindedly step on or in between a hurdle, do not allow him to finish, but quickly say, "No," and run him over the jump twice. Then ask him to jump in the formal manner.

There is one problem that may crop up later. Your dog may start cutting the right corner of the jump, jumping diagonally instead of straight. If he does, try this. As he leaps over the jump, hold your right leg out straight: he will veer to the left to avoid it. If you time this correction properly, your dog will soon remember to jump straight.

Throughout this exercise praise should be spontaneous whenever the dog is responding to your commands. Always give praise quickly and naturally.

THE LONG SIT (3 MINUTES) (30 POINTS)
and
THE LONG DOWN (5 MINUTES) (30 POINTS)

These exercises have already been explained in the Novice chapters.

18

Voice versus Signal Commands

A handler has the choice throughout these exercises, with the exception of the Utility Signal exercise, of using either a verbal command or a signal.

Throughout this book I have recommended a verbal command simply for the psychological effect it has upon your dog. Although dogs have not been afforded the privilege of speaking the way we do, it is a distinct pleasure for them to listen to our voices. Have you ever noticed how a dog becomes alive at the sound of his master's voice? One minute asleep and the next fully alert on his feet, eyes sparkling, tail wagging, his whole being trembling with joyful anticipation.

If you have trained your dog with your heart in your voice, don't deny him the joy of listening to it.

An expertly trained dog will work for verbal or signal commands, but the considerate handler will use verbal commands most of the time.

19

The Utility Exercises

The Utility exercises consist of the Signal exercise, the Scent Discrimination, the Directed Retrieve, the Directed Jumping, and the Group Stand for Examination. It will be necessary for you to qualify at three shows, under three different judges, in order to obtain your UD (Utility degree). This is comparable to a college degree.

In order to train your dog for the Utility work, you will need the high jump that you used in the Open work, and a bar jump that consists of a square, wooden horizontal bar resting on pegs that fit into two uprights. This bar is between two and two and a half inches square and can be adjusted to the height that your dog should jump. You will need three white work gloves for the Directed Retrieve exercises. The Scent Discrimination exercise calls for ten articles, two sets of five each, of leather and metal, already fully described, in the earlier section on Equipment.

All work in this class is done off leash. When you enter the Utility ring with your dog on leash at a show you tell the steward what height your dog is at the withers; then you place your leash and your Scent Discrimination articles (which should be in a box of some kind) and your three white gloves on the judge's table.

The Signal Exercise (40 points)

This exercise can be taught at any time after the dog has learned to Retrieve. It is done entirely by hand signal, and no verbal commands may be given at any time. During the first part of the exercise, the Heel Free routine is used and a Left Turn, Right Turn, Slow, About Turn, Fast, and Halt are included in the judge's commands. Then, when the handler and his dog are at one end of the ring, the judge will order the handler to "Stand his dog," and "Leave him." The handler will carry out these orders by signaling his dog to Stand and then to Stay. Then he will leave his dog and walk to the far end of the ring, turn, and face him. The judge will signal the handler to Drop his dog, Sit his dog, Call him in, and then Finish, in that order. The dog should be alert and respond to his handler's signals willingly and quickly.

Your dog has been learning all the signals except the Sit signal since you first started your Novice work, and now all you have to do is put them together.

With your dog sitting at Heel Position, give him the Heel signal (scoop your left hand forward over his head), and walk along briskly. Try a few Halts to be sure he will respond instantly to the Heel signal. Do a short Heeling routine, and then give your dog the Stand signal (quickly bring your right hand down in front of the dog's nose, fingers outstretched and pointing down), and return your hand to your right side. After a second, give your dog the Stay signal with your left hand (the same signal as the Stand signal but with the left hand). Walk about five feet from your dog, turn around, and face him; and place your hands down by your sides as in the Recall exercise. Give your dog the Down signal (raise your right arm quickly over your head and hold it there until the dog starts to drop). Later when the dog responds, hold the Down signal for just an instant. Praise him. Next, give your dog the Sit signal (raise your left arm quickly from your side in a lifting motion), reach forward, and lift the dog to a sitting position with his collar, saying, "Sit," and praise him. Tell him to "Stay," and step back a few paces. Give the dog the Come signal (sweep your hand out sideways and then in to your chest), and praise him when he sits in front of you. Then give your dog the Finish signal (sweep your left hand down by your side and back, then place it down by your side), and praise him again.

You should start the series of signals with your hands down by your sides, and after each signal you should return your hands to the same position. If you follow this same procedure in all the exercises, your whole performance will be smooth and integrated. Notice that this same routine is used consistently throughout the Novice, Open, and Utility exercises; and at this point you are probably doing it so smoothly that you are not even thinking about it.

In the beginning, it may be necessary to give your dog the verbal commands along with the signals, in order to make him respond more quickly.

"Stand."

"Stay."

If you have not taught your dog any signals, you will need to keep him on leash until he has learned all of them. He will learn the signals more easily if you guide him with the leash. Be especially patient with him when teaching him the Sit signal; it generally takes a dog longer to learn this signal than the others. If he seems a little slow to grasp the idea, put him on leash, and as you give the signal lift him up with the leash. Praise him each time he does it for you. If you have him off leash and he fails to respond to the Sit signal, say, "Sit," as you run up and lift him into a sitting position with his collar. Encourage him by praising him as he carries out the signal.

Your dog will learn the signals by constant repetition. Gradually increase the distance between you as your dog responds. When you have progressed to the point where you have left him on the Stay signal and walked about twenty feet away, you may have a problem. Many dogs purposely look away as you are about to give the signals. If this is the case, do not repeat the signal more than once, but run up to your dog and make him carry out the command. This will force him to be alert and watch for the signals.

"Down."

"Sit."

Place hands down by sides after each signal.

"Come."

Gradually increase the distance between you to fifty feet. Praise your dog after each signal when he responds correctly. Teach him to respond to each signal quickly but wait a few seconds before giving each signal so that he won't perform automatically.

Sooner or later when you give your dog the Stay signal, leave him standing, and walk to the other end of the ring, he will anticipate the Down signal and drop before you give him the signal. This is a normal

Above, left: "Heel." *Above, right:* Dog turns toward you into Heel Position. *Right:* Dog sits straight and smiles happily.

reaction you can expect, and it is easily corrected. Try returning to your dog every other time you leave him instead of dropping him. Walk around your dog once or twice, then stop in the heel position and signal him to heel. If he should go down before you have a chance to do anything say, "No, stand," and run up to him and lift him into a stance.

In the beginning vary your routine so that your dog will learn to wait for your signals. Once he understands the routine you should hesitate before each signal. Try practicing the signals where there are distractions so that your dog will make mistakes and you can correct him. He will become reliable as he gains more experience.

Scent Discrimination (each article—30 points)

The judge will take two articles (one from each set) from your box and place them on his table. He will then tell you where to stand with your dog at Heel Position while he or his steward handles and places the remaining articles on the ground. You will be facing him, and your dog should be watching the procedure. The articles should be placed about six inches apart, and you should be standing about fifteen feet from them. The judge will ask you to take an article from his table, and upon doing so you should show both the judge and his steward the number and type of article so that they can make a note of it. Some dogs dash up to a pile of articles and scatter them around so much that it is difficult to keep track of the correct article. When a record is kept of the number there is no question whether the dog retrieves the correct article. You then turn around so that both you and your dog have your backs to the articles. At this time you place your hand scent upon the article by rubbing it. After several seconds the judge takes it and places it in the pile. Then he orders you to "Send your dog," and you command your dog, "Hussan, get it," as you turn around and face the articles. Your dog should trot out briskly and search continuously for the scented article until he finds it. Then he should pick it up and return it to you briskly without mouthing it, and Sit straight in front of you, holding it patiently. Upon order from the judge, you take the article. Your dog should relinquish it willingly. The judge will say, "Finish," and you will tell your dog, "Hussan, heel," which he should do quickly and with precision. The judge and his steward will then check the article that your dog retrieved to be sure it is the correct one. You will follow this same procedure for the remaining article.

You are ready to teach your dog the Scent Discrimination exercise when he is proficient at retrieving the dumbbell. You will not have any difficulty in teaching your dog Scent Discrimination if you do so in easy stages.

The following method has proven to be so fast and easy to teach that I use it exclusively. Any breed of dog will learn this exercise very quickly if you use this method. The length of time it takes varies with the individual dog—some will learn in one week and others will take three. However, even when your dog has learned the exercise, and is doing it correctly, you should practice it every time you put him through the other Utility exercises.

A week before you decide to start practicing put one leather and one metal article in your pocket. Carry them around with you and rub your hand scent on them occasionally so that they will be impregnated with your scent.

First of all you should set up a Utility ring about forty by fifty feet long. Occasionally you should work in a ring larger than this because many show-giving clubs, particularly breed Specialty Clubs, make the obedience rings far too big. Unfortunately the judges accept the oversized rings and the Utility dogs are forced to work at a disadvantage. It would be better for the exhibitors if the judges would adhere to the regulations and insist upon the correct size ring. The Obedience Specialty Clubs run very efficient trials with everything geared to the regulations and the exhibitors.

Place the jumps about eighteen feet apart in the center of the ring, one on each side, and about six feet in from the side of the ring. Be sure that the jumps are in line with each other by sighting them both as you stand on the ring side of one jump.

The easiest articles for a dog to retrieve are the two, or three, bar dumbbells as one bar is always high enough for the dog to grasp. The single bar dumbbell is also easy for the dog to retrieve but the ends will eventually loosen and become a nuisance. I have used both in the illustrations.

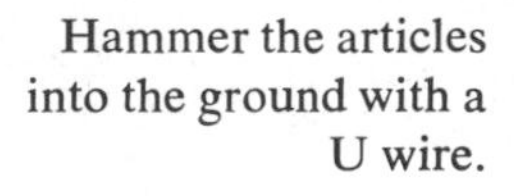
Hammer the articles into the ground with a U wire.

Cut the ends off six metal coat hangers and make them three inches long. This will give you twelve wire ends shaped like U's. Before you take your dog into the ring take two clean, unscented metal articles and hammer each one into the grass with a U wire. Use a corner of the ring. Do not touch the articles; place them on the ground with tongs, and space them ten inches apart.

Have a small stool or chair in the ring and place your articles and gloves on it. The chair should be centered at one end of the ring. Have your dog sitting at heel position, hand him the heavily scented metal article and tell him to "Get it." When he takes it, praise him. Now tell him to Stay and go place the scented article about ten inches from the other two articles. Let your dog see you do this. Return to your dog and command him "Get mine," or whatever you want to say. You will find that your dog will do one of several things: He may trot up to the articles and pick up the first article he comes to which could be the scented one. Praise him if he does this. If he goes to the unscented article first, he may try to pick

Left: Your dog sniffs the article. *Right:* As he starts to pick it up, praise him.

it up, but if he is unable to do so he will go on to the scented article and retrieve it. Praise him. Or he may reach the unscented article first, try unsuccessfully to pick it up, then stand there wondering what to do next. In this case repeat your command to get it, and if necessary go up to him, take him over to the scented article and encourage him to get it. When he does pick it up praise him.

You will find that your dog will be sniffing for the scented article the first day that you try this. The next day try the same procedure. If your dog does well add two more articles. Be sure to encourage him with well-timed praise.

When your dog is sniffing carefully and choosing the heavily scented article each day from five articles you may now add one clean leather article to the group. When your dog sniffs the scented leather article encourage him to pick it up. After this first attempt do not praise him until he has the article in his mouth. Encourage your dog to return to you quickly and sit straight in front of you. Then insist upon a straight sit at heel position.

If you have a stubborn, hardheaded, or stupid dog you might have to take him up to the articles on leash, push his head down so that his nose is close to an unscented article, and say "Is that it?" and if he tried to pick it up you would say "No." Then you would do the same thing to two other clean articles. And last of all you would hold his head over the heavily scented article and say, "Is that it?" and if he tried to pick it up you would quickly say, "Yes, yes, that's it," and make a fuss over him. If you are patient and don't lose your temper, you will have this dog sniffing for the scented article by the second lesson. It would be wise to keep him on leash for a few days.

Gradually add the rest of the unscented leather articles to the group and be sure to secure each one by hammering it to the ground with a U wire. Follow this procedure for at least a week and try practicing this exercise in different parts of your yard, and your ring, with various distractions.

Now it is time to start working with the clean, unscented articles but continue to tie the others down with the U wires. Wash your practice articles that were heavily scented and air them for at least three days before you use them again. Practice each day with two different articles. The first few times you use all clean articles be sure to rub them well to give them a strong scent. As your dog becomes proficient reduce the time you rub your hand scent on the articles to about ten seconds.

When you feel that your dog is quite reliable and consistent in choosing the scented articles gradually reduce the number of articles that you tie down until you are working without the U wires. If you have followed

Above: Your dog turns with you as you pivot. You should not move more than one step toward the articles as you do this. Send your dog after the article with the command or signal to retrieve. *Right:* Without stopping, your dog hurries out to retrieve the scented article.

the aforementioned method carefully, your dog will have no difficulty retrieving the correct articles.

Now practice the exercise with your backs to the articles. You may give your dog the command "Get mine" as you pivot to the right and your dog turns with you and moves out briskly to the articles. Or you may command your dog to "Heel" as you turn. Then the dog may stop and sit at heel position, and upon your command "Get mine" move forward briskly to retrieve the article.

While the handler and his dog have their backs to the articles, the handler may give his dog his hand scent by pressing his palm against his dog's nose. This must be done gently or he will be penalized. While this is permitted it is quite unnecessary. Any dog who has been working with his handler will be fully aware of his scent in a day. Since it takes most people weeks, months, or years to reach the Utility work their dogs will have catalogued their scents long before this. While we remember people by their names or their appearances dogs remember by scent. A person can change his appearance to try to fool his dog but once the dog has got a whiff of his scent the mystery is over.

If you haven't followed the above method, you may find that your dog is making a wide swing before he gets to the articles. To correct this you should have him sit after you turn. Then when you send him he will

Left: Your dog picks the correct article from the pile. *Right:* He selects the correct metal article.

probably go straight to the articles. Other handlers who have used the above method will find it is faster to pivot and send the dog at the same time.

It is important to practice this exercise by sending your dog in a different direction each time you practice. If you place the articles between the jumps each time that you practice, your dog will head for that spot in a show even though the judge has placed the articles in a corner of the ring while your dog was watching. Dogs are creatures of habit and will fail an exercise if you don't anticipate their reactions and practice accordingly. This is one reason why I earn so many Obedience Titles in the shortest possible time. I have learned to read my dogs' reactions when I practice with them. By watching dogs work I can tell how they will react in a given situation. I can also tell handlers what method they used to train their dogs when I see them making mistakes. The errors are a direct result of improper training and handling, and although they can be corrected it takes a considerable amount of time to retrain the dogs, and teach him to work consistently, precisely, and happily.

It is quite possible to practice this exercise by yourself, but if there is a second person present, ask him to place the articles in the pile for you. Practice this exercise in different locations; a dog will often miss an article where the ground scent is heavy, for instance in thick grass after a rainstorm, until he is experienced.

Be consistent and extravagant with your praise so that your dog will work quickly and willingly. If he starts to slow down, it is either because you are making it tedious or you are not encouraging him enough. It is better to take three weeks to teach him this exercise than to dampen his spirits by long, tedious lessons. Make the lessons short but pleasant and to the point.

People who live in apartments, or those who live in areas where the winters are cold and the ground freezes, might want to practice the Scent Discrimination exercise indoors. Use the exact same method but instead of hammering the articles into the ground, use a piece of carpet. Buy an inexpensive four-by-six-foot washable shag rug. It should be at least this size so that the dog can walk on it as he approaches the articles. An inexpensive carpet will be loosely woven so it will be easy to poke the wires through it to tie the articles down. You will have to use a lightweight wire that is easy to twist.

You should place the articles in different positions every other day. The articles should be washed if there is any scent on them even though it is your dog's scent when he mouthed or tried to pick up an article. The rug should be washed after the second week when the dog knows the work. The practice sessions should then be on various types of flooring.

The Directed Retrieve (30 points)

Start this exercise the way you would any new retrieve exercise: hand your dog the glove and say, "Get it," and when he does this, say, "Hold it." If he doesn't take it readily, place it in his mouth and make him hold it for a few seconds. Repeat this until your dog does it correctly.

Next, have your dog sit at Heel Position with your backs to the glove, give him the Stay command, and go place the glove on the ground twenty feet away from you. Return to your dog and tell him to Heel as you turn toward the glove. Be sure he sits straight, then give him the Directed Signal to retrieve as you say, "Get it." The Directed Retrieve signal is given with your left hand and arm, and you may bend your knees and body if you wish. At first, exaggerate the signal by swishing your hand and arm down alongside your dog's head and out toward the glove. Take one or two steps toward the glove as you do this.

Your dog watched you place the glove down, he knows how to retrieve, so he will no doubt trot out after the glove. If he doesn't, repeat the signal. If he still doesn't move, take him by the collar with your left hand and run him out toward the glove a few steps as you tell him to "Get it."

Now place the other two gloves in line with the one you are using and place them about twenty feet apart. Keep sending your dog for a different glove each time.

If you practiced changing your position when you were teaching your dog to go to the Heel Position, you are all ready. If not, go back and read the instructions at the end of the section on Teaching Your Dog to Go to the Heel Position, which will be found in the chapter "The Novice Exercises." Your dog should change his position when you command him to Heel and you should not touch him at this time. It is extremely important that you practice these turns so that your dog will turn and sit straight when he faces the glove. If he doesn't sit straight he will probably go to the wrong glove. When your dog is fairly consistent about going out in the right direction give the signal without stepping forward.

Practice the retrieve at a distance of twenty feet until your dog is doing it perfectly. Now place the gloves twenty feet apart and send your dog from a distance of thirty feet. You will have to move your jumps back to be centered between them. Your dog will probably continue to do it correctly, but if he doesn't, help him. If he doesn't go in a straight line toward the selected glove bring him back and make him do it over again. Don't ever let him pick up the wrong glove; be quick to correct him if he attempts to do this. If he seems confused when you send him out, repeat and hold the signal as you run up to the glove with him. You may have

Above: You may bend over to give the Directed Retrieval signal if you wish.

Below: Joll retrieves the center glove.

to do this a good number of times before he gets the habit of going out straight. Whenever your dog veers from a straight line to the glove, prop up the glove you want him to retrieve by placing a clump of grass or a rock under it. If your dog can see it easily, he is more likely to head straight for it.

If you have a stubborn, hardheaded, or stupid dog who refuses to go out in a straight line, put him on a twenty-foot leash, send him out with the signal and verbal command, and follow behind him so that you can jerk him into line if he swerves off the straight route to the glove.

By teaching your dog to go out straight to retrieve the glove at a distance of thirty, then forty feet, you are also teaching him the Send Out in the Directed Jumping exercise. It will make it considerably easier for your dog when you start this exercise.

When you turn and face the gloves Number One is on your left, Number Two is in the center, and Number Three is on your right. When retrieving gloves One and Two, I suggest you turn to the right. When retrieving glove Three it is better to turn to the left. The distance to the gloves from where you are standing should be about twenty-two feet. The distance between the gloves should vary during practice sessions and be from fourteen to twenty feet. Every once in a while have your dog retrieve the center glove with the jumps in the center of the ring, from a distance of forty feet.

In a show with your backs to the gloves, you would stand in the center, between, and in line with the High Jump and the Bar Jump. On command of the judge who would call either "One," "Two," or "Three," you would turn to face the designated glove. As you turned you would tell your dog to Heel by giving him a verbal command and he should quickly go to Heel Position and Sit straight. You may not touch your dog but you may pivot toward the specified glove while you remain in the same spot. Then you should give your dog the Directed Retrieve signal as you say, "Get it." Your dog should trot out briskly in the direction of the designated glove, and return it to you at a brisk trot without mouthing or playing with it. He should Sit straight in front of you without touching you and close enough so that you do not have to step forward or stretch out to take the glove from him. Upon order from the judge to "Take it," you do so. Then upon order from the judge to "Finish," you send your dog to the Heel Position for a straight Sit.

Directed Jumping (40 points)

The exercise should look like this. Have your dog sit at the Heel Position about twenty feet from the jumps, and centered between them. Give him the signal and the command, "Go." The dog should trot out briskly until he is about twenty feet beyond the jumps. Then call his name and tell him to "Sit." After he has sat for a few seconds give him the command, "Hup," and signal him toward the jump. The dog should clear the jump without touching it, and while he is in mid-air you should turn in the direction in which he will come in to you. He should sit straight in front of you, and then he should be sent to Heel for another straight Sit, and be praised. You should repeat the exercise again using the other jump.

Wait until your dog knows the Directed Retrieve exercise before you teach him the send-out portion of this exercise.

A dog can become quite confused by this exercise if it is not taught properly. It should be done in two stages, and your dog should be rested when you teach him. Begin your practice session with this exercise so that your dog will be alert and responsive.

The first stage is to teach your dog to respond to a directed signal and the verbal command "Hup." Stand with your dog in Heel Position twenty feet back from the jumps and centered between them. Give your dog the command "Go" and run with him down to the end of the ring, or about

At first, bend way down to give your dog the signal to go out.

forty-five feet, give him the command "Hussan, sit," and as he turns toward you, step back and stand there as he sits. If he sits praise him. If he doesn't sit, or if he sits crooked, go up to him and push him into a straight sit as you repeat the verbal command Sit. Then praise him.

At this time you are not actually teaching the Send-out, but since your dog must be at the far end of the ring you might as well get him used to trotting out in a straight line. At this stage he will be learning to turn and sit on command, so teach him to sit straight. A dog does not have to sit straight in a show when he is sent out, but it is wise to practice straight sits. If this is neglected in the beginning, the dog will become careless and might sit with his back to a jump. This would make it harder for him

Left: Then bend over a little to give him the direction.

Right: When your dog understands the verbal command "Go out" and the signal, give the signal without bending over. *Below:* Follow behind him quietly.

Left: So that you will be close enough to help him turn.

Right: And sit.

to respond to your signal to jump the hurdle in back of him. Try to avoid such pitfalls during your training sessions.

Tell your dog to stay and go stand about ten feet from the high jump and about five feet back. Give your dog the command "Hussan, hup," as you signal in the direction of the high jump. Repeat the command and signal if necessary, and step toward the jump. The first time you might even have to touch the top of the jump as you stand beside, or behind, it, as you again repeat the signal and verbal command. Praise the dog happily as he responds.

Try the bar jump in the same way but in the beginning have both jumps set low. Later, when the dog is jumping consistently you should gradually raise them to the height he is required to jump in a show. During the first two lessons when you are teaching your dog the Directed Jumping signals, it won't be necessary to have him sit in front of you after he jumps. Quickly take him back and repeat the exercise. He will probably progress very quickly, as most dogs learn the signals within a week.

Remember to call cadence at the right moment as your dog approaches either the high jump or the bar jump; this will teach him to jump gracefully. In a show, if he climbs the high jump or knocks off the bar, he will be disqualified.

Above: At first stand close to the hurdle as you give the signal and the verbal command "Hup." *Right:* Finally have him sit forty-five feet from you.

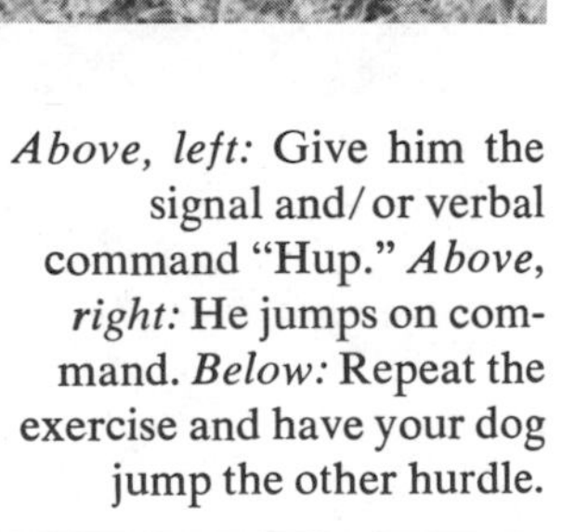

Above, left: Give him the signal and/or verbal command "Hup." *Above, right:* He jumps on command. *Below:* Repeat the exercise and have your dog jump the other hurdle.

Gradually increase the distance between you until you are twenty feet from the jumps and at least forty feet from your dog. If he should start in the wrong direction, say, "No," and walk toward the correct jump. Give the signal again, and say, "Hup." Never let him jump the wrong jump even if you have to run up to it and block his path. Now, when your dog jumps, have him come all the way in to you and Sit straight in front of you and praise him. Send him to Heel, and praise him again. As he is leaping over the jump, turn in that direction.

When you feel that your dog understands the Directed Jumping signals and works fast, willingly, and precisely it is time to make the exercise more difficult. Since you have been practicing with your dog sitting in the center of the ring, now try the signals with your dog way off center. Eventually try placing him behind the bar jump and give him the signal to jump the high jump, or vice versa. At first encourage him by repeating the signal and verbal command. Later he should obey the signal promptly without any extra commands. If he doesn't obey immediately, a verbal reprimand or a jerk on his collar might be necessary. Of course, when you place the dog off center, do so after he has trotted down the center of the ring and sat straight.

The second stage is to teach your dog to Go Out. If you have used my

Above: When he is in midair over the jump turn in his direction so that he will sit straight in front of you. *Right:* Then have him finish with a straight sit.

method to teach your dog the Directed Retrieve, you will find it a decided advantage now. Have your solid and bar jumps in line on opposite sides of your ring about eighteen feet apart, and about twenty-five feet from the end of the ring. Stand with your dog at Heel Position, in the center, about twenty feet back from the jumps. Place a white rock at the far end of the ring about twenty-five feet beyond the jumps and centered between them. Be sure that your dog sees you do this. Now give your dog the exaggerated Directed Retrieve signal as you say, "Go," and point straight ahead. When he is one third of the way there follow along behind him very quietly. Let him proceed to the rock, and when he reaches it, tell him to sit, and give your dog's name first. If he sits praise him. If he doesn't sit, quickly make him do so. If your dog doesn't go far enough, send him out again by repeating the signal and verbal command.

If your dog works fast, and if you have control of him, you might find it wise to omit his name when you tell him to Sit. Generally speaking, it is better to use a dog's name before the command to get his attention.

Repeat this procedure at least a dozen times each day for a week. Now try the exercise in different locations and every two or three times remove the rock and see if your dog will go out straight without it. As soon as a dog learns to go out it is normal for him to lie down instead of sitting. You should correct him quickly every time he lies down until he eventually learns to turn and sit.

Sooner or later your dog will veer to the left or right when he goes out. To correct this take him back to the starting point, hold his collar in your right hand, give the signal with your left, and run him out straight as you say, "Go." You may have to run out with your dog many, many times before he learns to go out straight every single time. Gradually give a less exaggerated signal without bending over to do so. When you are practicing always insist that your dog go out at least twenty-five feet. If he stops short of this, either command him to "Go back" or go up to him and send him on again.

There are some dogs who haven't had any Directed Retrieve training, who simply refuse to leave their handlers' sides to Go Out. The following method will help these dogs understand that they are to run out, and it will also cut their training time in half. Have this dog in heel position at the starting point, and have a forty-foot tracking leash attached to his collar. An assistant should be standing outside the center of the ring at the far end, holding the end of the tracking leash.

When the handler gives his dog the signal and the verbal command "Go," the assistant should quickly run forward about forty feet, jerking the dog forward as he does so. The handler should follow his dog quickly and quietly and command him to sit when he is at the far end of the

A good square stance.

The wrong stance —feet not together.

ring. The dog should be praised. The handler should then hold the leash about a foot from his dog's collar so there will be no pressure on it as they go back to the starting point. After two or three times the dog will go out so fast that the assistant will not be able to run fast enough to keep ahead of the dog. The handler must be quick to control his dog when he reaches the far end. He should be ready to have him sit straight, and praise him. This method should be repeated several times for two or three days. After this the dog should be willing to go out by himself.

When your dog has mastered both stages of this exercise, combine them into one. The exercise should be practiced in different locations, with various distractions, until your dog can perform it correctly wherever he is.

Group Examination (30 points)

The Group Examination is the last exercise in the Utility Class. This takes place when a group of dogs have all completed the individual Utility exercises. If the class consists of more than fifteen dogs there will be more than one Group Examination. The dogs are lined up in the center of the ring, and upon instructions from the judge to "Stand your dogs," the handlers stand their dogs in a square stance. When the judge says, "Leave them," the handlers leave their dogs and cross to the opposite side of the ring, turn, and face their dogs. The judge then examines each dog individually. If, at the expiration of three minutes, he has finished examining all of them, he orders the handlers, "Back to your dogs." When the handlers are in Heel Position he calls out, "Exercise finished." During this time the dogs are not supposed to move, and when they are examined

Group stand for Examination. Class practice makes reliable workers.

they should not show any shyness or resentment. The handlers should not signal or speak to their dogs once they have left them and until the judge says, "Exercise finished."

In this exercise it is best to pose your dog in a square stance so that his weight is evenly distributed on all four legs. He will have to remain standing without moving his feet for at least three minutes, and this will be the most comfortable position for him. If your dog is standing squarely, he is less likely to move than if he has one foot ahead of the other. When you have your dog standing comfortably, give him the command, "Stand, stay," and leave him. Give him the command in a quiet, firm tone of voice. If you have trained your dog properly, you will not feel impelled to raise your voice at a show.

Stand facing your dog, about twenty feet away, and, if it is a comfortable stance for you, fold your arms across your chest, using the same position you would assume in the Long Sit or the Long Down exercises. After your dog has stood there for two minutes, go back to him, and go over him as they do in the Conformation Classes. Approach the dog from the front, and stroke his head; run your hands down his shoulders, legs, back, and hindquarters. Some judges will examine the dog's teeth, and lift the dog's tail, so do this occasionally to let him become accustomed to it. Walk around your dog, and go back to your first position. Wait another minute and then walk around the dog and into the Heel Position. Wait a few seconds, and then praise your dog.

Your dog is not supposed to move, so be quick to correct him if he does. If you say, "No, stay," just as your dog is lifting his foot, it is more effective than if you wait until he has already moved. If he walks away, breaking his position, put him back exactly where you left him. As he

breaks say, "No, bad dog." When you leave him again tell him to "Stand, stay." Most dogs will sit after a minute or so when they are learning this exercise. If your dog should sit, run up to him and as you stand him again say, "No, stand." As you are posing him in the square stance, push down on his back and hindquarters to be sure he is standing firmly. If the dog has any inclination to sit he will do so when you push down on him, and you can correct him immediately.

Some handlers have difficulty preventing their dogs from whining during the Stand. If a voice correction does not work, an effective means of stopping this is to walk up to him and squirt him in the face with a water pistol, saying, "No, stop." This will also control barkers.

When your dog will stand for three minutes, try to get a friend to examine him for you during the exercise.

In a show your dog will be lined up in the center of the ring with the other dogs. It will be wise to practice the Group Stand for Examination exercise with other dogs before entering a show.

20

Brace Competition

This competition is open to any brace of dogs or bitches, or combination of both, of the same breed. It is not a regular class, and no credit toward any Obedience title will be given. This class is generally found at Obedience Trials sponsored by a training club.

The Novice routine is employed, and a tandem chain is used to clip the two dogs together. This is a short chain, about ten inches long, with a clip at both ends. You can make it yourself or buy one.

The dog that works the fastest, or the one that heels the closest, should be on the outside, since he will have to hurry on the turns. The other dog will work the inside position next to you. The first exercise is Heeling on Leash with the Slow, Fast, Halt, Normal, About Turn, Left Turn, and Right Turn commands given at different intervals. The Figure 8 is employed, but the stewards will stand farther apart since two dogs will require more room to turn.

During the Stand for Examination exercise the judge will examine each dog individually by touching his head, back, and croup. This is done off leash.

Heeling off Leash should be done with the same precision as the Heeling on Leash.

The Recall exercise is next, and the dogs are expected to come in at a trot and Sit straight in front of the handler. Upon command they should go to Heel smartly.

The Long Sit for one minute, and the Long Down for three minutes will be executed with the Braces lined up together in a row on one side

Heeling on Leash. A beautiful brace. Leash should be attached to collar of the dog nearest to the handler.

The Stay signal and verbal command as the dogs walk into a perfect stance.

of the ring. At the judge's command the handlers will leave their dogs, cross the ring, turn, and face them, and stand there for the allotted time. When the judge orders the handlers to "Return to your dogs," they will do so.

The Brace that works with the most precision stands the best chance of winning. It is desirable that the dogs work as if they were one, keeping in step at all times while heeling, making turns, and sitting.

Brace work is very interesting and a great deal of fun. If you have trained two dogs that work equally well, you have good material for a Brace. Each dog should understand the Novice work perfectly before you try the Brace work. They should work at about the same speed, and should sit quietly. Their response to commands should be identical. This type of Obedience work is not worth watching unless it is nearly perfect. Precision and teamwork must be in evidence.

I have used the name "Boys," for Brace work commands since my first Brace competition in the spring of 1952. Since they were used to being called "good boys," they readily understood the name. Of course you may choose any name you wish, but it should have character.

Perfectly straight sits in front after a recall.

Heeling on Leash. Use just one leash, and clip it to the collar of the dog nearest to you. Practice the regular Novice Heeling, and on your turns call the name of the dog that lags, and tell him to Heel. If one dog forges ahead, reach down and jerk him back by using the tandem chain. Do not jerk the good dog—praise him. If both dogs are perfectly trained, your only problem will be to keep them in step, and see that they sit together. If one sits more slowly than the other, tap him for a faster sit. Praise them at every opportunity so that they will think it is fun, and enjoy working together.

Figure 8. You will have to watch the outside dog on the Figure 8 and make him hurry around the outside turn. When working the inside turn, caution the dogs with the word, "Easy." Your posts will have to be slightly farther apart than in the Novice Class.

Stand for Examination. You may pose the dogs singly or walk them into the pose. It looks smooth and impressive to walk both dogs into a pose and stand them with a hand signal. It is a sign of expert handling. If the dogs are Heeling with precision, they will stop in step with each other. Practice this until you have it down perfectly.

Heeling off Leash. The dogs are still attached with the tandem chain, or not, as you wish. I prefer to use it. This exercise is not very difficult for trained dogs. You must watch carefully to see that every change of pace, every turn, and every Sit is performed with perfect precision. Too often in Brace work you will see a handler doing a fast pantomime instead of really running. If you practice, you can teach your dogs to do the fast pace, with as much precision as the normal pace.

Be careful that your dogs do not weave in and out as they are Heeling. They should not be wide one minute and crowd you the next. Practice to attain precision, and be quick to correct the dog that is making the mistake. Be equally fast with a word of praise when it is earned.

The Recall Exercise. You may remove the tandem chain in this exercise if you wish. When working off leash you must either keep the tandem chain on for all the exercises off leash, or leave it off. When you call your dogs say, "Boys, come," using the name first. If one lags behind, urge him to come in faster. As they come in, be sure that they sit directly in front of you. Practice the finish that they know, and repeat it until they can do it smoothly together. One dog will learn to wait for the other, and they will become adjusted to working shoulder to shoulder.

The Long Sit and the Long Down. These exercises are exactly the same as in the Novice Class except that the dogs are close together. They may or may not be connected with the tandem chain depending upon your choice in the Heel Free exercise.

If you are lucky enough to own two dogs, you will find this training most helpful. If you can handle both dogs at the same time, it will be no problem to take them places together. By teaching them the Brace work you will gain even more control over them, and they will be better behaved. The training will teach them to get along well together, to give a thought to each other, and to learn the technique of keeping in step.

It is very heart-warming to handle a Brace of dogs that has been precision trained. The pleasure you get from watching them respond is worth all the work you put into it.

21

Graduate Novice

The Graduate Novice Class is a nonregular class and is open to any dog or bitch that has not gained a leg toward the CDX title. This class is not provided at every Obedience Trial. It is generally included at Obedience Specialty Shows sponsored by Training Clubs. No credit is given toward any Obedience title.

In the Graduate Novice Class the Novice routine is used, except that the Figure 8 will be performed off leash, the Drop on Recall will be substituted for the straight Recall, and the Long Sit and the Long Down exercises will be as conducted in the Open Class work.

If your dog has already competed in the Novice Class you should have no problem. Heeling on Leash, Stand for Examination, and Heeling off Leash, including the Figure 8 exercise, should be simple for your dog. The Drop on Recall should be practiced a week before the show, but do not repeat this so often that it slows down your dog's Recall. The Long Sit and Long Down exercises should be practiced about three weeks prior to the show to get your dog used to seeing you disappear out of sight. These exercises should be practiced in different locations during this period.

This is just a fun class, and if you enjoy showing your dog in Obedience Trials this will appeal to you.

22

Versatility Class

The Versatility Class is a nonregular class and it is generally found at Obedience Trials given by Training Clubs. Dogs are permitted to enter this class irrespective of the number of training titles they hold.

The handler must bring his dumbbell, Scent Discrimination articles, and Directed Retrieve gloves into the ring with him. The High Jump, Bar Jump, and Broad Jump will be set up in the ring.

The handler will select a piece of paper from the judge that will tell him what exercises his dog will perform. These exercises are taken from the Novice, Open, and Utility exercises, and there are different combinations for the different handlers. It is a matter of luck whether you choose a slip that contains the most difficult exercises or the easiest ones. If your dog knows the individual exercises from all three classes you will have no problem. Since everyone has different exercises it doesn't prove anything.

It is not a popular class, as most handlers find it quite boring. However, some Training Clubs offer nice trophies that might be worth winning, so if you enjoy show work you might want to try this.

23

The Working Class

There are many, many people who have won Utility titles for their dogs who would like to continue from there and teach their dogs something new.

I am one of those people who enjoy training and I find it fun to teach my dogs different things that make them more interesting and better companions. I am introducing a set of exercises in this chapter that is not beyond the reach of an intelligent Utility dog. Not only will you have fun teaching these exercises, but you will find that they will develop your dog's mind.

I have devised these exercises exclusively for Obedience enthusiasts. They are new and exciting and a challenge to every handler and every dog. All the dogs I have trained love this new work. Spectators find every exercise fascinating to watch. Your dog needs just his nylon or chain choke collar and a leash. You can train your dog successfully by using this method, a little patience, and a great deal of praise. It is not uncommon in the other fields of dog training for trainers to use shock collars, spike collars, and shock sticks. Such equipment will be completely unnecessary in teaching your dog these Obedience exercises.

The new jumps can be homemade, or you can have them made to order for about $70. The jumps that I have designed are simple in principle and safe to use. Your dog will not be required to clear more than a three-foot-high jump so will not acquire the habit of climbing these jumps. For instance, if you have a German Shepherd whom you want to continue showing in both Open B and Utility but would love to try this new class, rest assured that this work will improve the other. The High Jump, Bar Jump, and Window Jump are three feet high and will have to be cleared. The Barrier is entirely different and must be climbed, so your dog will learn to differentiate between them. I designed the Barrier so that Breed Champions could compete without the danger of injuring themselves. The platform on the back will break their jump to the ground and make it reasonably safe. The largest dogs will be jumping down from a height of four feet, which is not difficult for a physically sound dog. The Long Jump is designed to improve a dog's jumping ability. The individual hurdles will fall over if a dog does not clear them and this is a good reminder to him to pick his feet up.

These new exercises are listed below.

1. Search Exercise—40 Points. A practical exercise that will teach your dog to recover your lost articles, and that is a useful form of Scent Discrimination.
2. Vocabulary Exercise—40 Points. If your dog understands everything you say, this will be a cinch. If not, this will teach him to listen to you.
3. Control Exercise—40 Points. Devised to give you even better control of your dog—combining new and old with the "new look."
4. The Long Jump—40 Points. A Long Jump that is a challenge to every handler and every dog.
5. The Agility Exercise—40 Points. A series of hurdles that will develop your dog's agility.

Not every dog will be able to do these exercises. Only the most intelligent and the most agile will succeed. Not every dog could earn a Tracking title and fewer still could earn an Advanced Tracking title (if there was one), for many would be handicapped either mentally or physically. But to those who meet the mental and physical requirements here is a new challenge. And to you handlers who are looking for new fields to conquer I say, "Try it."

The Search Exercise

The handler will stand with his dog in the Heel Position, and on order from the judge will execute such portions of the Heel Free exercise as the judge may direct. Upon order from the judge the handler will surreptitiously drop a small key case that is dark brown in color and about two by three inches in size. The judge will have the handler and his dog continue heeling until they are at the opposite end of the ring and will give them an order to "Halt." While the handler and his dog have their backs turned the judge will now place his own key case about two feet from that the handler dropped. The judge's case will be the same size and color. The judge will then direct the handler to "About Turn and halt." On order from the judge to "Send your dog," the handler will give his dog the command or signal to "Seek Back." If the handler elects to use a signal it will be with one hand and arm only; body signals will be penalized. The handler must remain in the same spot and may not turn toward the key case.

The dog may check the judge's case by sniffing it but will be marked Failed if he picks it up. He should trot out briskly, find his handler's key case, and return at a brisk trot. He should return the case to his handler without mouthing or playing with it, and should relinquish it immediately without any command. His Sit in front should be perfectly straight, and his Finish should be as precise.

The first step in teaching this exercise is to have all of your jumps set up in the practice area. The High Jump, Bar Jump, Window Jump, and

Joll finds a key case and sniffs it to be sure it belongs to his handler.

Barrier should be placed in that order eighteen feet apart in readiness for your dog to jump them in succession. They will be erected parallel to the left side of the ring fifteen feet in from the rope. The Long Jump will be placed parallel to the right side of the ring and fifteen feet in from the rope.

Have your dog Sit at Heel, offer him the key case, saying, "Get it." When he takes it tell him, "Hold it," and after a few seconds take it from him. If your dog does not take the case when you command him to do so, open his mouth and put the case in it. Tell him, "Hold it," and praise him. He will probably take it the next time you ask him. Now throw the case on the ground in front of you, and tell your dog to "Get it, Seek Back." Discourage him from mouthing or playing with it when he gets it by saying, "No, hold it."

Next have your dog Heel in a straight line out beyond the jumps, and as you turn around drop the case, allowing the dog to see you do so. Walk back to your original position, turn around, and be sure your dog Sits. Then command your dog to "Get it, Seek Back." When he reaches for the case say, "Good, come." Do not let him play with the case. Clap your hands, and praise him to make him return to you quickly. Have him Sit straight in front of you and hold the case, without mouthing it, for a few seconds. Take the case away from him and praise him. Have him go to Heel and praise him if he Sits straight. Repeat this procedure several times. Now drop the "Get it," and just say, "Seek Back."

Now you can drop the case surreptitiously, in various places, to accustom him to search for it. Drop it behind the jumps occasionally so that he will get used to looking for it anywhere. Keep him searching for the case. If he stops because he cannot find it, run out immediately and encourage him to keep working. Show him the case, if necessary, and repeat the exercise until he learns to keep searching for it until he finds it. It is only a matter of repetition and he will learn if you are patient.

When a dog is learning this exercise he may become discouraged if he doesn't see the case after glancing around once or twice, and he may then lie down. When this happens run out to him and take him by the collar for a few steps as you take him over to the case. If you let him go out in front of you he will see the case and think that he found it himself, so praise him. Then run back, telling him to "Come," and praise him if he responds. If he drops the case say, "No, get it," and when he picks it up again caution him to "Hold it."

As soon as you feel your dog understands this exercise it is time to drop a strange key case near yours. Since the strange key case must carry a stranger's scent try this. Buy a key case similar to your own, give it to a friend, and ask him to keep it in his pocket for a week and occasionally rub it between his hands. At the end of that time have him place the case in a glass jar that has a cover you can screw down (like a peanut butter jar). Now you can use the case whenever you like, and it will carry a foreign scent. Just be careful you don't touch it yourself. You can always pick it up with the jar cover. Keep the strange case in an airtight glass jar when you are not using it. If both of these cases are identical in size and color be sure to put your initial on the one you want your dog to retrieve.

At first, work the dog near you so that you can correct him immediately if he tries to pick up the strange case. Since he is familiar with Scent Discrimination he will catch on very quickly. The dog that will fail this exercise is the one that has searched diligently for the case, spots one of them, and picks it up quickly without checking. With a case this small, and an area this large, plus the Scent Discrimination factor, a dog will have to be working and thinking in order to do the exercise correctly. It is not easy, for there are many hiding places. The dog will be using his eyes and his nose to aid him in his search.

The important thing is to keep your dog working fast by encouraging him, and as he improves, keep making it harder to find the case. If you make a game of it he will be eager to learn.

Vocabulary Exercise

How many times have you heard people say, "My dog understands every word I say to him." When you try this exercise the first time you will be in for a surprise. Your dog will be more interested in retrieving the first thing he comes to more than he will be in obeying your specific command. No matter how familiar he is with these articles, he will likely draw a blank when he is called upon to get one of them.

The articles you will need for this exercise are a dumbbell, a leather leash, a leather glove, and a basket with a rigid handle that is the correct size for your dog, not too small or too large.

You will be standing with your dog at Heel Position while the judge places your four articles on the ground eight inches apart and twenty feet in front of you. The judge will tell you to send your dog. Your dog will make four separate retrieves in this order: the basket, the dumbbell, the glove, and the leash. You will give your dog the verbal command for each article by naming the article, then ordering him to get it. It will be like this, "Basket, get the basket." Your tone of voice must be moderate as any loud tones will be penalized. Your dog should trot out briskly, choose the correct article, return it to you at a brisk pace, and Sit straight in front of you without mouthing or playing with it. When the judge orders you to "Finish" your dog should do so in the proper manner. Then your dog must retrieve the remaining three articles in the aforementioned order.

To train your dog to designate between these articles, the first step is to start with just two articles. For instance, if you use the glove and the basket at first, keep working on these until he will retrieve either one without any difficulty. When he reaches this point, take one of the articles, such as the basket, which he can now retrieve by name, and add a new one, such as the leash, and work on these two. He will understand that if you do not say, "Basket," you must want him to retrieve the other object. When he has this down, try the leash with the dumbbell. Never work with more than two articles at the same time until he is proficient at retrieving any one of the four articles in this set of two.

Now you may work with any three articles trying different combinations, but always including the four articles at one time or another. If he makes a mistake and selects the wrong article such as a glove, when he has been sent for a leash, say, "No, get the leash," and put your hand on the leash. Praise him immediately when he gets the leash.

When your dog has reached the point where he will retrieve a specific object each time you give him the verbal command, and you are practicing with a combination of three articles, you may now add the fourth article.

If you have followed this method of instruction carefully the addition of the fourth article will not make any difference.

Joll correctly selects the basket after his handler has given him the verbal command to do so.

Pull your dog toward you as you give the Down signal and say, "Down, crawl."

Give your dog the Crawl signal as you say, "Crawl."

Control Exercise

The handler will stand with his dog in the Heel Position, and upon order from the judge to "Start," the handler will give his dog the following commands, which the dog will execute at a smart pace. "Go—Sit—Come—Down—Crawl—Stand—Come—Heel." The handler may give his dog verbal commands or signals each time but not a combination of both. The dog that misses one command or signal fails the whole exercise. The dog must Go out about sixty feet, Crawl at least ten feet, Sit or Down quickly, and Sit straight in front of the handler and at Heel Position.

Your dog already knows some of these commands and signals so we will work on the new ones and then combine all of them.

To teach your dog to Crawl have him on leash and give him the Down signal. Call him to you and pull a little on the leash as you hold the Down signal, and control him by saying, "Down, crawl." Make him Crawl about ten feet, then have him Stand as you praise and pet him. When you say Stand to your dog, give him the Stand Signal. Start with your hands down by your sides, then swing your hand up toward your dog, bending your elbow to do so, and finish by swinging your hand out to your right side waist high, showing the dog the palm of your right hand all the while. Do this in a sweeping motion.

As soon as it is feasible combine the Crawl signal with the verbal command Crawl, even though you still have to use the Down command and signal to keep him down. To execute the Crawl signal, hold your right hand down by your side with the back of your hand toward your dog and flick your hand back and forth twice by bending your wrist, then return your hand to its original position.

Be patient but firm, don't let your dog get up and walk one step when you tell him to Crawl. A verbal correction should be all that is necessary to teach him this exercise. Your dog may be taken off leash when you feel you have sufficient control over him to guide him with the verbal command, "Crawl," or the Crawl signal.

Now you can combine the whole exercise in the proper sequence. On command or signal your dog should Go out about sixty feet, Sit promptly, Come toward you half the distance, Down quickly, Crawl about ten feet, and Stand. He should be at least fifteen feet from you when he is standing. Then he should Come to you and Sit straight and Finish by sitting straight at Heel Position. A dog that disobeys one of these commands will fail and a dog that does not stay down while he is crawling will fail.

This is an interesting exercise to teach or watch, and the handler who succeeds in teaching his dog this exercise will gain more control over his dog. You may alternate the verbal commands and signals.

The Long Jump

The Long Jump will be executed the same way as the Open Class Broad Jump except that the jump will be seven feet long for dogs twenty-two inches or over at the withers, six feet long for dogs sixteen through twenty-one inches at the withers, and a five-foot jump for all other dogs. The jump will be three feet wide, two feet high for all dogs over fifteen inches high, and one foot high for all other dogs.

Your dog already knows how to jump the Open Broad Jump and this knowledge will be a help to him when you start to teach him this Long Jump. I designed this jump with the intention of improving a dog's jumping ability and this is exactly what it does. Any dog that masters this type of jump will find it much easier to jump any other type of hurdle or obstacle.

This is a difficult hurdle to jump but it can be mastered if you teach your dog to do it in simple stages. There are three reasons why this hurdle is difficult and why it is a challenge. First, it is a long jump. Second, although it is two feet high (or one foot high depending upon the size of your dog), your dog must jump considerably higher than that in order

Joll clears the Long Jump.

Joll clearing eight feet at a height of three feet three inches. This is a practice jump the author designed to improve his jumping ability.

to clear the full length. Third, it is what I call a blind jump because your dog will be able to see only a quarter of it until he is in the air. This means he must learn to gauge his distance by your position.

The first lesson will be an introduction to this type of jump. Have your dog jump over one hurdle, then two, and then three. Stretch them out until your dog is jumping half of the required length. Run up to the jump with your dog and say, "Hup," as he approaches the jump. Try this several times and praise your dog every time he does it. Build up his confidence at this time, let him think this new jump is easy and great fun. A Utility dog should be able to do this easily off leash but if your dog balks try him on leash. Your dog should be jumping half the required distance off leash before you try the next step.

Now add another hurdle and leave your dog sitting about twenty feet from the jump. Tell him to stay and go stand about two feet beyond the Long Jump. Call your dog by name and when he gets to the most advantageous position for a takeoff say, "Hup." If he clears the jump add another hurdle and space them an equal distance apart so that your dog will now be jumping three quarters of the required jump. Work on this length for two or three lessons.

Now you will try a longer jump and this type of hurdle should be taken

In this practice jump Joll actually cleared thirteen and one half feet at a height of three and one half feet. The handler must stand three feet beyond the jump so that his dog can gauge the distance correctly.

with the dog going at a fast trot or gallop. It is a running jump, and the dog should build up enough momentum in his dash to the jump and his subsequent leap into the air to clear the hurdles. The principle is the same as that employed by an athlete or a pole vaulter taking a fast sprint to clear a jump. You should leave your dog thirty feet back but in a direct line with the jump. For two or three weeks start your dog at three quarters of the required length and work up to the full length each day. Continue this practice until you are quite certain that your dog can clear the full length on his first attempt. Don't rush your dog into this, but play it safe and give your dog the chance to build up his confidence in his jumping ability. Above all, remember this is a difficult jump that will require considerable practice and patience. Do not practice this jump unless your dog has dry, firm footing for the takeoff and landing. Never practice when there is any danger of your dog slipping. The ideal place to practice is a level stretch of lawn as the grass will cushion your dog's landing.

Have your dog Sit at Heel Position thirty feet from the Long Jump and in a direct line with it. Tell him to "stay" and go stand three feet beyond the hurdle and two feet out from it and face it. Say, "Joll, ready," and give your dog's name. You may give the Hup portion of the command when the dog is near the jump. When your dog is in midair make a right-angle turn. Your dog should come in to you and Sit straight and upon command he should Sit straight at Heel Position.

The Agility Exercise

This exercise will consist of four hurdles that are placed ahead of each other but directly in line, so that by running and jumping the dog will be able to clear all four hurdles in succession. The hurdles will be set up in this order—the High Jump, the Bar Jump, the Window Jump, and the Barrier. The jumps will be placed a distance of eighteen feet apart, and they will be painted a flat white. The width of each jump is four feet, with the exception of the Window Jump, which is twenty-eight inches wide. The inside measurement of the window is twenty by twenty inches.

The height of the High Jump, Bar Jump, and Window Jump will be three feet, and the Barrier will be six feet high for all dogs twenty-two inches or over at the withers. The first three jumps will be set at thirty inches and the Barrier at five feet for all dogs fifteen through twenty-one inches at the withers. For all other dogs the first three jumps will be set at two feet and the Barrier will be four feet high.

Joll jumps through the window hurdle without touching it.

The first two jumps must be jumped clear. The dog must then jump through the window portion of the third jump without touching the hurdle with his feet. The Barrier must be climbed on the dog's first attempt.

The handler will be standing with his dog at Heel, and the judge will instruct the handler to leave his dog. The handler will take a position between the first and last jump, about five feet out from them, and facing them. Upon order from the judge to "Send your dog," the handler may give his dog a verbal command or signal. When the dog has jumped three hurdles, the handler will take a right-angle turn but remain in the same spot. After the dog has jumped all the hurdles, he will Sit straight in front of the handler and then Finish smartly upon command or signal.

Your dog already knows how to jump the High Jump and the Bar Jump, so the first lesson will be to teach him the Window Jump. Stand behind the jump so that you can place your hand on the bottom section of the window when you ask your dog to jump. By placing your hand there he will understand that you want him to jump through the opening. Simply repeat this until your dog jumps smoothly without touching the lower portion of the window with his feet.

When he has accomplished this, stand off to the side, give him the command, "Hup," and praise him when he jumps. Don't let him go around

this jump at any time; be fast with your corrections if he doesn't jump or if he tries to climb it.

As soon as you think he understands this hurdle and is jumping smoothly, combine the first three hurdles. Practice on just these three hurdles until your dog will take all three jumps on one command. At first you will have to give several commands and signals to accomplish this, but your dog will soon be doing it on his own.

The next step is to teach your dog to climb the Barrier. This can best be done in two stages. Set your jump up apart from the other hurdles and adjust the side brackets so that the jump is more slanted and about two feet lower than normal. Have your dog on leash and run up to the jump with him as you say, "Hup, climb." When you encourage your dog with your voice and lift him a little with the leash he will realize that he is expected to climb the Barrier. Quickly move over in back of the jump so that you can teach him to step onto the platform before he jumps to the ground. This will have to be repeated a few times before he is ready for the next step.

When you have reached the final stage, set the jump to its full height, which is just five degrees short of being vertical, and make certain that it is strong and steady. Your dog realizes at this point that he must climb

Joll jumping through the Window Jump after clearing the other two hurdles.

Joll learning to climb the six-foot barrier with the jump in the Number Three Position. He is on leash and the author is standing by ready to assist him if necessary.

the Barrier, so run him up to the jump as you say, "Climb." If he balks, try it again, encouraging him with your voice. Most dogs will attempt the high Barrier once they have learned to do it at a lower level. For stubborn dogs you may have to keep lowering the Barrier until they get up enough courage to try it. A few dogs will stop at the jump and refuse to try. If this happens, put your dog on leash and throw the leash over the top of the Barrier. As you pull your dog up another person should be giving him a boost by pushing him up (not lifting him) so that he can get the idea of scrambling up himself. It will take only one or two such experiences and he will understand what to do. If you persevere, your dog will climb it quite swiftly. The more you praise him the more eager he will be to climb.

Once your dog has acquired the knack of climbing this jump barrier you may combine all four jumps. At first when you give the command, "Hup," run alongside the hurdles as he is jumping and encourage him to take each one. Be sure to praise him after each jump. Eventually you will

Above: Joll scales the barrier with the jump in the Number Two Position. *Below:* Joll jumps to the platform and then to the ground.

Now that he has learned to jump all four hurdles, they are combined. The barrier is in the Number One, or Vertical Position. On one command or signal Joll takes the four hurdles in succession, sits straight in front of the author, then goes to Heel upon command. Everyone seems to enjoy this exercise more than any other.

be able to stand alongside the jumps, and when you call, "Hup," he will jump all four hurdles.

If you want to set up a ring for these exercises you will need a level piece of ground ninety by sixty feet. This new class is best suited for outdoor dog shows run by specialty clubs.

When you have taught your dog these exercises you will get a great deal of satisfaction and pleasure watching him do them. The people who have watched my dogs do this work claim that it is the most interesting and enjoyable Obedience work they have ever seen. It is certainly exciting and thrilling to watch, often amusing as well as fascinating, but above all else it unquestionably displays your dog's intelligence.

You might like to think of it as getting your dog's master's degree. I daresay the number of dogs capable of earning such a degree would be equivalent to the number of students earning a similar degree.

24

Competing in Shows

I list a few suggestions which may be helpful to you in preparing for show competition.

When your dog works perfectly for you at home and in several other locations, he is ready for show competition. If you have tried him out at a Sanction Match you know how he will react to show conditions. Your dog, at this time, should work very well for you with just a few words of praise and some gentle patting between exercises. The time will never arrive for you to stop praising your dog, but occasionally you should try working him without this, because this is what you will have to do at a show.

Feed your dog early in the morning on the day of the show so that he will not have his mind on dinner. Some shows last all day, and the dog that normally eats in the afternoon will become impatient to be fed.

Groom your dog carefully before leaving for the show so that his appearance will be a credit to you. Spray an insecticide all over his coat to discourage insects from bothering him. Hold your hand over his eyes and face to avoid the chance of getting any spray there. A dog that has been sprayed in this way is less likely to pick up fleas from another dog.

Carry an extra leash and collar, a bench chain, and a water dish with you. Provide your dog with fresh water several times a day; they get very thirsty at dog shows. Often a change of water will have an adverse effect upon a dog, so it is wise to carry a gallon jug of water from home. Take a folding chair for yourself.

Be certain that your dog is protected against distemper and hepatitis by having your doctor give him a booster inoculation each year.

Stay with your dog at the show to keep him contented. If you have trained him by my methods he will not be tired with your company, but will be eager to please you.

Exercise your dog about twenty minutes before you are scheduled to go into the ring so that he may relieve himself.

When it is time for your Class to be judged, report to your ring steward and obtain your armband, and ascertain the approximate time you will be judged. Later, when you have been judged, ask the steward when they are going to do the Long Sit and Down exercises. Then be at the ringside at the proper time so that the steward will not have to go looking for you. It is a source of annoyance to everyone concerned, when the judging of the Long Sit and Long Down exercises are delayed because one inconsiderate handler has disappeared. If you are showing your dog in the Conformation Classes, be sure to let the steward know where you will be. As your turn approaches, watch the judging procedure so that you will be familiar with the judge's routine.

While the person ahead of you is handling his dog in the ring, give your dog a warm-up, Heeling him, so that he will be alert.

At practically all Obedience Trials there is a long waiting period before it will be your turn to take your dog into the ring. While you are waiting, your dog will probably lie down and go to sleep. Don't expect him to do his best if you wake him up and march him right into the ring. It takes a dog a few minutes to become fully awake and alert, just as a human being requires a certain amount of time after he wakes up to become fully conscious.

Some Obedience people feel that this warm-up is unnecessary, but these people do not compete in shows with their dogs. They think that a dog should be obedient at all times. This is true, but in Obedience Trials today obedience alone is not enough to win. The dog must be fully alert and awake in order to work with precision, and this can only be gained by a short warm-up period.

Dogs are creatures of varying moods, and different show conditions can affect them. I like to put my dogs through a short routine, not for the sake of practicing, but to understand the dog's mood on that particular day and so be prepared to handle him wisely. A slight variation in your method of handling, in compliance with your dog's mood, is often the difference between winning or losing. This is one of the finer points to acquire in training, and one that will come to you in time if you make it a habit to study your dog's reactions to places, weather, other animals, and so forth. Do not let your thoughts dwell on winning, when you should be concentrating upon your dog and your handling.

Whether you win or lose, try to rectify your errors at home, and resolve to do better next time. Remember that it is by trial and error that you will become an expert handler; it will not come to you overnight. You might just as well relax and have fun getting there.

25

Tracking

If you enjoy working outside with your dog, and love to take long walks in all kinds of weather, you will enjoy Tracking. It is fascinating to watch a trained dog follow a track that is invisible to your eyes, making turns after checking each direction, and gaily discovering the article at the end of the trail. It is exciting and invigorating to pursue a dog working swiftly and surely at the end of a forty-foot tracking leash, as you try to keep your footing up hills, down hills, through puddles and briar patches. But it is worth every breathless moment when your dog triumphantly snatches the object of the search from its hidden place and proudly carries it back to your outstretched arms. Until you have experienced the exultation of that precious moment you cannot imagine the enchantment that is Tracking.

The Tracking title, TD, is bestowed upon your dog by the American Kennel Club when he has successfully passed a Tracking Test.

A Tracking Test is conducted by an accredited Obedience Training Club, and there are very few tests in one area in the course of a year. Each month the Tracking Tests are listed in the leading dog publications. Not many handlers train their dogs to Track because it is time-consuming work and there are very few qualified trainers who can help them.

Several large fields are required for a Tracking Test. Each contestant will work a track that is no less than 440 yards or more than 500 yards long. It is easy to see why Tracking Tests are not held at dog shows. The scent left by the tracklayer should be not less than half an hour old or more than two hours old. The length of the leash used in tracking must be 20 to 40 feet, and the dog must work at this length with no help from the handler.

Two judges will judge the Tracking Test and keep duplicate charts of each track showing the length in yards of each leg, major landmarks, and boundaries. The course the dog pursues is to be marked on the charts and both judges will forward a signed copy to the American Kennel Club with a notation "Passed" or "Failed" on each copy.

If the dog is not tracking and taking the turns correctly, it will not be marked "Passed," even though it may come upon the article while it is wandering around. The object of the test is for the dog to follow the tracklayer's scent as closely as weather conditions permit.

I believe it is best to start a dog tracking after he has learned to retrieve, but it isn't absolutely necessary. Even if a dog has had no obedience training at all, he should be able to comprehend the tracking lessons and go on to earn his tracking title. Tracking may be started during the sixth month of training, which should give you sufficient time to earn your Tracking degree within the year. It will take considerable time and practice to accomplish this. Check the dates of the Tracking Test scheduled in your area, so that you may plan to have your dog ready. You must plan several months ahead in order to be ready. To enter a Tracking Test, your entry must be accompanied by a certificate signed by a qualified Tracking judge, stating that the dog is considered ready for such a test. The AKC can give you the names of the Tracking judges in your area. The judge will want to see your dog work an actual Track to determine if he is ready for a test.

Tracking is not the great mystery that many people claim it to be. The dog is simply following a scent that has been left by someone walking over the ground. Most of this scent clings to the ground, but some of it is wafted away on the wind and adheres to anything in its path. The scent is carried on air currents, and if you study these you will have a good idea how the scent is carried along. You don't have to be a meteorologist or have any special scientific knowledge in order to teach a dog to track. All it requires is a little common sense.

When I go walking in the woods after a rainstorm the scent all around me is very strong and pungent, which is a sharp contrast to the light fragrance I enjoy on a sunny day. My common sense tells me when I am Tracking that the scent is stronger on wet grass, low boggy areas, shady spots, sheltered valleys, or the leeward side of the hills. These, then, will be the easiest places for the dog to pick up the scent.

If you have ever noticed how the air currents carry along the smoke from the rubbish you are burning it will give you an idea what it could do with scent. When the wind changes capriciously the smoke is tossed around helplessly. It is no wonder a dog will work off the track on a windy day, and it is a matter of common sense to train the dog to work as close to the actual track as you can determine. It is wiser to keep bringing him back on it by guiding him with the leash than to let him follow the scent which is being scattered by the wind. If you do this the first month or so you will get him in the habit of sticking close to the track.

The training method that I used in 1952 to earn my first two Tracking titles is basically the same one I use today. By observing and studying my dogs I have concluded that this method is a sound one. Any opinions I have on tracking have been formed as a result of watching my dogs; I'm sure if anyone were to observe his own dog he would reach the same conclusions.

It is perfectly natural for a dog to use his nose in the same manner in which humans use their eyes. A person is never satisfied to have something described to him; he must see for himself. A dog is never satisfied to look at something; he wants to sniff it. A dog sees with his nose. Dogs do not accept what they see; they believe what they smell. They use their noses throughout their lives to help them make decisions. A dog will catalogue a person's scent in his mind for years and eventually when he meets this old friend or foe he will recognize him by scent alone.

Dogs differentiate between members of a family by scent alone. Even when one tries to fool a dog by having two members of a family exchange clothes the dog finds it a very elementary test to distinguish between them. Everyone has a different scent just as everyone has a different set of fingerprints.

When following a trail a dog is following a total scent. In other words, the scent of crushed vegetation and the tracklayer's clothing, personal articles, body odor, hair, and breath are mingling together. The dog will follow this scent in two ways: by finding it on the ground and by sniffing it in the air.

With a no-wind condition scent will remain in the air for hours at a time. I have noticed this many times and the following incident is just one example. One morning when my dog and I were visiting my mother I called a friend and asked him to stop by my home at noontime and pick up some papers I needed. That evening when I returned and opened the door my dog dashed through the house barking angrily. It gave me a start at first until I realized he had picked up the scent of my friend who had stopped in earlier. The person was a stranger to the dog and his scent was that of an intruder. No one had been in the house all day so the scent remained undisturbed.

I believe that scent flies off a person whether he is sitting or walking. I have seen a dog go up to a chair where a friend of his was sitting an hour earlier and start wagging his tail. He hadn't known that his friend was visiting us until he came in the house later and smelled the chair.

When a person is walking scent particles fly out from him in all directions. The heaviest of these particles fall close to him and those that are of medium weight fly out from him and settle to the ground a little farther away. The lightweight scent particles are airborne for different lengths of time depending upon the weather conditions at the time. It is my opinion that the scent that a dog picks up on the ground is a combination of the total scent that I mentioned earlier and not just a shoe or foot odor scent. It has never seemed to make any difference to a good tracking dog what kind of footwear, if any, the tracklayer wore. I found a dog would follow a scent even if the tracklayer wore plastic bags over his shoes. The dog appeared to be following the total scent which was present both on the ground and in the air.

The scent that is in the air is the same as that on the ground. To believe this one must realize that a moving body is enveloped by an air current and as one strides along the body, arms, and legs create a certain amount of turbulence. I believe that the body creates small parallel shoulder vortices that are agitated by the arms swinging back and forth. The amount of turbulence caused by every stride forces the scent particles that are flying out from the body, and up from the ground, to be tumbled around in the air. The scent is therefore scattered along a track that could be twenty or more feet wide. Wind currents play a part here in depositing the scent particles on anything in their path. The scent that lasts the longest is the one that falls to the ground or adheres to some stationary object. The lightweight scent particles never reach the ground but remain airborne until they fade away or are dispersed by wind currents or weather conditions. It is my opinion that different kinds of vegetation absorb the heavy scent particles more than others. Dogs very often will take more time to sniff certain weeds as if the scent is stronger on them than others.

The older the track the harder it is for the dog to find it. This might be for several reasons. Heavy rain will wash out a track but a light drizzle, humidity, or early morning fog will preserve it. Direct sunlight seems to dry up the scent just as an exposed drop of perfume will fade away quickly in the sun. A strong wind seems to eradicate the air scent in a short time.

Years ago I used to do all the preliminary Tracking work myself. This included laying all the different kinds of tracks until I had reached the point where the tracks had been laid (aged) twenty minutes. Then I would have a stranger lay the tracks for me. You can do it yourself if you have no one around to help you, but it will take a few weeks longer.

Point to the scuff mark, or the starting point, but do not put your hand ahead of your dog's nose where he would get your scent.

The first problem is to get the dog to start using his nose and keep it on the trail. If you have laid your own track there is not much incentive except his natural desire to please you and the fact that you are continually urging him on, saying, "Track," and pointing to the trail. By pointing to the trail and saying, "See, track," the dog will sniff where you are pointing and go on farther.

One way to get the dog to start using his nose faster is to let him find a reward in the glove at the end of the track. Leave a piece of cooked liver in the glove when you drop it at the end of the track; then, when he finds the glove and brings it to you, praise him excitedly and say, "See, see," and give him the liver. He will catch on very quickly and will be more than anxious to find the glove. Do not let him take the liver from the glove himself; make him bring the glove to you and then hand him the liver. This method works fine if you are laying your own tracks. When your dog has had enough experience and is using his nose at the beginning of the track stop giving him food. He will be interested enough to work now and will not need food as an incentive. This just gets him off to a fast start.

The best way to teach a dog Tracking at the very beginning is to have someone he loves lay the track, leave his glove, and hide either on the ground or behind some object about twenty feet beyond the end of the track. The dog will be so anxious to find his friend that he will start working naturally with little urging.

Find a good field where the grass is from eight to twelve inches high and, if it is possible, lay the early tracks out in the open away from natural boundaries. Try to practice in the early morning or evening when it is less windy. Take your dog to the field on the leash and do not put his harness on him until you get there so that he will associate the harness with Tracking. Use a twenty-foot leash and clip it to the harness. Let your dog sit and watch the tracklayer lay the track and disappear out of sight. Before he starts he should pet your dog and tell him to be a good boy, or say something he understands. At the start of the track he should plant a stake in the ground and scuff his feet for the first twenty feet and then plant another stake. He should then walk in a straight line about two hundred feet, plant another stake, continue on another ten feet, and then take a slight turn to the right, like the hands of a clock pointing to five past six. He should go straight for fifty feet, drop the glove, continue straight on for twenty feet to a hiding place and just lie and wait for you.

When he is laying the first 200 feet of track he should stop occasionally to wave to your dog and say something to arouse the dog's interest, such as, "Good-bye, Hussan," using your dog's name. Your dog would be sure he was missing something and want to follow him.

In order for the tracklayer to walk a perfectly straight track he should keep his eye on some tree or object on the horizon and walk toward it. If he looks at the ground his track will weave all over the place. The tracklayer's job is important—try to impress this upon him.

After waiting five minutes, take your dog up to the first stake, make him lie down with his nose close to the scuffed earth. Point to the spot without putting your hand in front of the dog's nose where he would get your scent, and say excitedly, "See, track." As soon as the dog takes a good sniff let him start Tracking. Keep him about ten feet in front of you and encourage him to go out and pull you. If it is necessary, keep urging him to go track. When he reaches the glove insist that he pick it up and bring it to you and then send him on again to find his friend. If he is terribly excited when he reaches the glove, let him pick it up and carry it on to his friend, and at this point you should both make a tremendous fuss over him.

By working on tracks of this kind with either a left or right turn for a few days, the dog will think it is great fun. It is not necessary to give your dog food if you use this method, for he has all the incentive he needs —he is finding someone he loves, and this is what he wants to do.

Now try a track with a slightly sharper turn, say, at ten past six. Many

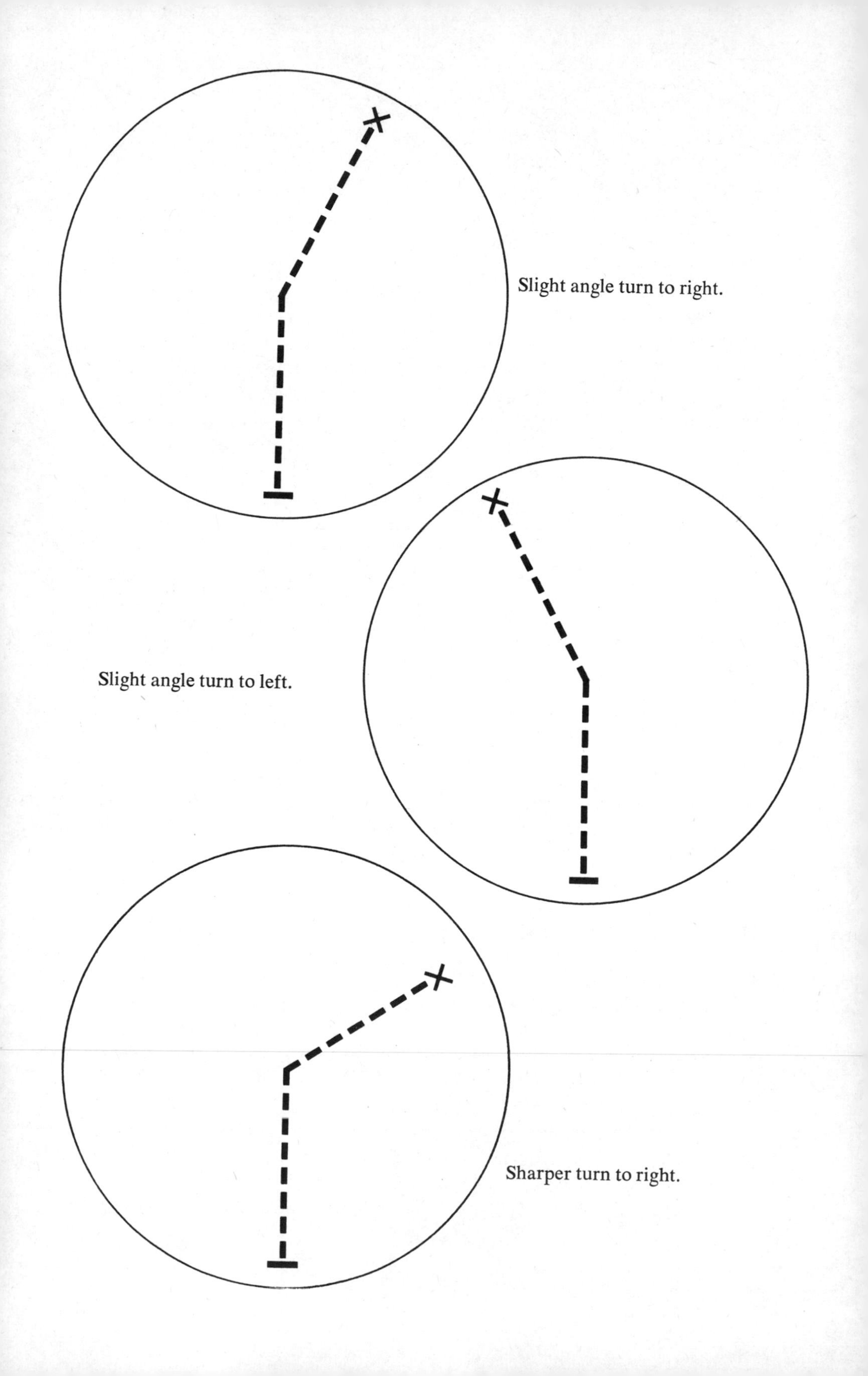
Slight angle turn to right.
Slight angle turn to left.
Sharper turn to right.

dogs zigzag back and forth across a track when they are following a scent. Repeat this type of track several times until your dog does it well without your help.

Next day try the same track with a left turn. This would be like the hands of a clock pointing to ten minutes to six.

Practice tracks of this type with either right or left turns, and age them for different periods. Start with five-minute tracks and go on to ten- and fifteen-minute tracks as your dog improves.

Now you should be able to try your first right-angle turn which on the clock would be at a quarter past six. Encourage your dog to work at the end of the leash. When he approaches the corner, be prepared to give him enough leash so that he can overrun the turn, come back, circle around until he finds the track, and continue on. Do not let him pass you and retrace his steps back to the starting point. If you stand about twenty feet from the turn, your dog should be able to circle and find the continuation of the track. Later, when you are following a blind trail, you will recognize a turn by the individual manner in which your dog searches for it. Dogs differ a great deal in this respect. Study yours so that you can eventually recognize a turn by the signal that he gives you. He may whine, lift his head, drop his tail, circle, or give you some other indication of a change in direction. Praise him when he takes the turn correctly.

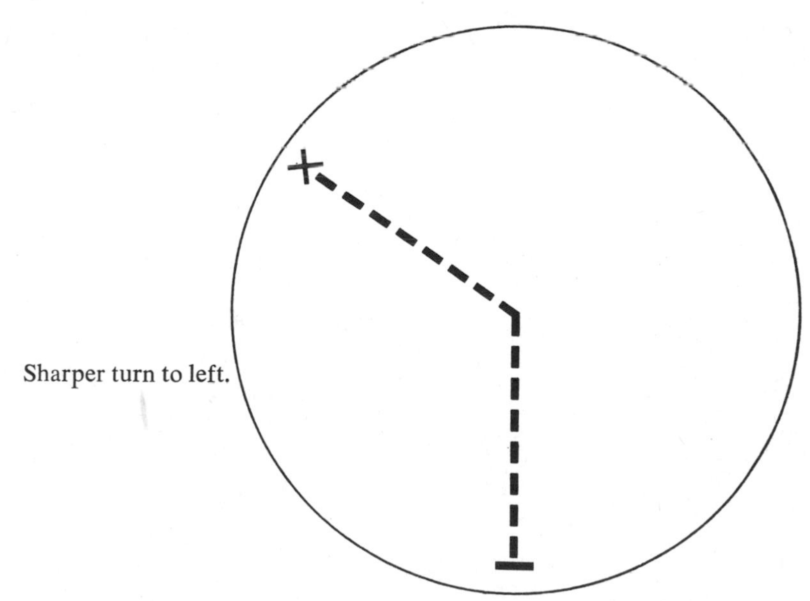
Sharper turn to left.

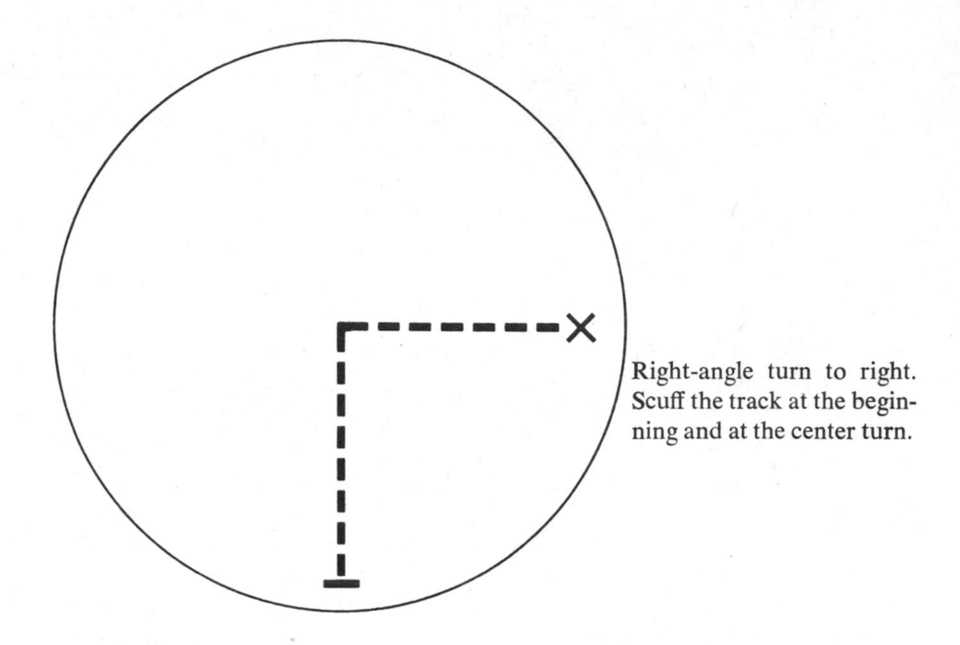

Right-angle turn to right. Scuff the track at the beginning and at the center turn.

Do not always expect him to make a turn at the exact point of the right angle. Most dogs overrun the turn about twenty feet before they realize they are no longer on the track. Then they return to the turn and start checking before striking out again on the right track. If the wind is blowing toward you, your dog will probably pick up the turn much sooner than you expect, and will then work parallel to the actual track. When he is opposite the tracklayer's wallet or glove, he will pick up the scent in the air and make a left turn toward it. If you have a cross wind, the dog will work alongside the actual track, and the distance will vary according to the wind direction, wind velocity, and the terrain. If he turns with his tail to the wind he will stay close to the track.

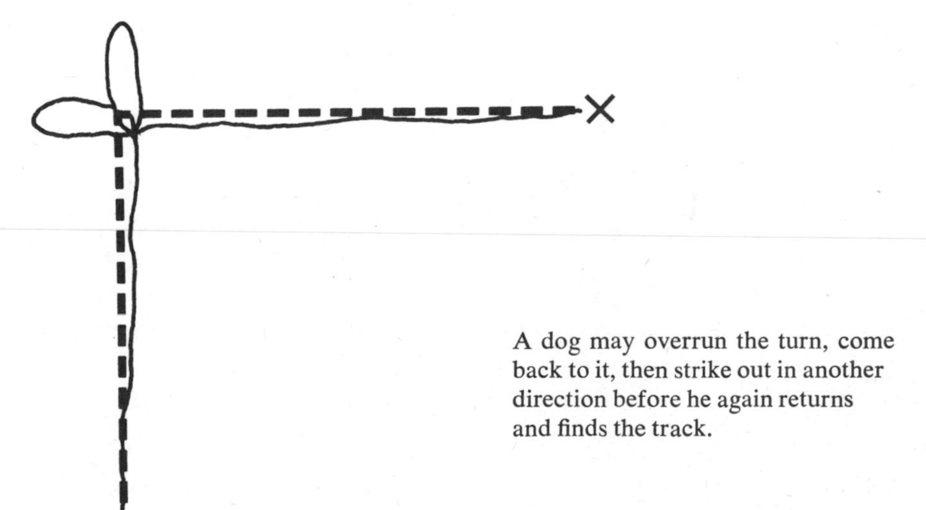

A dog may overrun the turn, come back to it, then strike out in another direction before he again returns and finds the track.

The exception to this is the perfect tracking dog that keeps his nose down on the track every inch of the way. Wind makes no difference to this dog, for he is working close to the ground with his nose in the grass. I have seen dogs like this take right-angle turns without any hesitation whatever. The work was so flawless that they did not have to stop at any point to double-check. Dogs can be taught to work close by starting on closely cropped grass and by working on a ten-foot lead. When the dog has become accustomed to keeping his nose to the ground you can lay tracks in fields where the grass is longer. You can gradually play out your tracking leash until you are thirty feet back. The important thing is to wait until the dog is doing an excellent track on the ten foot lead. This type of training takes longer and requires an experienced handler.

When you feel that your dog has mastered the right angle turn follow the same procedure to teach him the left-angle turn. Picture a clock again; the track will look like a quarter to six. Spend a week or more on this until you are certain your dog understands. If you get this down perfectly before you go on to the next step, you will save yourself trouble later on. Practice these right- and left-angle turns when the track has aged five minutes, ten minutes, and fifteen minutes.

From now on your tracks should be 300 yards in length and should incorporate at least three turns. Practice this type of track, and use different turns each time. Start practicing when the track is five minutes old, and gradually work up to a track that has aged twenty minutes. Use a forty-foot leash, put a knot at twenty feet and one at thirty feet. Try to work at thirty feet, holding the rest in abeyance in case you need it on a turn.

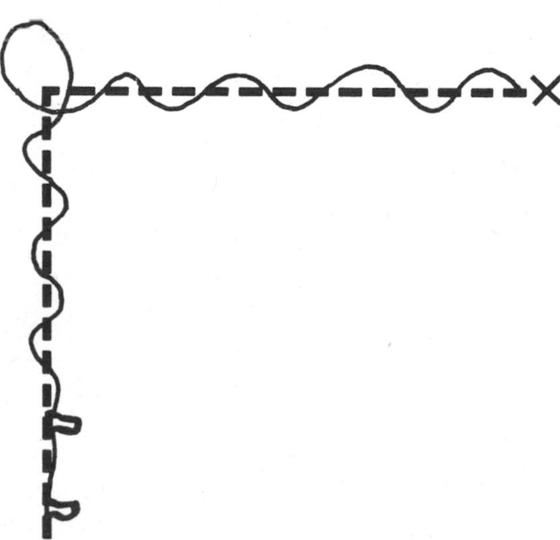

A dog may cross the track repeatedly all the way to the article.

Some of the tracklayer's scent is still on the actual track, but most dogs will follow the scent that the wind has carried some distance from it. These examples (pp. 218 and 219) illustrate what could happen.

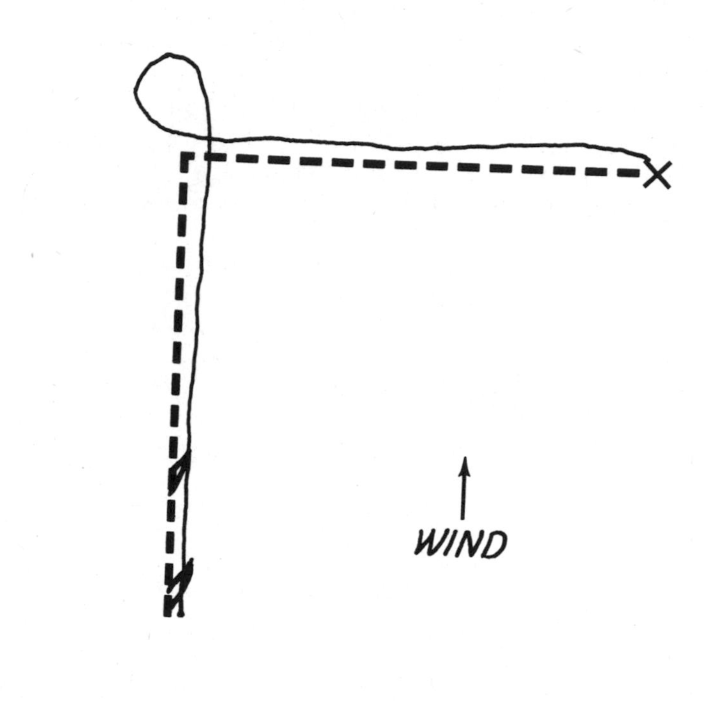

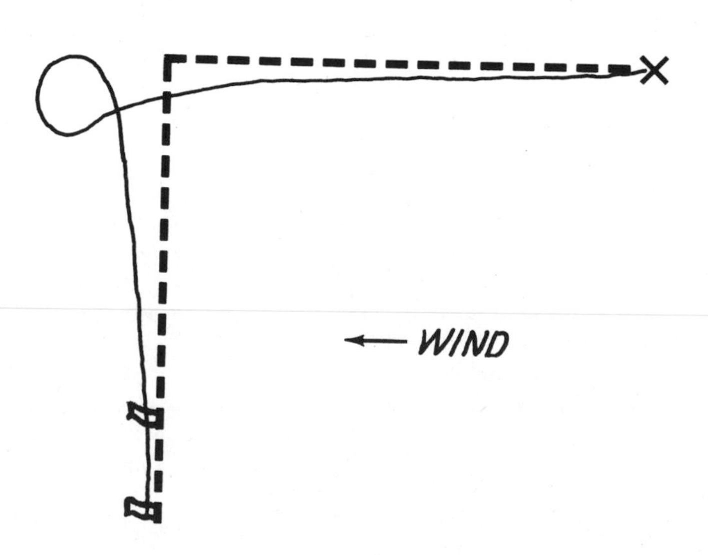

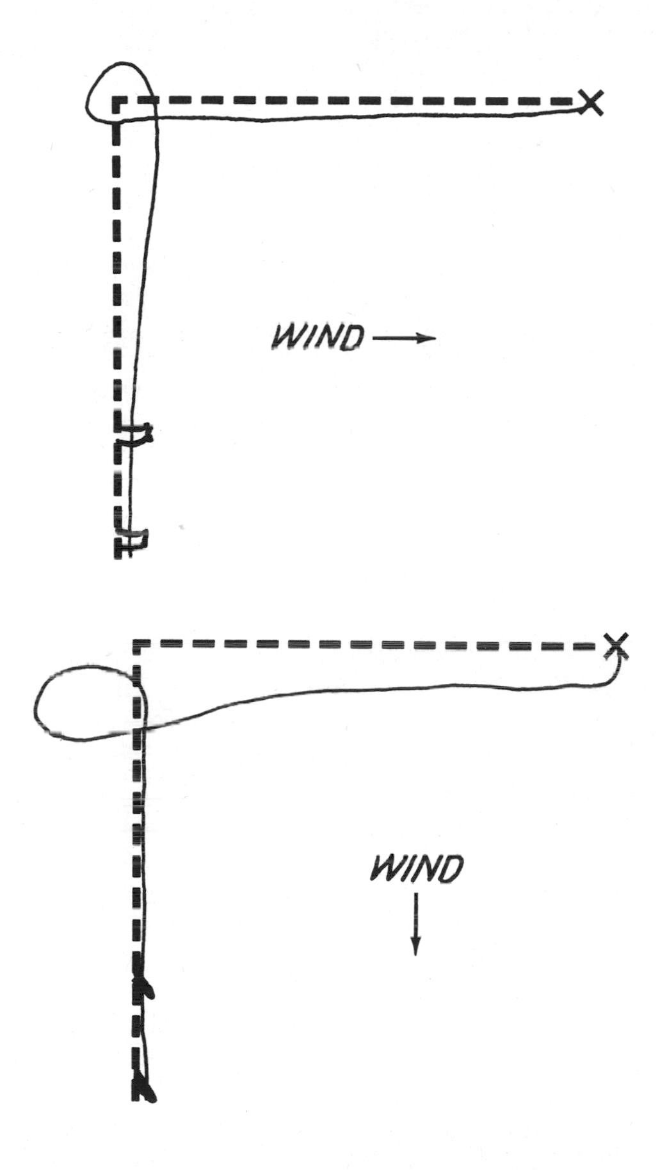

Discuss the track with the tracklayer before he starts. If there are any landmarks, such as a tree, shrub, large boulder, etc., that are visible at a distance, use them for turning points instead of stakes. Use stakes only when there is nothing else to mark the turn. Never turn right at the landmark, as the dog would eventually get wise to this. Make your turns about twenty feet past the landmark and have your tracklayer follow the proposed track accurately so that you can guide your dog correctly.

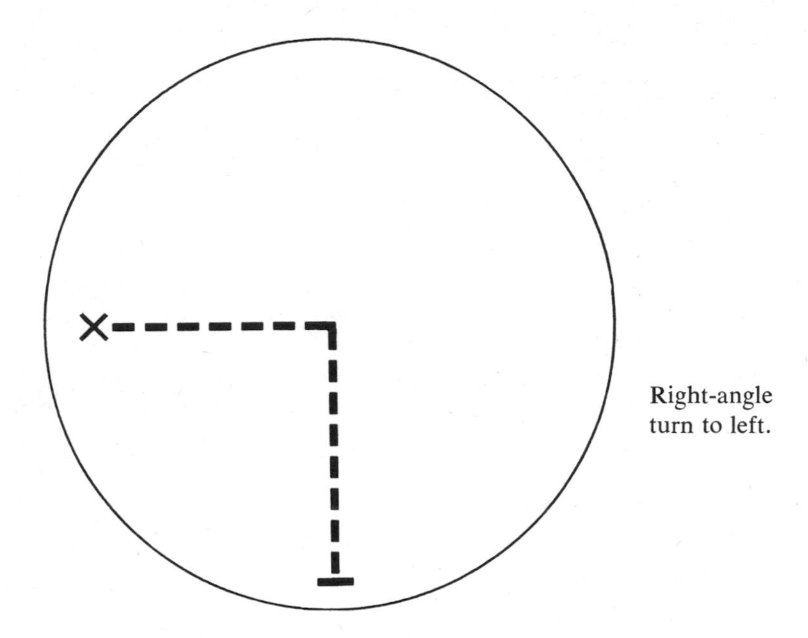

Right-angle turn to left.

Your dog must be convinced that you know where the track leads, for this will encourage him to try harder. It isn't any different than throwing a dumbbell that lands hidden in a hollow. If the dog doesn't see it he might quit, so you show him where it is, and the next time this happens he will look around for it. In tracking he will occasionally go off the track, and it will be up to you to show him where it is (and be sure you point to a portion of the track that is heavy with scent) so that he can continue on by himself. He is depending on you to help him when he gets confused, so it is of the utmost importance that you always know where the track lies, where each turn should be made, and when to find the glove.

At the start of each track you should now use two flags just as in an actual Tracking Test. (Tack a twelve-inch square of material on one end of a three-foot pole, and sharpen the other end with a knife so that it will stick firmly in the ground.) The flags should be placed thirty yards apart, and the tracklayer should scuff the ground near the first flag. The dog should be encouraged to take the scent at the first flag, and keep his nose to the ground up to the second flag. This distance should be sufficient for the dog to retain the scent and follow the trail. A dog is permitted to return to the first flag to take the scent again, providing he has not gone beyond the second flag. Do not let your dog retrieve the flag or play with it. At first, when laying tracks, scuff your feet along the ground between the two flags.

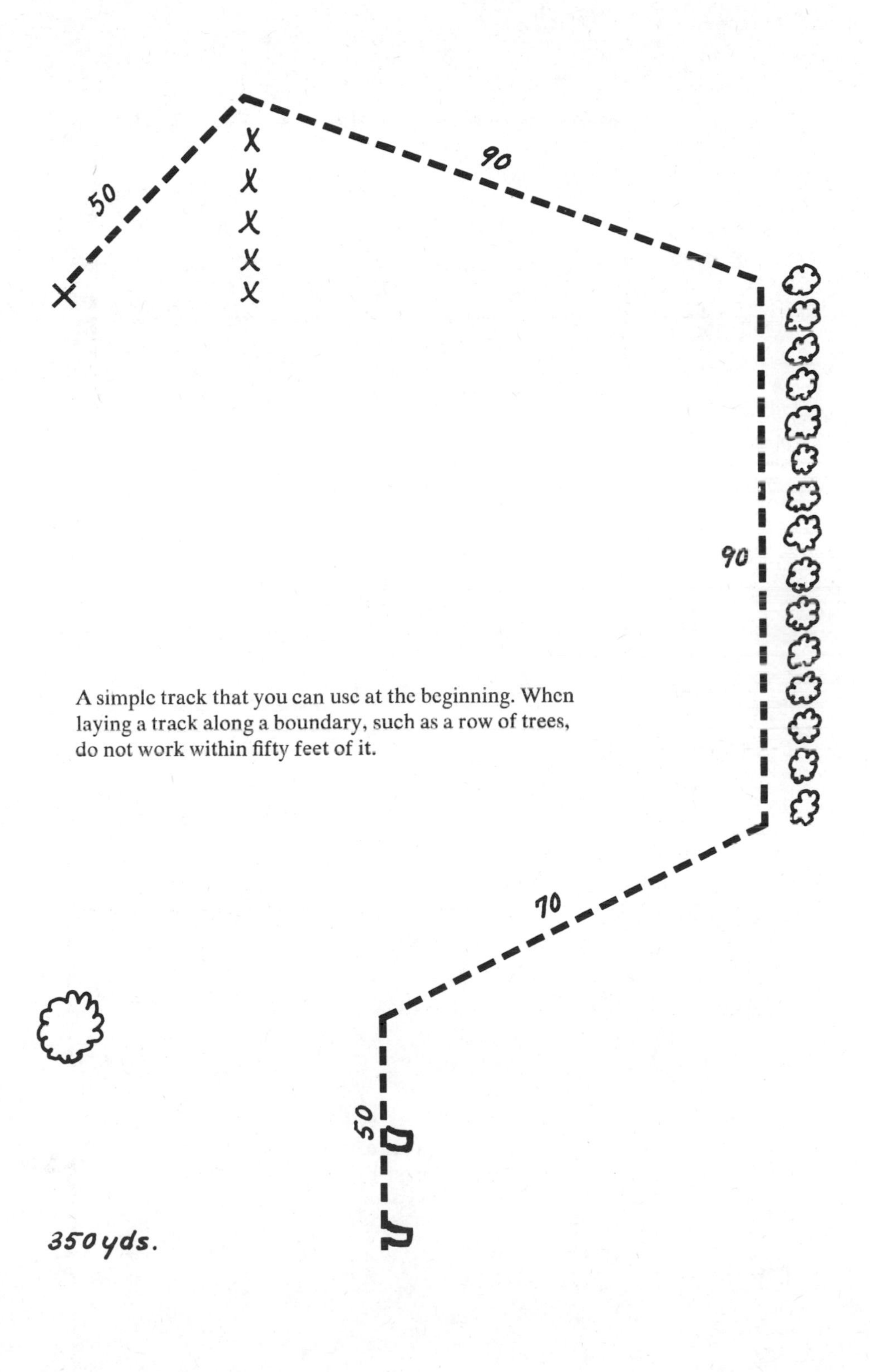

A simple track that you can use at the beginning. When laying a track along a boundary, such as a row of trees, do not work within fifty feet of it.

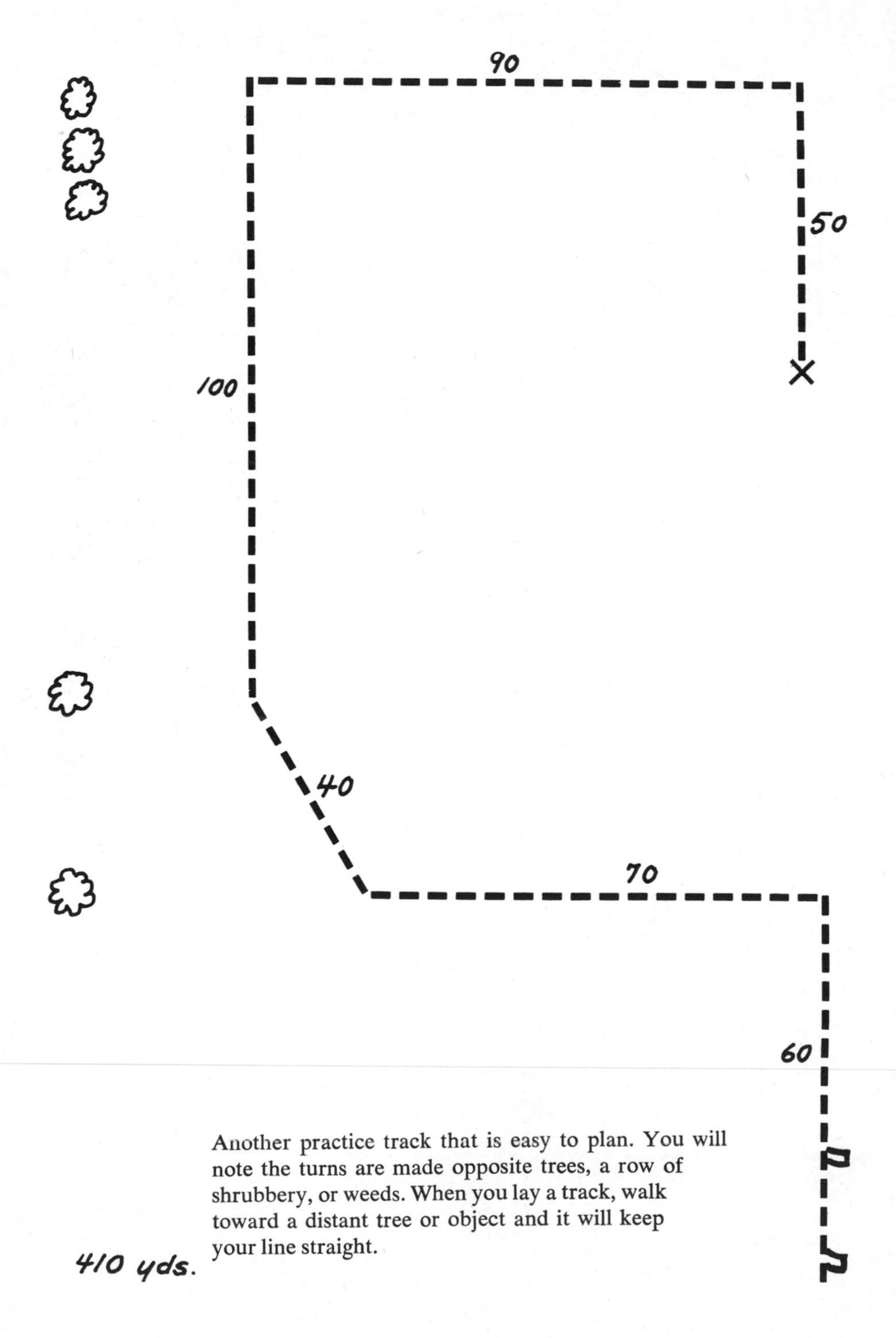

Another practice track that is easy to plan. You will note the turns are made opposite trees, a row of shrubbery, or weeds. When you lay a track, walk toward a distant tree or object and it will keep your line straight.

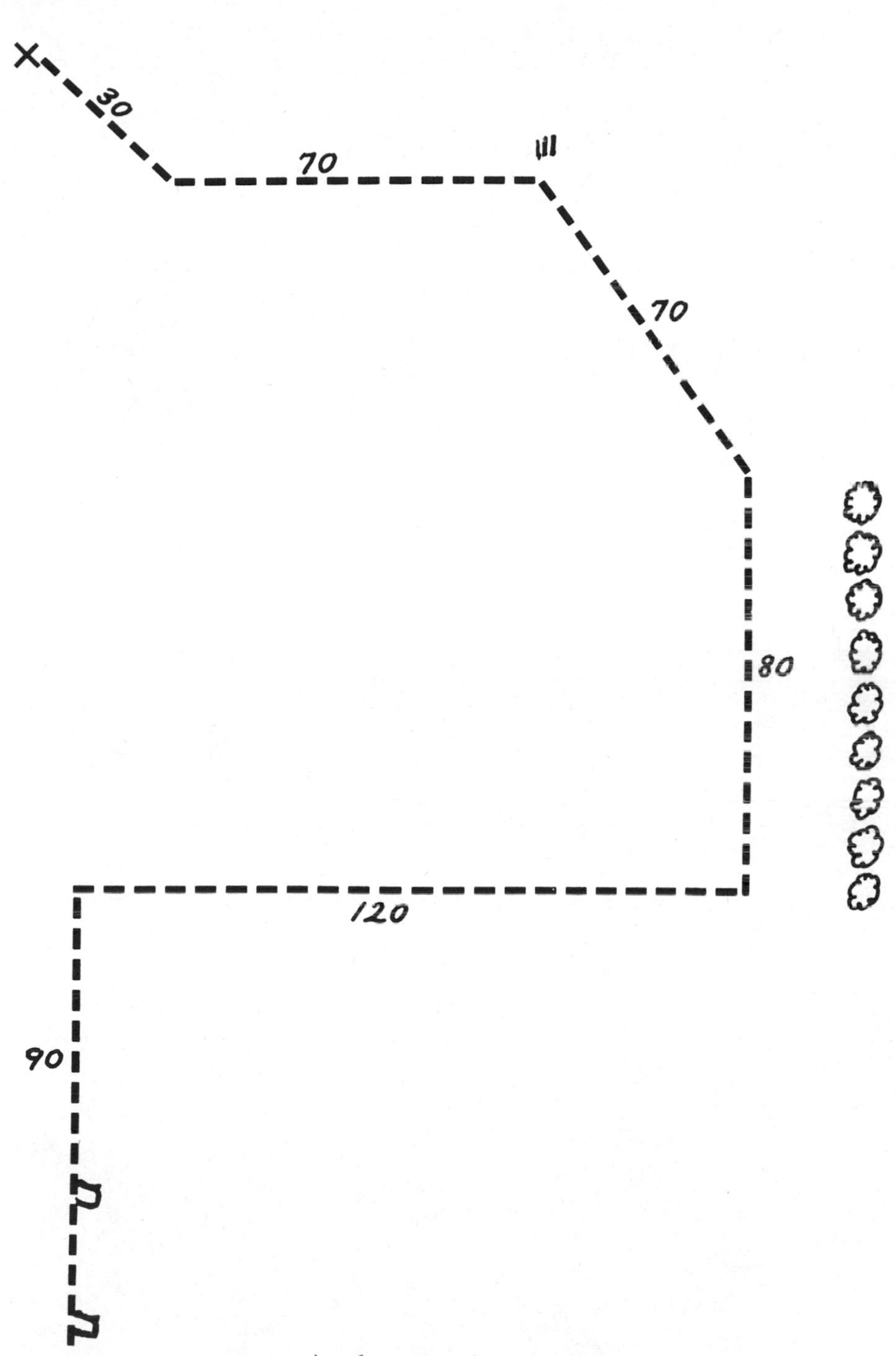

Another example of a well-planned track. This is the type of track you might find at a Tracking Test.

When your dog is doing this well, increase the length of the track to 550 yards and incorporate seven or eight turns. You will have to plan your track carefully so that you will end up near an exit from the field. Don't become so engrossed in laying the track that you find yourself stuck in a corner of the field with no way out except over the freshly laid track. Never make a turn narrower than a right- or left-angle turn, or the dog will cut over to the other portion of the track. Your objective is to keep the dog as close to the actual track as possible. Therefore avoid laying any tracks that prevent this.

Tracking fields are generally to be found in the country, and it is quite probable that your dog will flush a pheasant or some other game while

Play out your leash slowly, and hold your dog back so that he will take the time to keep his nose to the ground and get a strong scent.

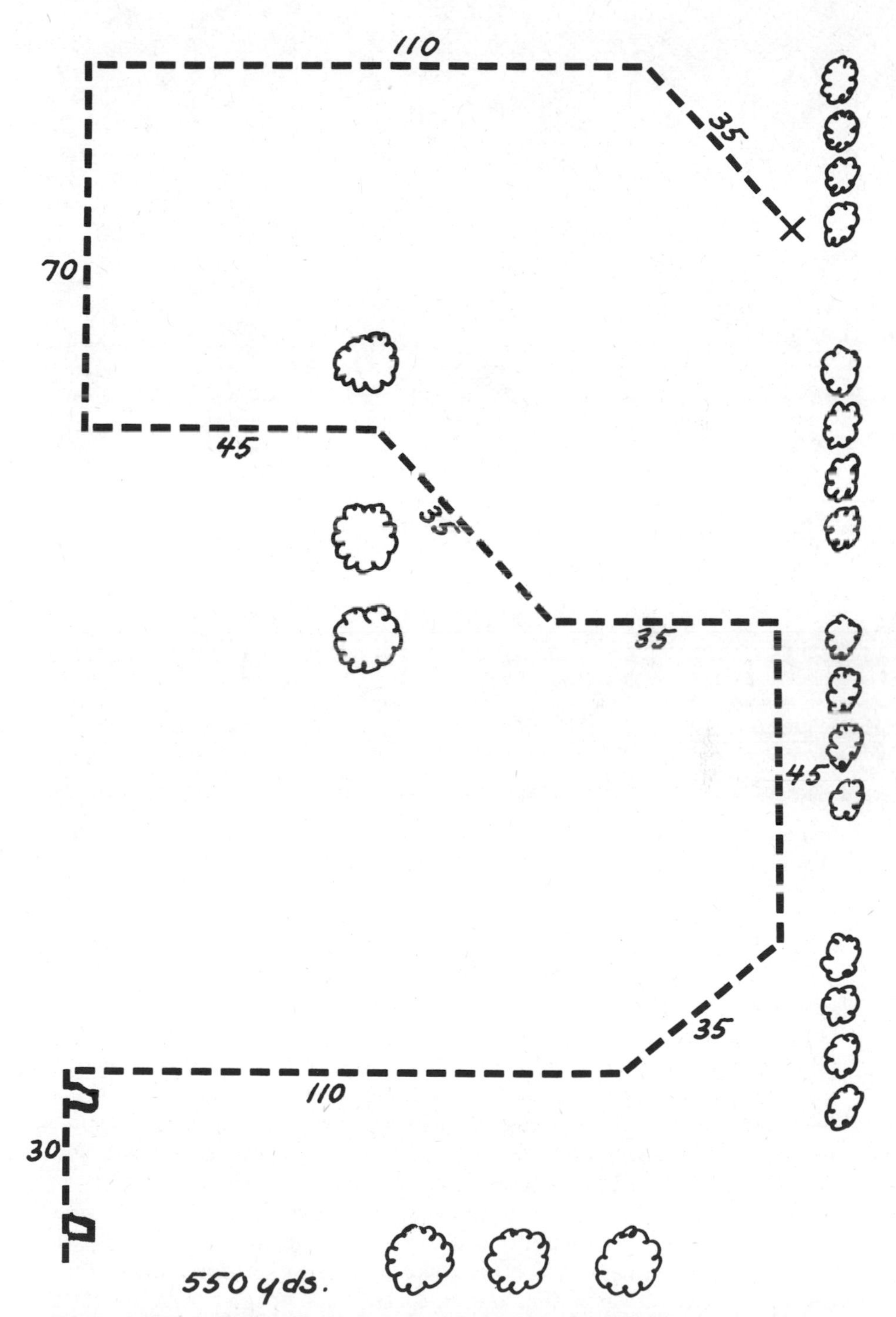

This is a difficult track but planned according to the terrain. When you and your dog can follow a blind track like this you are ready for a Tracking Test. The actual test will be much easier than this.

Stand at the second flag and let twenty feet of your leash play out. Place a knot in your leash at thirty feet also so that you may hold the remainder in abeyance until you need it.

he is tracking. Caution him to "Track," and insist that he continue to work and ignore the interruption. When you lay a track you may come across woodchuck holes or rabbit nests, and many of these creatures are bold enough to sit there and watch you approach. However, when you take your dog out they will be nowhere in sight. Try to give your dog the experience of working near cows or horses. Some tracks are laid in fields that adjoin cow pastures. If there are cows or horses grazing in a nearby field they will all come over to the fence to watch you and your dog Track. They are naturally inquisitive, and they will clop noisily up and down the fence, or stick their heads over and create a general commotion. A dog must be well trained to resist the temptation to dash over and inspect them; it is good experience for him to get this kind of thing during a practice session. The dog that can work under trying conditions is the dog that will pass.

If you wish to lay tracks on private property, have the courtesy to obtain permission to do so. Do not trespass on anyone's property; it may be freshly planted, animals may be loose, or you may simply not be welcome. As a rule, however, you will find that owners are willing to let you use their fields, provided you keep your dog under control.

When the tracks you use are twenty minutes old, then it is advisable to have a stranger lay them for you. Your dog will pick up the stranger's scent between the first two flags; encourage him to follow it with the verbal command, "Track." Since there will be just one human scent on the field, your dog will readily follow it. Once you find someone who is willing to lay the tracks, you must teach him how to do it, and then you must watch carefully to be sure he does it right. A poorly laid track will not only confuse your dog, but so discourage him he will not even try. Your friend must lay the track carefully so that no part of the line crosses another part, and the turns should either approximate a right angle or be wider. The track should not cross a road, brook, body of water, or follow a fence or boundary within fifteen yards of it.

Your tracklayer should also be extremely careful to note landmarks and the direction of the wind, so that you know the exact conditions before you take your dog out on the track. When you are teaching your dog to Track you must be in complete control of every situation that arises. Your dog must have the utmost confidence in you, and you must strive to impart your knowledge to him in the most subtle and astute ways. He cannot realize that you cannot smell the track, and fully expects you to show him where it is if he misses a turn. At first encourage him with your voice, and guide him with the leash. As you progress, and your dog becomes interested in Tracking, you should gradually fade into the background and let him take the initiative to forge ahead and find the track in his own way. Your part will be to interpret his signals correctly, and try to prevent him from Tracking too fast. A good tracker gets excited when he knows he is on the trail, and is apt to want to rush ahead exuberantly. Try to check your dog's speed from the beginning so that he will not overrun the turns. Have the tracklayer leave his own glove or wallet.

When you check the wind direction, be sure to do so at the dog's height and not your own. The unevenness of the terrain cuts down the wind velocity. Test this fact by standing in a field on a windy day and note the degree of wind at your height, then lie down and note the amount of wind about fourteen inches off the ground. Most dogs will be taking the scent at a height of fourteen inches or less, from the ground.

For the first week only have the tracklayer scuff the ground on the sharp turns. Start with fifteen-minute tracks and gradually work up to sixty minutes. At the end of the track have the tracklayer continue straight on for about fifty feet beyond the article, then leave the field without approaching within 100 yards of any part of the track. Your dog should practice four days a week with two or three tracks at each lesson. Try to get a few friends to lay tracks for you.

The final stage in teaching your dog to Track is to follow a blind track. Have an experienced tracklayer lay at least five tracks a week for you, without your observing him. Get used to relying upon your dog's nose. The tracklayer may follow you at a discreet distance, and advise you if the dog goes astray. When you have conquered this last stage you are ready for a Tracking Test.

I hope that you get the enjoyment from Tracking that I have. Topper and Hussan were entered in the same Tracking Test and both passed that day. I was so excited and pleased that my expression for the next two days was a very wide grin.

Topper had made several turns, when suddenly the leash dropped off his harness. It was the type of snap that closes with a tiny bar, and some dirt had got into it so that it didn't close. With the permission of the judges, I called him back and snapped the leash on again. I thought we were finished, since I had to interrupt his Tracking to do it, but he got right back to business and completed the track.

Half an hour later, Hussan started on his track. He weighed almost as much as I did—there was five pounds' difference—and he loved to Track. When he got started, he made me run to keep up with him. He was so strong that he got going like a freight train and didn't stop until he had the article. I had all I could do to keep my footing, and I remember splashing through a wide puddle and laughing aloud at the amusing spectacle we made. It was a very happy occasion.

Arry was working fast the day he passed his Tracking Test. I remember him taking a left turn into a grove of trees, and as he threaded his way between them, I hoped he knew what he was doing. At the end of the track he headed for some tall grass, and then I was sure he was wrong, for we had been working on very short grass, but he dashed right along and found the article without any trouble.

All this proves that it is better to leave the Tracking to the dog on the day of the test. When you get out there, it will seem to you that the dog is mistaken in his judgment, but it is wiser to let him prove that he is right.

The day that Max passed his Tracking Test he was very businesslike, and checked all the turns carefully. He didn't hesitate along the way, but went straight to the article. Each dog has his own way of Tracking; and whatever that way is, it is most exhilarating to be on the other end of the leash.

Don't try to help your dog on the day of the test. You will not be able to see the track, so make up your mind to let him take the initiative and do the work. All you have to do is hold on to the leash and make sure that it does not get tangled up in rocks or shrubs.

Judges plan the tracks the day before the Tracking Test, using tracking poles on the turns and at the end of the track. On the day of the test the poles are removed by the tracklayer as he lays the actual track and leaves an article of his own at the end of the track for the dog to find.

It takes a great deal of time and effort on the part of the judges to prepare a Tracking Test. Therefore be quite certain that you and your dog can follow a blind track before you enter him in a Tracking Test.

The tracking method described here will enable you to pass an AKC Tracking Test and get your Tracking title. This is the preliminary work necessary if you wish to teach your dog the more serious business of finding lost persons. It is a good foundation on which to build, as your dog now realizes that he must follow the given scent until something is found.

The leash will be taut like this when your dog is working on the track.

It is not too difficult to continue from here and give the dog an article of clothing belonging to the lost person and let him search for him. If you try this out with members of your family, your dog will be eager to cooperate. The "lost" person should always make a big fuss over him when "found" to create more interest and excitement. This type of Tracking is fun and good exercise for all concerned.

26

Advanced Tracking

The purpose of this Tracking is to teach your dog to find lost persons. That person might be a child who has wandered away from his home, a camper who has become lost in the woods, or an escaped criminal. In most cases a search is started by the interested parties, and they only succeed in fouling the ground with assorted scents. After several hours have elapsed a dog is brought in to help with the search. There are so few reliable tracking dogs in the country that one generally has to be flown to the scene from another state. If there were more dogs situated throughout the country who were qualified to do this type of work, it would save many hours of valuable time in starting the search, and more lives would be saved.

In order for a dog to find a lost person successfully he must be able to distinguish between the tracklayer's scent and all the other distracting scents that are both confusing and tempting to him. An Advanced Tracking Test should include any problems a dog would have if he was actually tracking a lost person. Any test that fails to do this is neither practical nor realistic.

If your dog can pass the following test he deserves to receive what I would call an AT title (Advanced Tracking). At this writing there is no Advanced Tracking Test or title given by the American Kennel Club.

The test will require one stake, one tracking flag, four tracklayers, and one companion dog. The track will be no less than one-half a mile and no more than three-quarters of a mile in length, and it will cross open fields, a dirt road or footpath, a shallow brook no less than four feet in width but no wider than eight feet, and end in some woods where the dog will find the tracklayer. There will be at least one ninety-degree turn out in the open field, and the track will be laid in such a manner that no portion of it will cross any other portion.

The main track laid by Tracklayer Number One will be no less than six hours old and no more than seven hours old. The first diversionary track laid by Tracklayer Number Two will be two hours old, the second diversionary track laid by Tracklayer Number Three will be one hour old, and the third diversionary track laid by Tracklayer Number Four and his dog will be one-half an hour old. The tracklayers and this dog will be strangers to the handler's dog.

The tracks will be staked out by the judges two days before the test, and the stakes will be numbered so that the tracklayer can collect them in numerical order on the day of the test. The stakes for Tracklayer Number One will be painted bright red, Tracklayer Number Two will have yellow stakes, Tracklayer Number Three will have blue stakes, and Tracklayer Number Four will have orange stakes. The stake marking the 100-yard point will be alternately striped black and white.

The dog will work on a harness or a leather collar and the leash will be ten feet long. The dog will be given the scent from an old shoe that has been worn that week by Tracklayer Number One. It must belong to him. The dog may be given this scent before he reaches the starting flag and once more if the handler deems it necessary, before they reach the 100-yard stake. At this point the handler must then leave the shoe on the ground and continue on without it. The handler may encourage the dog at any time with his voice, or restrain him if he thinks he is working too fast; however, if the dog is not working, or if the handler is trying to aid his dog forcefully, he will be marked Failed.

One tracking flag will mark the starting point. Tracklayer Number One will lay a straight track for the first 100 yards. The 100-yard stake will not be placed on the main track. When the main track is four hours old Tracklayer Number Two will lay a semicircular track that will start some distance to the right of the starting flag, cross the main track within fifty yards of the flag, and end some distance off to the left. It will not parallel the main track at any time, by fifteen yards. Nor will tracks three and four.

When the main track is five hours old Tracklayer Number Three will lay a semicircular track that will start at some distance to the left of the starting flag, cross the main track within eighty yards of the flag, and end some distance off to the right. It will not parallel the main track at any time.

As soon as the main track is five and a half hours old Tracklayer Number Four and his dog will enter a field that contains the main track, and

Joll finding the track across the brook.

they will walk over it, cross the main track without walking parallel to it, and leave the field from the other side. The tracklayer's dog will be kept on leash at Heel.

This test is designed to teach a dog to differentiate between the lost person's tracks, those of people walking around the beginning of the track, or those made by a stranger and his dog when they cross the track at a later time. It will teach your dog to recognize the difference between an old track and a new one. If you train your dog to do this correctly you will be able to rely on him if his services are actually needed in an emergency.

Your dog should be quite reliable on an hour track before you start. Try several very long tracks that are one hour old, and generate a little more excitement by having someone the dog loves lay the track. Gradually work the age of the tracks you use up to eight hours and confine the tracks to fields.

Now take your dog to a wooded area that is not too overgrown with brush or briars. The first track you lay should age about twenty minutes. You will see why anything more than a ten-foot leash is impractical when you try this. Be patient with your dog, for he will encounter all kinds of interesting animal and vegetation odors in the woods that may distract him. You will probably find it necessary to keep urging him on. Always show him the track by pointing to it; let him think you know where it is. I have found that a good way to mark the trail in the woods is to have the tracklayer stick feathered darts into the trees at least five feet from the ground. The feathers should be painted a bright orange so they will be visible at a distance. Work these tracks until the dog is doing it well, then combine the tracks in the open fields with these.

At this point the tracks will be half a mile long and six hours old, and I believe it is best for the tracklayer to be someone the dog loves until he has this work down perfectly. When you feel he understands it take him down to a brook.

Work on the brook crossing separately until your dog will search around eagerly for the track. Start with a short track leading to the brook and crossing over it, and have the tracklayer hide behind a tree some fifty feet beyond the brook. Make a tremendous fuss over the dog when he finds the tracklayer. Start with a twenty-minute track to make it easy for him and work the time up again when he responds. You will have to show the dog the track until he realizes he must cross the brook in order to find the tracklayer. This is really not too difficult, because most dogs love the water and will not hesitate to go in it. You must keep your dog's mind on the track at this time and not let him play in the brook. Any time the dog seems confused when you are teaching him Advanced Tracking give him a sniff of the tracklayer's shoe which you should be carrying in a plastic bag. This will remind him of the scent he is following. In the beginning you will have to show it to him quite frequently, but these instances will lessen as his proficiency increases.

Now try a combination of the three kinds of tracks. Lay a half-mile

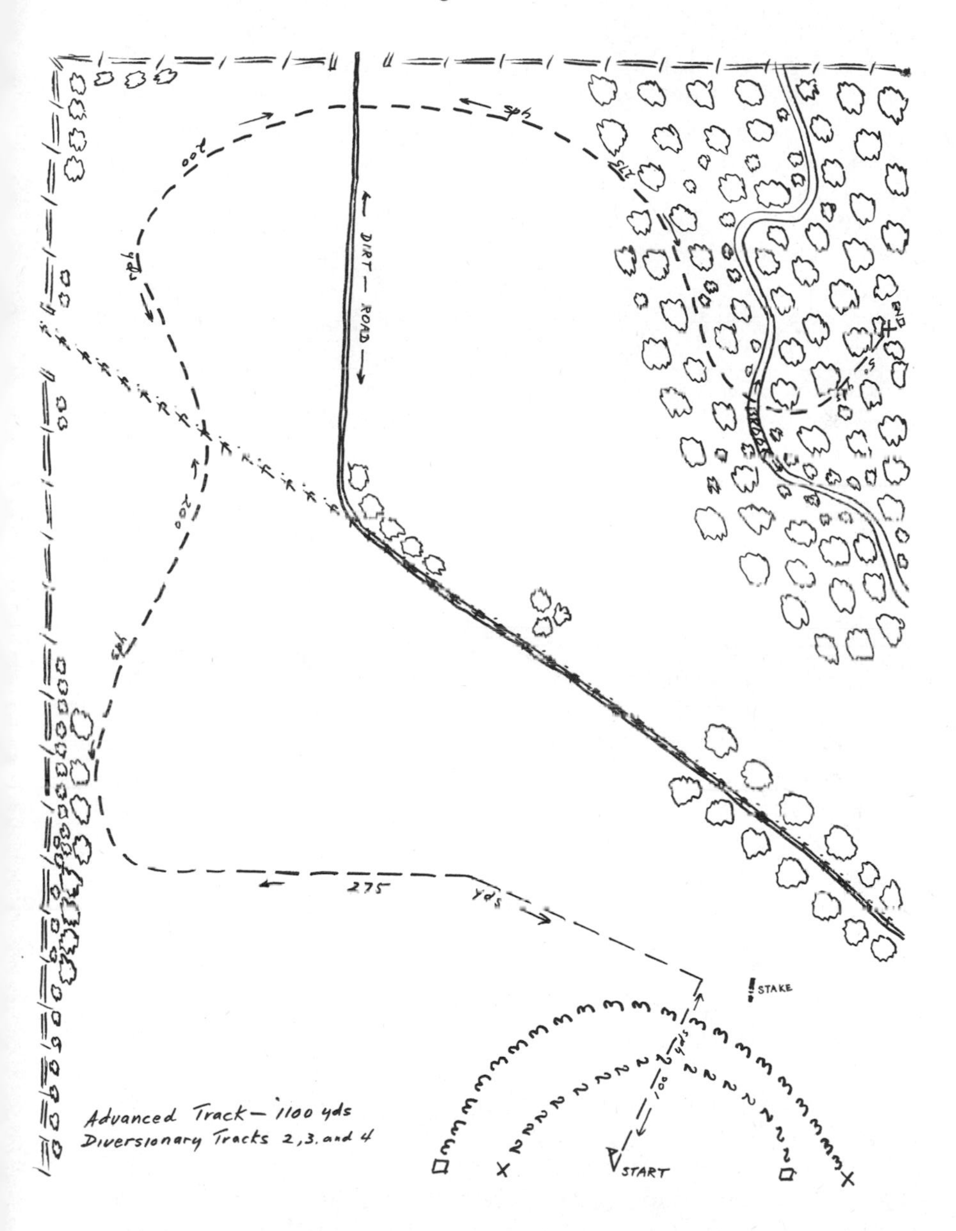

track through the fields, over a brook, and end it in the woods. Try several of these with the same tracklayer until the dog is very steady.

When you have reached this point it is time to have strangers lay the tracks. It is much more difficult getting a stranger to lay these tracks than it is to teach your dog to track. Poorly laid tracks can completely confuse your dog, so it is better to spend some time advising your tracklayers how you want the track laid than to assume they will do it right. If you want to be certain they will do it correctly use the numbered stakes and mark it out yourself two days before you plan to practice.

There is one important thing to remember when practicing tracks that have aged several hours. The tracklayer will not want to wait in the woods for six or more hours while the track is aging, so the spot where he is to wait must be marked with two stakes, then he can leave the woods by walking in a straight line from the track. He should place stakes as he leaves, so that he can retrace his steps twenty minutes before you start out at the beginning of the track with your dog.

Teaching your dog to follow this type of track is like anything else—if you take it slowly and carefully at first your dog will learn. If you encourage him from the beginning by showing him what you want, you will build up his confidence in his ability to find the lost tracklayer.

Once your dog will track a stranger successfully on an eight-hour-old track it is time to introduce the diversionary tracks. It is quite likely that some animals have crossed the tracks during these weeks that you have been practicing but you will never know. Have a second tracklayer cross the track an hour before you start. You should know exactly where this occurs so that you can notice your dog's reaction. Give him a chance to investigate this new scent but do not let him follow it more than twenty feet, caution him to "Track," and help him to get back on the main track if necessary.

Try a good number of similar tests with different time periods, but always be in command of the situation by knowing exactly where the tracklayer crosses the main track. This is very important, as you must be ready to assist your dog. When he has it down pat, get two or three tracklayers to cross the main track at the beginning. Again you must know where they cross each time.

At this point of the training you will have a great respect for your dog's ability to use his nose. Now you can rely on him to follow a blind track and try a few tests similar to the one in the illustration. It is sometimes uncanny the way a dog can find a person or an object just by scent and intuition. I had an amazing experience with Joll that still fills me full of wonder and admiration whenever I think of it.

I had to go down to Georgia on business, so I decided to fly down and take Joll with me. I had a pilot's license so I rented a plane at the local airport near my home in Delaware, invited Joll to hop in behind the pilot's seat where he had plenty of room, and off we flew. Joll loves to fly, and curls up and takes a nap unless I talk to him. On take-offs and landings he sits up and watches the proceedings, and many a person has been surprised to see him watching out his window.

It was sunny all day long and we had a head wind most of the way. I stopped twice to refuel, and both times walked a considerable distance with Joll to the office to pay for the gas. Both times on my return to my plane I noticed several planes had come in and parked near us. Joll would dash on ahead and wait for me next to our plane, and I thought at the time that he was being rather bright. It happened that none of these other planes were Cessnas.

The plane that I had rented was brand new, I had never flown it, and Joll and I had never seen it before. It was an all-day flight to Atlanta, and we touched down at 6:00 P.M. After landing, I taxied up to the hangar and asked the attendant to fill the plane with gas. He advised me to lock the plane and take the key and he would fill it with gas and park it somewhere else later on. It is quite simple to move a plane by rolling it, not like trying to move a locked car. So I got my luggage, asked Joll to jump out, locked the plane, and left it parked there near the hangar office.

This was a Friday night, and the next day it was very hot and sunny all day long. On Sunday it rained steadily all day but cleared enough in the evening for me to decide to leave the next morning. Monday morning our flight home was delayed until 11:00 A.M. because of the poor weather farther north. Finally we got the green light from the weather bureau, and I drove out to the airport with Joll. I left Joll in the car while I went into the office to pay my bill and find out where they had parked my plane. The attendant stood at the door and pointed in the general direction and mentioned that it was in one of the front rows. The whole field was a sea of planes, all sizes and shapes, all private planes, and many Cessnas just like mine. However, I knew the number and color of my plane so didn't anticipate any trouble finding it.

I got Joll out of the car and had him Heel by my side until we got to the hangar office, then I said, "Jolly, let's go home." He got all excited and went dashing off ahead of me, leaving me way behind. I ran to catch up with him, and we went the length of a long city block, zigzagging in and out of the rows of planes before I saw him standing near a plane way up ahead of me. I couldn't even read the plane's number from where I stood, so wasn't sure it was mine. When I got close enough I saw it was our plane and Joll was all smiles, hopping up and down and turning in little circles. He was waiting in front of the pilot's door, the only one we had used.

I saw it, but I couldn't believe that he knew *that* was our plane, so I tested him. I said, "No, Joll, that's not the one, it's over *here*," and I walked over to another Cessna that was the same model but a different color. He wouldn't budge, but jumped up against our plane door, wagging his tail like mad and flashing his brown eyes at me with a "Yes, it is, yes, it is," expression. So I laughed and said, "You're right, that's it." I opened the door and he jumped in behind the pilot's seat and sat there. His expression said very clearly, "O.K., let's go home."

I've seen dogs do some very remarkable things in my lifetime but I think this was fantastic. There were over three hundred-odd planes on this field, and what little scent there was on the outside of our metal plane was seventy-one hours old. This had been subjected to high winds, a dry, hot sunny day, and twelve hours of steady rainfall.

I know Joll has a keen nose and a remarkably high degree of intelligence, as he has demonstrated these qualities before. I also believe that dogs can distinguish colors. What astounded me was his ability to combine these talents with his intuition.

So this six-hour track is really just a beginning. I am convinced that a keen dog could follow a three- or four-day-old track if he had the incentive and the proper training.

27

Traveling with Your Dog

Whenever I travel anywhere I enjoy taking my dog with me because he is such good company and so well behaved. He takes a great interest in everything I do and as a result of his behavior I get more enjoyment out of whatever I am doing.

For instance, when I am driving, Joll watches everything going on, somewhat like a back-seat driver but without the nagging. When I apply the brakes he looks down at the brake pedal and then quickly looks around to see why I put on the brakes. He has watched me drive for such a long time that I'll bet he could drive the car himself if he were physically able. He nudges my shoulder if I complain aloud when someone takes a left turn from the right hand lane, etc., as if in complete accord. One time on the turnpike when I was passing someone who was in the middle lane he suddenly swerved out right into the side of my car, as I was nearly parallel with him. I averted an accident by veering over onto the left shoulder, blowing my horn in protest as I did so. The other driver realizing he had goofed, swerved back again into the middle lane, thus giving me a chance to get back on the road. Joll had been watching this and got quite upset about the whole thing. He stared out the side window at this driver, and when I passed him, Joll turned around and stared back at him out the back window, came up and nudged me, and stared back up the road again. It was just as if he were saying, "Did you see that dumb driver . . .?" and started calling him a few choice names

The co-pilot listening to last-minute instructions.

that I missed. It made an anxious moment rather funny. Joll does many things to relieve the tension of a long drive.

I can't understand the people who keep their dogs in crates, like animals. They miss so much by not treating their dogs as part of the family. I suppose they feel it is less nerve-racking to carry untrained dogs in crates. We generally have anywhere from two to six dogs in our station wagon when we go to a show, and they all lie down and behave themselves. It is so much better to train your dogs so that they can travel with you.

When I have to ship a dog to another part of the country I like to send it by air. I try to choose a flight that is direct, or one that doesn't involve two airlines. When a dog is transferred from one airline to another there is always a chance that someone will goof and forget to transfer the dog to the second flight. If you call the airline and make a reservation you can be assured of kennel space for your dog. You may take your own crate, buy one from the airline, or in some cases rent one. All dogs must travel in a crate (except guide dogs). You may ship your dog alone or he may accompany you on the same flight.

If your dog has never been in a crate before, introduce him to one at home by having him walk into one and lie down. Make it a pleasant experience by praising him and petting him when he is lying down, and don't make him stay in it for more than a few minutes at a time. Be sure that the crate is large enough for your dog to move around comfortably.

You will need a health certificate and proof of rabies inoculation when you ship your dog. If he is an older dog, give him something to eat the morning that he is to be shipped, let him exercise just before you take him to the airport, and offer him a drink of water before you place him in the crate. Stay with him at the airport until the crate is put aboard the plane. Be sure to attach an identification tag to his collar, with your name, address, and telephone number on it, and be sure to write "Reward—if found."

I have never put identification tags on my dogs because I always keep them with me or in my car when we are traveling. At home they don't need tags, for life is very interesting for them, and although my property is completely fenced in I know they wouldn't dream of leaving it. My dogs are all trained to jump and could scale the fences; the thing is, they are happy here and a contented dog will not run away. When we take them to shows they are not permitted to have any tags on their collars. However, I strongly advise you to attach an identification tag to your dog's collar if for any reason you have to ship him somewhere. The following is a good reason why it is necessary.

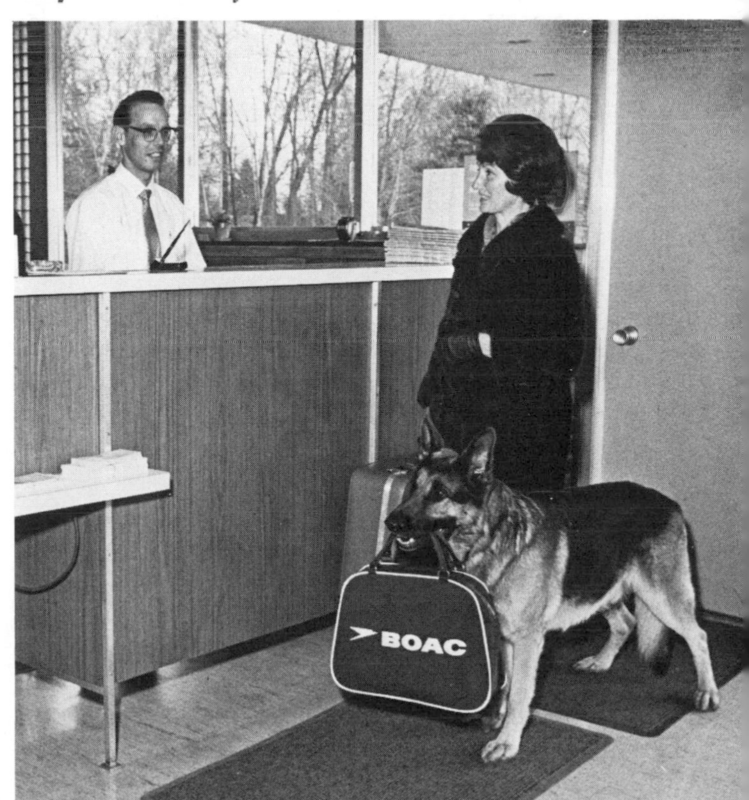

Checking in at a motel.

I had sold one of my dogs to a woman in Denver, Colorado, who had convinced me that he would be given a good home and would be her companion. This dog meant a lot to me, as I had trained him myself and had handled him to two Highest Scores in Trial with 199 and 199½. The fact that I had his litter brother and sister, and the thought that he would be getting a good home, led me to sell him. I kept reminding myself that a breeder has got to be realistic when running a kennel or he will end up with two zillion dogs. Some inner voice told me to put an identification tag on him, so I attached a red-leather tag that held my name, address, etc. I shipped him by air on Friday and stayed with him until his plane left. The next night after I had returned home from a show I called to see if he was adjusting to his new home and was told he had run away. I was quite upset at this news—a country dog lost in the middle of a large city—and offered to fly out to help look for him, but his new owner didn't like the idea and told me there was nothing I could do. So I took the next plane out there to find him. Upon my arrival I alerted the radio stations, dog pounds, newspapers, and police department. I hired a car and searched all that day and night and again the next morning. The police officials were most cooperative and I was in their office on the second day when a call came in that a dog had been picked up on the airport grounds. They mentioned that it was a German Shepherd wearing a red-leather identification tag. My bright CD dog had decided he didn't want to live in Denver and would go home to his friends. He was right in his decision, too—it wasn't the place for him. He knew the last place he had seen me was at an airport, so he had enough sense to go back to one. Needless to say I was very happy to get him back, Randy was happy to be with me, his would-be owner got her check back in full, and all those fine people in Denver who had been so kind to us were pleased to see us reunited. Randy won't be sold again, and I'll probably end up with two zillion dogs. A month later Randy won Highest Scoring Dog in Show three times.

Most hotels and motels will accept dog guests if they are well mannered. Many motels have accepted my dogs when I have shown them my dogs and mentioned their credentials. I am completely sympathetic with the views motel owners have about dogs. Many dog owners take advantage of other people's property and let their dogs do things they wouldn't permit them to do in their own homes. I think every trained dog should have an identification card with his picture on it, and his training titles, and a statement signed by his owner that guarantees him to be housebroken, well mannered, and trained, and these cards should be honored by all motels and hotels everywhere. Then our companion dogs would be welcome wherever we traveled.

A well-mannered dog is a joy to own.

28

Exhibition Work

If you have a congenial group of people in your Obedience Training class, or your club, you may be interested in forming an Exhibition Group. This can consist of nine handlers with their dogs, or sixteen handlers with their dogs. In either case, you will need three or four extras to learn the routine with you so that they can fill in at the last minute in case someone in the regular group falls ill; when you are working with a large group this can happen more frequently than you realize.

When the dogs in the group are all the same breed, it is most impressive. However, if you belong to an all-breed class, use only the dogs that are well trained.

Groups that work with precision and have a great variety of Obedience routines and tricks are greatly in demand. The performances never fail to appeal to everyone who watches them. Dogs that are expertly trained and work happily become the good-will ambassadors for Obedience. They can give the public the impression, in just one performance, that Obedience Training is not just fun alone, but is to be recommended to everyone.

A few years ago I organized an Exhibition Group of nine handlers and their German Shepherds, which has been very successful. The girls wear red skirts, white blouses, and black shoes. The boys wear red vests, white shirts, black trousers, black shoes, and black ties. The dogs wear red coats trimmed with black grosgrain ribbon, with the club emblem on their coats. The red in every case is exactly the same shade. These colors are gay and festive, but in forming your own group you can choose some other color scheme, more suitable to the breed of dog in your group, for instance, green for Irish Setters.

Joll got mixed reactions from his friends the first time he tried an eight-foot jump over them.

You will need a conscientious leader to give the commands for the routines and see that precision is maintained throughout the exercises. These should follow each other like clockwork so that the performance as a whole will be smooth and integrated.

Our ring is seventy feet square. The entrance is at the lower lefthand corner. These are the routines that I use for our Exhibition work as an example of what can be done: we march through the entrance in single file, two yards apart, dogs on leash, take a sharp right turn, and continue on around the square. I usually lead the group, and when I reach the entrance corner, the fifth person in line has reached the top left corner; we both turn toward the center simultaneously, and I pass the center first and head for the right top corner as the fifth person in line heads for the lower right corner. This is called the Cross, and each person in line follows through the center, crossing alternately with the other line. When each handler reaches the opposite corner he takes a left turn back into the square. Then the Cross is executed a second time.

When the leader reaches the entrance corner the third time, he takes a left turn and the group lines up at the bottom of the ring one yard apart. The leader then calls, "Left turn," and the group steps to the left with their left feet and halts on the next step. If everyone in the group will take two steps on every turn before a halt it will keep everyone in

line. On precision work when we all must keep in step, we start off with our left feet. Next, everyone praises his dog.

Then we march in formation, nine abreast, to the top of the ring, as I call, "Forward, march." At the top of the ring I call, "About turn," and everyone turns as usual on the second word of the command, and we take two steps and halt. Now we remove the leashes.

Next we break the group into threes, the three handlers at my end of the line step forward one step, then take a right turn until they are each in front of the middle three handlers. At this point they take a left turn, and as we all move forward the three handlers at the other end of the line fall in behind the middle three. We are now in formation three abreast in three rows. We then execute left turns, right turns, and about turns, all in perfect precision. It is good to watch this when it is done properly. We end the precision work by marching up to the top of the ring and forming a single line once more. We halt two yards apart, take a left turn and halt.

Next, handlers, 1, 3, 5, 7, and 9 leave their dogs on a Sit Stay command, and march in line to the bottom of the ring. Handler Number 1 calls his dog first and drops him in the center. The rest follow suit until all the dogs are lying down in a line across the center of the ring. Then handlers, 2, 4, 6, and 8 leave their dogs on a Sit Stay and march in formation to the bottom of the ring. They call their dogs in to them one at a time on a straight recall. Next the dogs lying down are called in to their handlers one at a time. Everyone finishes in unison.

The handlers are now lined up at the bottom of the ring. Each handler takes his dog to the center of the ring, and performs some unusual exercise or trick.

After this a high jump is set up on either side of the ring, and a broad jump is set up on the two remaining sides. Each dog has a baton with red flags hanging from it which he carries in his mouth. Each dog now jumps the four hurdles carrying his baton. When the first dog jumps the fourth hurdle the second dog should start on the first hurdle. When each is finished, he lines up in the center of the ring.

The leader's dog is now sent after the leashes which were left in a heap at the side of the ring. He returns the leashes to his owner, who in turn passes them down the line. The leashes are black to match the costumes. The handlers snap the leashes on their dogs and march out of the ring in single file.

Here is a list of a few of the exercises and tricks that appeal to the public: Shaking Hands, Sitting Up, Saying His Prayers, Playing Dead,

Joll jumping through a hoop.

Rolling Over, Speaking, Jumping over a Baton, Jumping through the Handler's Arms, Jumping over the High Jump, Bar Jump, and a Hoop, Crawling, and Jumping Rope with the Handler as he runs along.

A few exercises you can use in a demonstration of this kind are:

The Scent Discrimination exercise, in which fifteen articles are used: five wood, five metal, and five leather.

The advanced Scent Discrimination exercise, in which three handlers step forward and place an article in the center of the ring. The dog then sniffs the article and picks it up. The dog carries the article down the line until he comes to the owner of the article and sets in front of him. The owner takes his article from the dog. The dog then returns the other two articles to their rightful owners.

The Signal exercise.

The Seek Back, in which two small articles are dropped during a Heeling routine. The articles should be a key and a ring. The dog should search for the articles and return them one at a time.

Another advanced exercise is one in which the dog is asked to sniff a glove and commanded to find the owner. The dog should check the handlers in line and bark when he reaches the owner of the glove.

A Drop on Recall will enable the handler to show his skill by dropping the dog on a line placed there for that purpose. The handler should call out where he intends to drop his dog before doing so.

Another exercise shows the dog's skill in Sitting straight in front of his handler. The dog should be called from different angles, never a straight Recall, which should include one Recall where he is at the end of the ring with his back to his dog.

One of the dogs can demonstrate his versatility by carrying an egg without cracking it, and then a basketful of groceries, and finally a pail of water without spilling it.

29

Teaching Your Dog to Be Useful

Now that you have trained your dog and he has earned his Obedience degrees, you can derive both benefit and pleasure from the hard work of all the training. Use your ingenuity and take advantage of the exercises you have taught him. Teach him to be useful.

A dog can easily be taught to retrieve your slippers or shoes, if you show him where they are the first few times and praise him for getting them. If you keep your leash and dumbbell in one special place, your dog will delight to retrieve them for you when you wish to use them.

It is my firm belief that dogs learn the names of articles just by hearing them mentioned occasionally. In the case of one of my own dogs, I never taught him what a sweater was, but he knew just the same. One evening when we were having dinner I felt cold and wanted my sweater. I called him over to me and said, "Arry, go get my sweater." He trotted upstairs to my room and came back with it in his mouth. It was something of a shock to the rest of the family who had been betting he would not know what I wanted.

If you have a large dog, you can teach him to carry a basket so that when you go shopping he will help you carry packages. When you get home, let him help you carry the packages in from your car. If you do this frequently, he will soon learn that "shopping" means carrying packages. Arry could carry a ten-pound bag of potatoes with the greatest of ease. He picked a bag up one day and was so pleased with himself for carrying it into the house that he insisted from then on to be the one to carry in the potatoes.

For several years we lived on a farm that had a long, pine-bordered lane leading up to the house. It was quite a walk to get the newspaper or the mail, so I trained my dogs to do this errand.

In the same way, if you are gardening, your dog can help you by carrying the equipment you need.

When I endeavor to improve my golf game by practicing with my short irons, I hit a dozen balls and then let Topper retrieve them. He loves this and waits eagerly for the word so that he may dash out and bring the balls back to me two at a time.

At Obedience Trials I always had my dog carry his own bag, containing his things, in and out of the show. On trips Joll would also carry one of the small suitcases. If I went to the closet to get a suitcase, Joll would select his own bag with the assumption that he would be going. He accompanied me everywhere.

Topper had a quality I admire—initiative. If I sent him after something that was not there, he would substitute another article just to accomplish his mission. Occasionally I would send him after my handbag, thinking it was on a chair, when actually I had put it in a drawer, so he would bring something else instead. I could figure that if he did not return with the correct article, it was locked away somewhere. An amusing incident resulted as a sequel to his never-say-die spirit.

A friend called to say he had lost his wallet, and wondered if he had dropped it in my yard. I called Topper and Hussan to aid in the search. They searched diligently, as did all of us, without finding a trace of the missing wallet. As we were about to give up, Topper came trotting across the yard to me carrying a huge trashcan by one handle. It was larger than he was, but he made a gallant effort to carry it high and off the ground. He carried it some fifty yards and held it until I took it from him. The yard was bare, there was nothing retrievable except the trashcan, so, unwieldy as it was, he was determined not to come back empty-handed. I would have considered the feat impossible if I had not seen it. I only wish I could have recorded it on film. The wallet, incidentally, was recovered from a theater where it had been lost.

When Arry finishes his dinner, he picks up his dish and takes it over to the sink to be washed. He has always loved to carry ladies' handbags. He will greet guests at the door and take their handbags and carry them into the living room. They are a little apprehensive at first, but never give him an argument. He always carries them by the handle and relinquishes them upon command. Topper, on the other hand, confines his love for retrieving to my own personal belongings.

Another great convenience is to teach your dog to carry messages to the rest of your family. If some member is off somewhere, either in or

Joll, Bar, and Randy help the author carry in the groceries.

outside the house, give your dog a note and tell him, "Give to it to Ron," or whomever you name. Teach your dog the names of the family first, and have him deliver messages or articles, at close range, until he becomes adept. This feat has saved me much time and energy. I have lived in the country most of my life and our family spends a great deal of time out-of-doors. It is much more interesting to use a messenger dog than to search or call for someone.

If you have a big, strong dog, it is great fun to teach him lifesaving in the water. The person teaching him should be himself a strong swimmer; a dog that gets easily excited can climb on you in the water and push you under. Until they are taught water manners, some dogs can be a menace.

Hussan had the ideal disposition and physique for this type of work. He was very calm and deliberate, he could swim like a seal, very fast but effortlessly, he was unusually strong and could swim around for hours

Joll gets the newspaper.

without tiring. He hardly rippled the water, and it was a lovely sight to watch his black head gliding along smoothly above the water.

With his natural love for swimming he enjoyed retrieving anything. I taught him to Heel beside me in the water and we would swim out quite a distance together. On the way back, if I tired, I would put my arm gently around his neck, and he would pull me back to shore.

Next, I tied a cloth around a truck tire tube and had him retrieve it by holding on to the cloth. Then I tied the cloth around my arm and had him hold that and pull me in to shore. When he became expert, I removed the cloth, and he would hold my arm, above the elbow, very firmly but without hurting me, and push me toward shore. I would be in a floating position on my back. The fact that he was so strong and gentle is what made the whole feat possible. I always felt that the children and I were perfectly safe near the water when he was with us.

A friend of mine who owns a German Shepherd called me the other day. He had been to my classes, earned his Novice degree with high scores, and was ready to compete in Open work.

He was quite excited and pleased, and I could sense that something unusual had occurred. He had taken his dog hunting with him and they had discovered a duck on the far side of a large pond. When the duck flew away he shot it, and it fell into the water. He immediately alerted the dog and sent him after the duck with the command "Get it." The dog raced into the water, swam across the pond, retrieved the duck, and came back to Sit in front of his owner, gently holding the bird. This is an excellent example of Obedience Training. This dog had never been in the water before, but when his master gave him a command, he carried it out without hesitation. Incidents like these prove time and time again that Obedience Training is a completely worthwhile project.

Nowadays when I have several dogs to train each day, I let Joll be my errand boy. He brings me a leash or a dumbbell whenever I need it. When I am ready to practice a Figure 8 I yell, "Figure eight," and two or three dogs come dashing over to be posts. I also call "Long Sit and Down" when I am ready for those exercises, and all the dogs that are out with me come running over to line up just like a class. They love to do it.

Life has been made much richer for me and also for my whole family because I wanted my first dog to be "obedient." I hope that Obedience Training will be an equal source of enjoyment to you.

AMERICAN KENNEL CLUB OBEDIENCE REGULATIONS

PURPOSE

Obedience trials are a sport and all participants should be guided by the principles of good sportsmanship both in and outside of the ring. The purpose of obedience trials is to demonstrate the usefulness of the pure-bred dog as a companion of man, not merely the dog's ability to follow specified routines in the obedience ring. While all contestants in a class are required to perform the same exercises in substantially the same way so that the relative quality of the various performances may be compared and scored, the basic objective of obedience trials is to produce dogs that have been trained and conditioned always to behave in the home, in public places, and in the presence of other dogs, in a manner that will reflect credit on the sport of obedience. The performances of dog and handler in the ring must be accurate and correct and must conform to the requirements of these regulations. However, it is also essential that the dog demonstrate willingness and enjoyment of its work, and that smoothness and naturalness on the part of the handler be given precedence over a performance based on military precision and peremptory commands.

CHAPTER I
GENERAL REGULATIONS

Section 1. **Obedience Clubs.** An obedience club that meets all the requirements of The American Kennel Club and wishes to hold an Obedience Trial at which qualifying scores toward an obedience title may be awarded, must make application to The American Kennel Club on the form provided for permission to hold such trial. Such a trial, if approved, may be held either in conjunction with a dog show or as a separate event. If the club is not a member of The American Kennel Club it shall pay a license fee for the privilege of holding such trial, the amount of which shall be determined by the Board of Directors of The American Kennel Club. If the club fails to hold its trial at the time and place which have been approved, the amount of the license fee paid will be returned.

Section 2. **Dog Show and Specialty Clubs.** A dog show club may be granted permission to hold a licensed or member obedience trial at its dog show, and a specialty club may also be granted permission to hold a licensed or member obedience trial if, in the opinion of the Board of Directors of The American Kennel Club, such clubs are qualified to do so.

Section 3. **Obedience Classes.** A licensed or member obedience trial need not include all of the regular obedience classes defined in these Regulations, but a club will be approved to hold Open classes only if it also holds Novice classes, and a club will be approved to hold a Utility class only if it also holds Novice and Open classes. A specialty club which has been approved to hold a licensed or member obedience trial, if qualified in the opinion of the Board of Directors of The American Kennel Club, or an obedience club which has been approved to hold a licensed or member obedience trial may, subject to the approval of The American Kennel Club, offer additional nonregular classes for dogs not less than six months of age, provided a clear and complete description of the eligibility requirements and performance requirements for each such class appears in the premium list. However, the nonregular classes defined in these Regulations need not be described in the premium list. Pre-Novice classes will not be approved at licensed or member obedience trials.

Section 4. **Tracking Tests.** A club that has been approved to hold licensed or member obedience trials and that meets the requirements of The American Kennel Club, may also make application to hold a Tracking Test. A club may not hold a tracking test on the same day as its show or obedience trial, but the tracking test may be announced in the premium list for the show or trial, and the tracking test entries may be included in the show or obedience trial catalog. If the entries are not listed in the catalog for the show or obedience trial, the club must provide, at the tracking test, several copies of a sheet, which may be typewritten, giving all the information that would be contained in the catalog for each entered dog. If the tracking test is to be held within 7 days of the obedience trial the entries must be sent to the same person designated to receive the obedience trial entries, and the same closing date should apply. If the tracking test is not to be held within 7 days of the obedience trial the club may name someone else in the premium list to receive the tracking test entries, and may specify a different closing date for entries at least 7 days before the tracking test.

The presence of a veterinarian shall not be required at a tracking test.

Section 5. **Obedience Trial Committee.** If an obedience trial is held by an obedience club, an Obedience Trial Committee must be appointed by the club, and this committee shall exercise all the authority vested in a dog show's

Bench Show Committee. If an obedience club holds its obedience trial in conjunction with a dog show, then the Obedience Trial Committee shall have sole jurisdiction only over those dogs entered in the obedience trial and their handlers and owners; provided, however, that if any dog is entered in both obedience and breed classes, then the Obedience Trial Committee shall have jurisdiction over such dog, its owner, and its handler, only in matters pertaining to the Obedience Regulations, and the Bench Show Committee shall have jurisdiction over such dog, its owner and handler, in all other matters.

When an obedience trial is to be held in conjunction with a dog show by the club which has been granted permission to hold the show, the club's Bench Show Committee shall include one person designated as "Obedience Chairman." At such event the Bench Show Committee of the show-giving club shall have sole jurisdiction over all matters which may properly come before it, regardless of whether the matter has to do with the dog show or with the obedience trial.

Section 6. **Sanctioned Matches.** A club may hold an Obedience Match by obtaining the sanction of The American Kennel Club. Sanctioned obedience matches shall be governed by such regulations as may be adopted by the Board of Directors of The American Kennel Club. Scores awarded at such matches will not be entered in the records of The American Kennel Club nor count towards an obedience title.

All of these Obedience Regulations shall also apply to sanctioned matches except for those sections in which it is specified that the provisions apply to licensed or member trials, and except where specifically stated otherwise in the Regulations for Sanctioned Matches.

Section 7. **American Kennel Club Sanction.** American Kennel Club sanction must be obtained by any club that holds American Kennel Club obedience trials, for any type of match for which it solicits or accepts entries from non-members.

Section 8. **Dog Show Rules.** All the Dog Show Rules, where applicable, shall govern the conduct of obedience trials and tracking tests, and shall apply to all persons and dogs participating in them except as these Obedience Regulations may provide otherwise.

Section 9. **Identification.** No badges, club jackets, coats with kennel names thereon or ribbon prizes shall be worn or displayed, nor other visible means of identification used, by an individual when exhibiting a dog in the ring.

Section 10. **Immediate Family.** As used in this chapter, "immediate family" means husband, wife, father, mother, son, daughter, brother, or sister.

Section 11. **Pure-Bred Dogs Only.** As used in these regulations the word "dog" refers to either sex but only to dogs that are pure-bred of a breed eligible for registration in The American Kennel Club stud book or for entry in the Miscellaneous Class at American Kennel Club dog shows, as only such dogs may compete in obedience trials, tracking tests, or sanctioned matches. A judge must report to The American Kennel Club after the trial or tracking test any dog shown under him which in his opinion appears not to be pure-bred.

Section 12. **Unregistered Dogs.** Chapter 16, Section 1 of the Dog Show Rules shall apply to entries in licensed or member obedience trials and tracking tests, except that an eligible unregistered dog for which an ILP number has been issued by The American Kennel Club may be entered indefinitely in such events provided the ILP number is shown on each entry form.

Section 13. **Dogs That May Not Compete.** No dog belonging wholly or in part to a judge or to a Show or Obedience Trial Secretary, Superintendent, or veterinarian, or to any member of such person's immediate family or household, shall be entered in any dog show, obedience trial, or tracking test at which such person officiates or is scheduled to officiate. This applies to both obedience and dog show judges when an obedience trial is held in conjunction with a dog show. However, a tracking test shall be considered a separate event for the purpose of this section.

No dogs shall be entered or shown under a judge at an obedience trial or tracking test if the dog has been owned, sold, held under lease, handled in the ring, boarded, or has been regularly trained or instructed, within one year prior to the date of the obedience trial or tracking test, by the judge or by any member of his immediate family or household, and no such dog shall be eligible to compete. "Trained or instructed" applies equally to judges who train professionally or as amateurs, and to judges who train individual dogs or who train or instruct dogs in classes with or through their handlers.

Section 14. **Qualifying Score.** A qualifying score shall be comprised of scores of more than 50% of the available points in each exercise and a final score of 170 or more points, earned in a single regular or nonregular class at a licensed or member Obedience Trial or Sanctioned Match.

Section 15. **When Titles Are Won.** Where any of the following sections of the regulations excludes from a particular obedience class dogs that have won a particular obedience title, eligibility to enter that class shall be determined as follows: a dog may continue to be shown in such a class after its handler has been notified by three different judges of regular classes in licensed or member trials, that it has received three qualifying scores for such title, but may not be entered or shown in such a class in any obedience trial of which the closing date for entries occurs after the owner has received official notification from The American Kennel Club that the dog has won the particular obedience title.

Where any of the following sections of the regulations require that a dog shall have won a particular obedience title before competing in a particular obedience class, a dog may not be shown in such class at any obedience trial before the owner has received official notification from The American Kennel Club that the dog has won the required title.

Section 16. **Disqualification and Ineligibility.** A dog that is blind or deaf or that has been changed in appearance by artificial means (except for such changes as are customarily approved for its breed) may not compete in any obedience trial or tracking test and must be disqualified. Blind means having useful vision in neither eye. Deaf means without useful hearing.

When a judge finds any of these conditions in any dog he is judging, he shall disqualify the dog marking his book "Disqualified" and stating the reason. He shall not obtain the opinion of the show veterinarian.

The judge must disqualify any dog that attempts to attack any person in the ring. He may excuse a dog that attacks another dog or that appears dangerous to other dogs in the ring. He shall mark the dog disqualified or excused and state the reason in his judge's book, and shall give the Superintendent or Show or Trial Secretary a brief report of the dog's actions which shall be submitted to AKC with the report of the show or trial.

When a dog has been disqualified under this section as being blind or deaf or having been changed in appearance by artificial means or for having attempted to attack a person in the ring, all awards made to the dog at the trial shall be cancelled by The American Kennel Club and the dog may not again compete unless and until, following application by the owner to The American Kennel Club, the owner has received official notification from The American Kennel Club that the dog's eligibility has been reinstated.

Spayed bitches, castrated dogs, monorchid or cryptorchid males, and dogs that have faults which would disqualify them under the standards for their breeds, may compete in obedience trials if otherwise eligible under these regulations.

A dog that is lame in the ring at any obedience trial or at a tracking test may not compete and shall not receive any score at the trial. It shall be the judge's responsibility to determine whether a dog is lame. He shall not obtain the opinion of the show veterinarian. If in the judge's opinion a dog in the ring is lame, he shall not score such dog, and shall promptly excuse it from the ring and mark his book "Excused—lame."

No dog shall be eligible to compete if it is taped or bandaged in any way or if it has anything attached to it for medical or corrective purposes. Such a dog must be immediately excused from the ring, and under no circumstance may it be returned later for judging after the tape, bandage or attachment has been removed.

With the exception of Maltese, Poodles, Shih Tzu and Yorkshire Terriers, which may be shown with the hair over the eyes tied back as they are normally shown in the breed ring, no dog shall be eligible to compete if it appears to have been dyed or colored in any way or if the coat shows evidence of chalk or powder, or if the dog has anything attached to it for protection or adornment. Such a dog may, at the judge's sole discretion, be judged at a later time if the offending condition has been corrected.

An obedience judge is not required to be familiar with the breed standards nor to scrutinize each dog as in dog show judging, but shall be alert for conditions which may require disqualification or exclusion under this section.

Section 17. **Disturbances.** Bitches in season are not permitted to compete. The judge of an obedience trial or tracking test must remove from competition any bitch in season, any dog which its handler cannot control, any handler who interferes willfully with another competitor or his dog, and any handler who abuses his dog in the ring, and may excuse from competition any dog which he considers unfit to compete, or any bitch which appears so attractive to males as to be a disturbing element. If a dog or handler is expelled or excused by a judge, the reason shall be stated in the judge's book or in a separate report.

Section 18. **Obedience Ribbons.** At licensed or member obedience trials the following colors shall be used for prize ribbons or rosettes in all regular classes and for the ribbon or rosette for Highest Scoring Dog in the Regular Classes:

First Prize .... Blue
Second Prize .... Red
Third Prize .... Yellow
Fourth Prize .... White
Qualifying Prize .... Dark Green
Highest Scoring Dog in the Regular Classes .... Blue and Gold

and the following colors shall be used for nonregular classes:

First Prize .... Rose
Second Prize .... Brown
Third Prize .... Light Green
Fourth Prize .... Gray

Each ribbon or rosette shall be at least two inches wide and approximately eight inches long, and shall bear on its face a facsimile of the seal of The American Kennel Club, the words "Obedience Trial," the name of the prize, the name of the trial-giving club, the date of the trial, and the name of the city or town where the trial is given.

Section 19. **Match Ribbons.** If ribbons are given at sanctioned obedience matches they shall be of the following colors and shall have the words "Obedience Match" printed on them, but may be of any design or size:

First Prize .... Rose
Second Prize .... Brown
Third Prize .... Light Green
Fourth Prize .... Gray
Qualifying Prize .... Green with Pink edges

Section 20. **Ribbons and Prizes.** Ribbons for the four official placings and all prizes offered for competition within a single regular or nonregular class at licensed or member trials or at sanctioned matches shall be awarded only to dogs that earn qualifying scores.

Prizes for which dogs in one class compete against dogs in one or more other classes at licensed or member trials or at sanctioned matches shall be awarded only to dogs that earn qualifying scores.

Prizes at a licensed or member obedience trial must be offered to be won outright, with the exception that a prize which requires three wins by the same owner, not necessarily with the same dog, for permanent possession, may be offered for the dog with the highest qualifying score in one of the regular classes, or the dog with the highest qualifying score in the regular classes, or the dog with the highest combined qualifying scores in the Open B and Utility classes.

Subject to the provisions of paragraphs 1 and 2 of this section, prizes may be offered for the highest scoring dogs of the Groups as defined in Chapter 2 of the Dog Show Rules, or for the highest scoring dogs of any breeds, but not for a breed variety. Show varieties are not recognized for obedience. In accordance with Chapter 2, all Poodles are in the Non-Sporting Group and all Manchester Terriers in the Terrier Group.

Prizes offered only to members of certain clubs or organizations will not be approved for publication in premium lists.

Section 21. **Highest Scoring Dog in the Regular Classes.** The dog receiving the highest qualifying score in the regular classes shall be awarded the ribbon and any prizes offered for this placement, after the announcement of final scores of the last regular class to be judged. The Superintendent or Show or Trial Secretary shall mark the catalog to identify the dog receiving this award.

In case of a tie between dogs receiving the highest qualifying score in two or more regular classes, the dogs shall be tested again by having them perform at the same time some part or parts of the Heel Free exercise. The judge for the run-off shall be designated by the Bench Show or Obedience Trial Committe from among the judges of the obedience trial. When the run-off has been completed, the judges shall record the results on a special sheet which shall identify the dogs taking part in the run-off by catalog number, class and breed. When the judge has marked and signed the sheet, it shall be turned over to the Superintendent or Show or Trial Secretary who shall mark the catalog accordingly and forward the sheet to The American Kennel Club as part of the records of the trial.

Section 22. **Risk.** The owner or agent entering a dog in an obedience trial does so at his own risk and agrees to abide by the rules of The American Kennel Club and the Obedience Regulations.

Section 23. **Decisions.** At the trial the decisions of the judge shall be final in all matters affecting the scoring and the working of the dogs and their handlers. The Obedience Trial Committee, or the Bench Show Committee, if the trial is held by a show-giving club, shall decide all other matters arising at the trial, including protests against dogs made under Chapter 20 of the Dog Show Rules, subject, however, to the rules and regulations of The American Kennel Club.

Section 24. **Dogs Must Compete.** Any dog entered and received at a licensed or member obedience trial must compete in all exercises of all classes in which it is entered unless disqualified, expelled, or excused by the judge or by the Bench Show or Obedience Trial Committee, or unless excused by the official veterinarian to protect the health of the dog or of other dogs at the trial. The excuse of the official veterinarian must be in writing and must be approved by the Superintendent or Show or Trial Secretary, and must be submitted to The American Kennel Club with the report of the trial. The judge must report to The American Kennel Club any dog that is not brought back for the Group exercises.

Section 25. **Judging Program.** Any club holding a licensed or member obedience trial must prepare, after the entries have closed, a program showing the time scheduled for the judging of each of the classes. A copy of this program shall be mailed to the owner of each entered dog and to each judge, and the program shall be printed in the catalog. This program shall be based on the judging of no more than 8 Novice entries, 7 Open entries, or 6 Utility entries, per hour during the time the show or trial will be open as published in the premium list, taking into consideration the starting hour for judging if published in the premium list, and the availability of rings. No judge shall be scheduled to exceed the rate of judging. In addition, one hour for rest or meals must be allowed if, under this formula, it will take more than five hours of actual judging to judge the dogs entered under him. No judge shall be assigned to judge for more than eight hours in one day under this formula, including any breed judging assignment if the obedience trial is held in conjunction with a dog show.

If any nonregular class is to be judged in the same ring as any regular class, or by the judge of any regular class, the nonregular class must be judged after the regular class.

Section 26. **Limitation of Entries.** If a club anticipates an entry in excess of its facilities for a licensed or member trial, it may limit entries in any or all regular classes, but nonregular classes will not be approved if the regular classes are limited. A club may limit entries in any or all regular classes to 64 in a Novice class, 56 in an Open class, or 48 in a Utility class.

Prominent announcement of such limits must appear on the title or cover page of the premium list for an obedience trial or immediately under the obedience heading in the premium list for a dog show, with a statement that entries in one or more specified classes or in the obedience trial will automatically close when a certain limit or limits have been reached, even though the official closing date for entries has not arrived.

Section 27. **Additional Judges, Reassignment, Split Classes.** If when the entries have closed, it is found that the entry under one or more judges exceeds the limit established in Section 25, the club shall immediately secure the approval of The American Kennel Club for the appointment of one or more additional judges, or for reassignment of its advertised judges, so that no judge will be required to exceed the limit.

If a judge with an excessive entry was advertised to judge more than one class, one or more of his classes shall be assigned to another judge. The class or classes selected for reassignment shall first be any nonregular classes for which he was advertised, and shall then be either the regular class or classes with the minimum number of entries, or those with the minimum scheduled time, which will bring the advertised judge's schedule within, and as close as possible to, the maximum limit. If a judge with an excessive entry was advertised to judge only one class, the Superintendent, Show Secretary, or Obedience Trial Secretary, shall divide the entry as evenly as possible between the advertised judge and the other judge by drawing lots.

The club shall promptly mail to the owner of each entry affected, a notification of any change of judge. The owner shall be permitted to withdraw such entry at any time prior to the day of the show, and the entry fee shall then be refunded. If the entry in any one class is split in this manner, the advertised judge shall judge the run-off of any tie scores that may develop between the two divisions of the class, after each judge has first run off any ties resulting from his own judging.

Section 28. **Split Classes in Premium List.** A club may choose to announce two or more judges for any class in its premium list. In such case the entries shall be divided by lots as provided above. The identification slips and judging program shall be made up so that the owner of each dog will know the division, and the judge of the division, in which his dog is entered, but no owner shall be entitled to a refund of entry fee. In such case the premium list shall also specify the judge for the run-off of any tie scores which may develop between the dogs in the different divisions, after each judge has first run off any ties resulting from his own judging.

Section 29. **Split Classes, Official Ribbons, Prizes.** A club which holds a split class, whether the split is announced in the premium list or made after entries close, shall not award American Kennel Club official ribbons in either division. The four dogs with the highest qualifying scores in the class, regardless of the division or divisions in which such scores are made, shall be called back into the ring and awarded the four American Kennel Club official ribbons by one of the judges of the class. This judge shall be responsible for recording the entry numbers of the four placed dogs in one of the judges' books.

If a split class is announced in the premium list, duplicate placement prizes may be offered in each division. If prizes have been offered for placements in a class that must be split after entries close, duplicate prizes or prizes of equal value may be offered in the additional division of the class.

Section 30. **Stewards.** The judge is in sole charge of his ring until his assignment is completed. Stewards are provided to assist him, but they may act only on the judge's instructions. Stewards shall not give information or instructions to owners and handlers except as specifically instructed by the judge, and then only in such a manner that it is clear that the instructions are those of the judge.

Section 31. **Ring Conditions.** If the judging takes place indoors the ring should be rectangular and should be about 35′ wide and 50′ long for all obedience classes. In no case shall the ring for a Utility class be less than 35′ by 50′, and in no case shall the ring for a Novice or Open class be less than 30′ by 40′. The floor shall have a surface or covering that provides firm footing for the largest dogs, and rubber or similar non-slip material must be laid for the take off and landing at all jumps unless the surface, in the judge's opinion, is such as not to require it. At an outdoor show or trial the rings shall be about 40′ wide and 50′ long. The ground shall be clean and level, and the grass, if any, shall be cut short. The Club and Superintendent are responsible for providing, for the Open classes, an appropriate place approved by the judge, for the handlers to go completely out of sight of their dogs. If inclement weather at an outdoor trial necessitates the judging of obedience under shelter, the requirements as to ring size may be waived.

Section 32. **Obedience Rings at Dog Shows.** At an outdoor dog show a separate ring or rings shall be provided for obedience, and a sign forbidding anyone to permit any dog to use the ring, except when being judged, shall be set up in each such ring by the Superintendent or Show Secretary. It shall be his duty as well as that of the Show Committee to enforce this regulation. At an indoor show where limited space does not permit the exclusive use of any ring for obedience, the same regulations will apply after the obedience rings have been set up. At a dog show the material used for enclosing the obedience rings shall be at least equal to the material used for enclosing the breed rings. The ring must be thoroughly cleaned before the obedience judging starts if it has previously been used for breed judging.

Section 33. **Judge's Report on Ring and Equipment.** The Superintendent and the officials of the club holding the obedience trial are responsible for providing rings and equipment which meet the requirements of these regulations. However, the judge must check the ring and equipment provided for his use before starting to judge, and must report to The American Kennel Club after the trial any undesirable ring conditions or deficiencies that have not been promptly corrected at his request.

CHAPTER 2

REGULATIONS FOR PERFORMANCE AND JUDGING

Section 1. **Standardized Judging.** Standardized judging is of paramount importance. Judges are not permitted to inject their own variations into the exercises, but must see that each handler and dog executes the various exercises exactly as described in these regulations. A handler who is familiar with these regulations should be able to enter the ring under any judge without having to inquire how the particular judge wishes to have any exercise performed, and without being confronted with some unexpected requirement.

Section 2. **Standard of Perfection.** The judge must carry a mental picture of the theoretically perfect performance in each exercise and score each dog and handler against this visualized standard which shall combine the utmost in willingness, enjoyment and precision on the part of the dog, and naturalness, gentleness, and smoothness in handling. Lack of willingness or enjoyment on the part of the dog must be penalized, as must lack of precision in the dog's performance, roughness in handling, military precision or peremptory commands by the handler. There shall be no penalty of less than ½ point or multiple of ½ point.

Section 3. **Qualifying Performance.** A judge's certification in his judge's book of a qualifying score for any particular dog constitutes his certification to The American Kennel Club that the dog on this particular occasion has performed all of the required exercises at least in accordance with the minimum standards and that its performance on this occasion would justify the awarding of the obedience title associated with the particular class. A qualifying score must never be awarded to a dog whose performance has not met the minimum requirements, nor to a dog that shows fear or resentment, or that relieves itself at any time while in an indoor ring for judging, or that relieves itself while performing any exercise in an outdoor ring, nor to a dog whose handler disciplines or abuses it in the ring, or carries or offers food in the ring.

In deciding whether a faulty performance of a particular exercise by a particular dog warrants a qualifying score, the judge shall consider whether the awarding of an obedience title would be justified if all dogs in the class performed the exercise in a similar manner. The judge must not give a qualifying score for the exercise if he decides that it would be contrary to the best interests of the sport if all dogs in the class were to perform in the same way.

Section 4. **Judge's Directions.** The judge's orders and signals should be given to the handlers in a clear and understandable manner, but in such a way that the work of the dog is not disturbed. Before starting each exercise, the judge shall ask "Are you ready?" At the end of each exercise the judge shall say "Exercise finished." Each contestant must be worked and judged separately except for the Group exercises, and in running off a tie.

Section 5. **No Added Requirements.** No judge shall require any dog or handler to do anything, nor penalize a dog or handler for failing to do anything, that is not required by these regulations.

Section 6. **A and B Classes and Different Breeds.** The same methods and standards must be used for judging and scoring the A and B Classes, and in judging and scoring the work of dogs of different breeds.

Section 7. **Interference and Double Handling.** A judge who is aware of any assistance, interference, or attempts to control a dog from outside the ring, must act promptly to stop any such double handling or interference, and shall penalize the dog substantially or, if in the judge's opinion the circumstances warrant, shall give the dog a score of zero for the exercise during which the aid was received.

Section 8. **Rejudging.** If a dog has failed in a particular part of an exercise, it shall not ordinarily be rejudged nor given a second chance; but if in the judge's opinion the dog's performance was prejudiced by peculiar and unusual conditions, the judge may at his own discretion rejudge the dog on the entire exercise.

Section 9. **Ties.** In case of a tie any prize in a Novice or Open class, the dogs shall be tested again by having them perform at the same time all or some part of the Heel Free exercise. In the Utility class the dogs shall perform at the same time all or some part of the Signal exercise. The original scores shall not be changed.

Section 10. **Judge's Book and Score Sheets.** The judge must enter the scores and sub-total score of each dog in the official judge's book immediately after each dog has been judged on the individual exercises and before judging the next dog. Scores for the group exercises and total scores must be entered in the official judge's book immediately after each group of dogs has been judged. No score may be changed except to correct an arithmetical error or if a score has been entered in the wrong column. All final scores must be entered in the judge's book before prizes are awarded. No person other than the judge may make any entry in the judge's book. Judges may use separate score sheets for their own purposes, but shall not give out nor allow exhibitors to see such sheets, nor give out any other written scores, nor permit anyone else to distribute score sheets or cards prepared by the judge. Carbon copies of the sheets in the official judge's book shall be made available through the Superintendent or Show or Trial Secretary for examination by owners and handlers immediately after the prizes have been awarded in each class. If score cards are distributed by a club after the prizes are awarded they must contain no more information than is shown in the judge's book and must be marked "unofficial score."

Section 11. **Announcement of Scores.** The judge shall not disclose any score or partial score to contestants or spectators until he has completed the judging of the entire class or, in case of a split class, until he has completed the judging of his division; nor shall he permit anyone else to do so. After all the scores are recorded for the class, or for the division in case of a split class, the judge shall call for all available dogs that have won qualifying scores to be brought into the ring. Before awarding the prizes, the judge shall inform the spectators as to the maximum number of points for a perfect score, and shall then announce the score of each prize winner, and announce to the handler the score of each dog that has won a qualifying score.

Section 12. **Explanations and Errors.** The judge is not required to explain his scoring, and need not enter into any discussion with any contestant who appears to be dissatisfied. Any interested person who thinks that there may have been an arithmetical error or an error in identifying a dog may report the facts to one of the stewards or to the Superintendent or Show or Trial Secretary so that the matter may be checked.

Section 13. **Compliance with Regulations and Standards.** In accordance with the certification on the entry form, the handler of each dog and the person signing each entry form must be familiar with the Obedience Regulations applicable to the class in which the dog is entered.

Section 14. **Handicapped Handlers.** Judges may modify the specific requirements of these regulations for handlers to the extent necessary to permit physically handicapped handlers to compete, provided such handlers can move about the ring without physical assistance or guidance from another person, except for guidance from the judge or from the handler of a competing dog in the ring for the Group exercises.

Dogs handled by such handlers shall be required to perform all parts of all exercises as described in these regulations, and shall be penalized for failure to perform any part of an exercise.

Section 15. **Catalog Order.** Dogs should be judged in catalog order to the extent that it is practicable to do so without holding up the judging in any ring.

Judges are not required to wait for dogs for either the individual exercises or the group exercises. It is the responsibility of each handler to be ready with his dog at ringside when required, without being called. The judge's first consideration should be the convenience of those exhibitors who are at ringside with their dogs when scheduled, and who ask no favors.

A judge may agree, on request in advance of the scheduled starting time of the class, to judge a dog earlier or later than the time scheduled by catalog order. However, a judge should not hesitate to mark absent and to refuse to judge any dog and handler that are not at ringside ready to be judged in catalog order if no arrangement has been made in advance.

Section 16. **Use of Leash.** All dogs shall be kept on leash except when in the obedience ring or exercise ring. Dogs should be brought into the ring and taken out of the ring on leash. Dogs may be kept on leash in the ring when brought in to receive awards, and when waiting in the ring before and after the Group exercises. The leash shall be left on the judge's table or other designated place, between the individual exercises, and during all exercises except the Heel on Leash and Group exercises. The leash may be of fabric or leather and, in the Novice classes, need be only of sufficient length to provide adequate slack in the Heel on Leash exercise.

Section 17. **Collars.** Dogs in the obedience ring must wear well-fitting plain buckle or slip collars. Slip collars of an appropriate single length of leather, fabric or chain with two rings, one on each end are acceptable. Fancy collars, or special training collars, or collars that are either too tight or so large that they hang down unreasonably in front of the dogs, are not permitted. There shall not be anything hanging from the collars.

Section 18. **Heel Position.** The heel position as used in these regulations, whether the dog is sitting, standing, or moving at heel, means that the dog shall be straight in line with the direction in which the handler is facing, at the handler's left side, and as close as practicable to the handler's left leg without crowding, permitting the handler freedom of motion at all times. The area from the dog's head to shoulder shall be in line with the handler's left hip.

Section 19. **Hands.** In all exercises in which the dog is required to come to or return to the handler and sit in front, the handler's arms and hands shall hang naturally at his sides while the dog is coming in and until the dog has sat in front. A substantial deduction shall be made if a handler's arms and hands are not hanging naturally at his sides.

Section 20. **Commands and Signals.** Whenever a command or signal is mentioned in these regulations, a single command or signal only may be given by the handler, and any extra commands or signals must be penalized; except that whenever the regulations specify "command and/or signal" the handler may give either one or the other or both command and signal simultaneously. When a signal is permitted and given, it must be a single gesture with one arm and hand only, and the arms must immediately be returned to a natural position. Delay in following a judge's order to give a command or signal must be penalized, unless the delay is directed by the judge because of some distraction or interference.

The signal for downing a dog may be given either with the arm raised or with a down swing of the arm, but any pause in holding the arm upright followed by a down swing of the arm will be considered an additional signal.

Signaling correction to a dog is forbidden and must be penalized. Signals must be inaudible and the handler must not touch the dog. Any unusual noise or motion may be considered to be a signal. Movements of the body that aid the dog shall be considered additional signals except that a handler may bend as far as necessary to bring his hand on a level with the dog's eyes in giving a signal to a dog in the heel position, and that in the Directed Retrieve exercise the body and knees may be bent to the extent necessary to give the direction to the dog. Whistling or the use of a whistle is prohibited.

The dog's name may be used once immediately before any verbal command or before a verbal command and signal when these regulations permit command and/or signal. The name shall not be used with any signal not given simultaneously with a verbal command. The dog's name, when given immediately before a verbal command, shall not be considered as an additional command, but a dog that responds to its name without waiting for the verbal command shall be scored as having anticipated the command. The dog should never anticipate the handler's directions, but must wait for the appropriate commands and/or signals. Moving forward at heel without any command or signal other than the natural movement of the handler's left leg, shall not be considered as anticipation.

Loud commands by handlers to their dogs create a poor impression of obedience and should be avoided. Shouting is not necessary even in a noisy place if the dog is properly trained to respond to a normal tone of voice. Commands which in the judge's opinion are excessively loud will be penalized.

Section 21. **Additional Commands or Signals.** If a handler gives an additional command or signal not permitted by these regulations, either when no command or signal is permitted, or simultaneously with or following a permitted command or signal, or if he uses the dog's name with a permitted signal but without a permitted command, the dog shall be scored as though it had failed completely to perform that particular part of the exercise.

Section 22. **Praise.** Praise and petting are allowed between and after exercises, but points must be deducted from the total score for a dog that is not under reasonable control while being praised. A handler shall not carry or offer food in the ring. There shall be a substantial penalty for any dog that is picked up or carried at any time in the obedience ring.

Section 23. **Handling between Exercises.** In the Novice classes the dog may be guided by the collar between exercises and to get it into proper position for an exercise. No other physical guidance, such as placing the dog in position with the hands or straightening the dog with the knees or feet, is permitted and shall be substantially penalized even if occurring before or between the exercises.

In the Open and Utility classes there shall be a substantial penalty for any dog that is physically guided at any time or that is not readily controllable.

Posing for examination and holding for measurement are permitted. Imperfections in heeling between exercises will not be judged. Minor penalties shall be imposed for a dog that does not respond promptly to its handler's commands or signals before or between exercises in the Open and Utility classes.

Section 24. **Orders and Minimum Penalties.** The orders for the exercises and the standards for judging are set forth in the following chapters. The lists of faults are not intended to be complete but minimum penalties are specified for most of the more common and serious faults. There is no maximum limit on penalties. A dog which makes none of the errors listed may still fail to qualify or may be scored zero for other reasons.

Section 25. **Misbehavior.** Any disciplining by the handler in the ring, any display of fear or nervousness by the dog, or any uncontrolled behavior of the dog such as snapping, barking, relieving itself while in the ring for judging, or running away from its handler, whether it occurs during an exercise, between exercises, or before or after judging, must be penalized according to the seriousness of the misbehavior, and the judge may expel or excuse the dog from further competition in the class. If such behavior occurs during an exercise, the penalty must first be applied to the score for that exercise. Should the penalty be greater than the value of the exercise during which it is incurred, the additional points shall be deducted from the total score under Misbehavior. If such behavior occurs before or after the judging or between exercises, the entire penalty shall be deducted from the total score.

The judge must disqualify any dog that attempts to attack any person in the ring. He may excuse a dog that attacks another dog or that appears dangerous to other dogs in the ring.

Section 26. **Training on the Grounds.** There shall be no drilling nor intensive or abusive training of dogs on the grounds or premises at a licensed or member obedience trial or at a sanctioned match. No practice rings or areas shall be permitted at such events. All dogs shall be kept on leash except when in the obedience ring or exercise ring. Special training collars shall not be used on the grounds or premises at an obedience trial or match. These requirements shall not be interpreted as preventing a handler from moving normally about the grounds or premises with his dog at heel on leash, nor from giving such signals or such commands in a normal tone, as are necessary and usual in everyday life in heeling a dog or making it stay, but physical or verbal disciplining of dogs shall not be permitted except to a reasonable extent in the case of an attack on a person or another dog. The Superintendent, or Show or Trial Secretary, and the members of the Bench Show or Obedience Trial Committee, shall be responsible for compliance with this section, and shall investigate any reports of infractions.

Section 27. **Training and Disciplining in the Ring.** The judge shall not permit any handler to train his dog nor to practice any exercise in the ring either before or after he is judged, and shall deduct points from the total score of any dog whose handler does this. A dog whose handler disciplines it in the ring must not receive a qualifying score. The penalty shall be deducted from the points available for the exercise during which the disciplining may occur, and additional points may be deducted from the total score if necessary. If the disciplining does not occur during an exercise the penalty shall be deducted from the total score. Any abuse of a dog in the ring must be immediately reported by the judge to the Bench Show or Obedience Trial Committee for action under Chapter 2, Section 29.

Section 28. **Abuse of Dogs.** The Bench Show or Obedience Trial Committee shall investigate any reports of abuse of dogs or severe disciplining of dogs on the grounds or premises of a show, trial or match. Any person who, at a licensed or member obedience trial, conducts himself in such manner or in any other manner prejudicial to the best interests of the sport, or who fails to comply with the requirements of Chapter 2, Section 26, shall be dealt with promptly, during the trial if possible, after the offender has been notified of the specific charges against him, and has been given an opportunity to be heard in his own defense in accordance with Chapter 2, Section 29.

Any abuse of a dog in the ring must be immediately reported by the judge to the Bench Show or Obedience Trial Committee for action under Chapter 2, Section 29.

Article XII Section 2 of the Constitution and By-Laws of The American Kennel Club Provides:

Section 29. **Discipline.** The Bench Show, Obedience Trial or Field Trial Committee of a club or association shall have the right to suspend any person from the privileges of The American Kennel Club for conduct prejudicial to the best interests of pure-bred dogs, dog shows, obedience trials, field trials or The American Kennel Club, alleged to have occurred in connection with or during the progress of its show, obedience trial or field trial, after the alleged offender has been given an opportunity to be heard.

Notice in writing must be sent promptly by registered mail by the Bench Show, Obedience Trial or Field Trial Committee to the person suspended and a duplicate notice giving the name and address of the person suspended and full details as to the reasons for the suspension must be forwarded to The American Kennel Club within seven days.

An appeal may be taken from a decision of a Bench Show, Obedience Trial or Field Trial Committee. Notice in writing claiming such appeal together with a deposit of five ($5.00) dollars must be sent to The American Kennel Club within thirty days after the date of suspension. The Board of Directors may itself hear said appeal or may refer it to a committee of the Board, or to a Trial Board to be heard. The deposit shall become the property of The American Kennel Club if the decision is confirmed, or shall be returned to the appellant if the decision is not confirmed.

(See Guide for Bench Show and Obedience Trial Committees in Dealing with Misconduct at Dog Shows and Obedience Trials for proper procedure at licensed or member obedience trials.)

(The Committee at a Sanctioned event does not have this power of suspension, but must investigate any allegation of such conduct and forward a complete and detailed report of any such incident to The American Kennel Club.)

CHAPTER 3
NOVICE

Section 1. **Novice A Class.** The Novice A class shall be for dogs not less than six months of age that have not won the title C.D. A dog that is owned or co-owned by a person who has previously handled or regularly trained a dog that has won a C.D. title may not be entered in the Novice A class, nor may a dog be handled in this class by such person.

Each dog in this class must have a different handler who shall be its owner or co-owner or a member of the immediate family of the owner or co-owner, provided that such member has not previously handled or regularly trained a C.D. dog. The same person must handle the same dog in all exercises. No person may handle more than one dog in the Novice A class.

Section 2. **Novice B Class.** The Novice B class shall be for dogs not less than six months of age that have not won the title C.D. Dogs in this class may be handled by the owner or any other person. A person may handle more than one dog in this class, but each dog must have a separate handler for the Long Sit and Long Down exercises when judged in the same group. No dog may be entered in both Novice A and Novice B classes at any one trial.

Section 3. **Novice Exercises and Scores.** The exercises and maximum scores in the Novice classes are:

1. Heel on Leash	40 points
2. Stand for Examination	30 points
3. Heel Free	40 points
4. Recall	30 points
5. Long Sit	30 points
6. Long Down	30 points
Maximum Total Score	200 points

Section 4. **C.D. Title.** The American Kennel Club will issue a Companion Dog certificate for each registered dog, and will permit the use of the letters "C.D." after the name of each dog that has been certified by three different judges to have received qualifying scores in Novice classes at three licensed or member obedience trials, provided the sum total of dogs that actually competed in the regular Novice classes at each trial is not less than six.

Section 5. **Heel on Leash & Figure Eight.** The principal feature of this exercise is the ability of the dog and handler to work as a team.

Orders for the exercise are "Forward," "Halt," "Right turn," "Left turn," "About turn," "Slow," "Normal" and "Fast." "Fast" signifies that the handler must run, handler and dog moving forward at noticeably accelerated speed. In executing the About turn, the handler will always do a Right About turn.

The orders may be given in any sequence and may be repeated as necessary, but the judge shall attempt to standardize the heeling pattern for all dogs in any class.

The leash may be held in either hand or in both hands, provided the hands are in a natural position. However, any tightening or jerking of the leash or any act, signal or command which in the judge's opinion gives the dog assistance shall be penalized.

The handler shall enter the ring with his dog on a loose leash and stand with the dog sitting in the Heel Position. The judge shall ask if the handler is ready before giving the order, "Forward." The handler may give a command or signal to Heel, and shall walk briskly and in a natural manner with his dog on a loose leash. The dog shall walk close to the left side of the handler without swinging wide, lagging, forging or crowding. Whether heeling or sitting, the dog must not interfere with the handler's freedom of motion at any time. At each order to Halt, the handler will stop and his dog shall sit straight and promptly in the Heel Position without command or signal, and shall not move until the handler again moves forward on order from the judge. It is permissible after each Halt, before moving again, for the handler to give a command or signal to Heel. The judge shall say, "Exercise finished" after this portion of the exercise.

Before starting the Figure Eight the judge shall ask if the handler is ready. Figure Eight signifies that on specific orders from the judge to Forward and Halt, the handler and dog, from a starting position midway between two stewards and facing the judge, shall walk briskly twice completely around and between the two stewards, who shall stand 8 feet apart. The Figure Eight in the Novice classes shall be done on leash. The handler may choose to go in either direction. There shall be no About turn or Fast or Slow in the Figure Eight, but the judge must order at least one Halt during and another Halt at the end of this portion of the exercise.

Section 6. **Heel on Leash & Figure Eight Scoring.** If a dog is unmanageable, or if its handler constantly controls its performance by tugging on the leash or adapts pace to that of the dog, the dog must be scored zero.

Substantial deductions shall be made for additional commands or signals to Heel and for failure of dog or handler to change pace noticeably for Slow and Fast.

Substantial or minor deductions shall be made for such things as lagging, heeling wide, poor sits, handler failing to walk at a brisk pace, occasional guidance with leash and other imperfections in heeling.

In scoring this exercise the judge shall accompany the handler at a discreet distance so that he can observe any signals or commands given by the handler to the dog. The judge must do so without interfering with either dog or handler.

Section 7. **Stand for Examination.** The principal features of this exercise are that the dog stand in position before and during the examination, and that the dog display neither shyness nor resentment.

Orders are "Stand your dog and leave when you are ready," "Back to your dog" and "Exercise finished." There will be no further command from the judge to the handler to leave the dog.

The handler shall take his dog on leash to a place indicated by the judge, where the handler shall remove the leash and give it to a steward who shall place it on the judge's table or other designated place.

On judge's order the handler will stand and/or pose his dog off leash by the method of his choice, taking any reasonable time if he chooses to pose the dog as in the show ring. When he is ready, the handler will give his command and/or signal to the dog to Stay, walk forward about six feet in front of the dog, turn around and stand facing the dog.

The judge shall approach the dog from the front, and shall touch only the dog's head, body and hindquarters, using the fingers and palm of one hand only. He shall then order, "Back to your dog," whereupon the handler shall walk around behind his dog and return to the Heel Position. The dog must remain standing until after the judge has said, "Exercise finished."

Section 8. **Stand for Examination, Scoring.** The scoring of this exercise will not start until the handler has given the command and/or signal to Stay, except for such things as rough treatment of the dog by its handler or active resistance by the dog to its handler's attempts to make it stand. Either of these shall be penalized substantially.

A dog that displays any shyness or resentment or growls or snaps at any time shall be scored zero, as shall a dog that sits before or during the examination or a dog that moves away before or during the examination from the place where it was left.

Minor or substantial deductions, depending on the circumstance, shall be made for a dog that moves its feet at any time or sits or moves away after the examination has been completed.

Section 9. **Heel Free, Performance and Scoring.** This exercise shall be executed in the same manner as Heel on Leash & Figure Eight except that the dog shall be off leash and that there shall be no Figure Eight. Orders and scoring shall also be the same.

Section 10. **Recall.** The principal features of this exercise are that the dog stay where left until called by its handler, and that the dog respond promptly to the handler's command or signal to Come.

Orders are "Leave your dog," "Call your dog" and "Finish."

On order from the judge, the handler may give command and/or signal to the dog to Stay in the sit position while the handler walks forward about 35 feet to the other end of the ring, where he shall turn and stand in a natural manner facing his dog. On judge's order or signal, the handler will give command or signal for the dog to Come. The dog must come straight in at a brisk pace and sit straight, centered immediately in front of the handler's feet, close enough that the handler could readily touch its head without moving either foot or having to stretch forward. The dog must not touch the handler or sit between his feet.

On judge's order the handler will give command or signal to Finish and the dog must go smartly to the Heel Position and sit. The manner in which the dog finishes shall be optional with the handler provided that it is prompt and that the dog sit straight at heel.

Section 11. **Recall, Scoring.** A dog must receive a score of zero for the following: not staying without additional command or signal, failure to come on the first command or signal, moving from the place where left before being called or signalled, not sitting close enough in front that the handler could readily touch its head without moving either foot or stretching forward.

Substantial deductions shall be made for a slow response to the Come, varying with the extent of the slowness; for extra command or signal to Stay if given before the handler leaves the dog; for the dog's standing or lying down instead of waiting in the sit position; for extra command or signal to Finish and for failure to Sit or Finish.

Minor deductions shall be made for slow or poor Sits or Finishes, for touching the handler on coming in or while finishing, and for sitting between the handler's feet.

Section 12. **Group Exercises.** The principal feature of these exercises is that the dog remain in the sitting or down position, whichever is required by the particular exercise.

Orders are "Sit your dogs" or "Down your dogs," "Leave your dogs" and "Back to your dogs."

All the competing dogs in the class take these exercises together, except that if there are 12 or more dogs they shall, at the judge's option, be judged in groups of not less than 6 nor more than 15 dogs. When the same judge does both Novice A and Novice B, the two classes may be combined provided that there are not more than 15 dogs competing in the combined classes. The dogs that are in the ring shall be lined up in catalog order along one of the four sides of the ring. Handlers' armbands, weighted with leashes or other articles if necessary, shall be placed behind the dogs.

For the Long Sit the handlers shall, on order from the judge, command and/or signal their dogs to Sit if they are not already sitting. On further order from the judge to leave their dogs, the handlers shall give a command and/or signal to Stay and immediately leave their dogs. The handlers will go to the opposite side of the ring, turn and stand facing their respective dogs.

If a dog gets up and starts to roam or follows its handler, or if a dog moves so as to interfere with another dog, the judge shall promptly instruct the handler or one of the stewards to take the dog out of the ring or to keep it away from the other dogs.

After one minute from the time he has ordered the handlers to leave their dogs, the judge will give the order to return, whereupon the handlers must promptly go back to their dogs, each walking around and in back of his own dog to the Heel Position. The dogs must not move from the sitting position until after the judge has said, "Exercise finished." The judge shall not give the order "Exercise finished" until the handlers have returned to the Heel Position.

Before starting the Long Down the judge shall ask if the handlers are ready. The Long Down is done in the same manner as the Long Sit except that instead of sitting their dogs the handlers shall, on order from the judge, down their dogs without touching either the dogs or their collars, and except further that the judge will order the handlers to return after three minutes. The dogs must not move from the down position until after the judge has said, "Exercise finished."

The dogs shall not be required to sit at the end of the Down exercise.

Section 13. **Group Exercises, Scoring.** During these exercises the judge shall stand in such position that all of the dogs are in his line of vision, and where he can see all the handlers in the ring without having to turn around.

Scoring of the exercises will not start until after the judge has ordered the handlers to leave their dogs, except for such things as rough treatment of a dog by its handler or active resistance by a dog to its handler's attempts to make it Sit or lie Down. These shall be penalized substantially; in extreme cases the dog may be excused.

A score of zero is required for the following: the dog's moving at any time during either exercise a substantial distance away from the place where it was left, or going over to any other dog, or staying on the spot where it was left but not remaining in whichever position is required by the particular exercise until the handler has returned to the Heel Position, or repeatedly barking or whining.

A substantial deduction shall be made for a dog that moves even a minor distance away from the place where it was left or that barks or whines only once or twice. Depending on the circumstance, a substantial or minor deduction shall be made for touching the dog or its collar in getting the dog into the Down position.

There shall be a minor deduction if a dog changes position after the handler has returned to the Heel Position but before the judge has said, "Exercise finished." The judge shall not give the order "Exercise finished" until the handlers have returned to the Heel Position.

CHAPTER 4
OPEN

Section 1. **Open A Class.** The Open A class shall be for dogs that have won the C.D. title but have not won the title C.D.X. Obedience judges and licensed handlers may not enter or handle dogs in this class. Each dog must be handled by its owner or by a member of his immediate family. Owners may enter more than one dog in this class but the same person who handled each dog in the first five exercises must handle the same dog in the Long Sit and Long Down exercises, except that if a person has handled more than one dog in the first five exercises he must have an additional handler, who must be the owner or a member of his immediate family, for each additional dog, when more than one dog that he has handled in the first five exercises is judged in the same group for the Long Sit and Long Down.

Section 2. **Open B Class.** The Open B class will be for dogs that have won the title C.D. or C.D.X. A dog may continue to compete in this class after it has won the title U.D. Dogs in this class may be handled by the owner or any other person. Owners may enter more than one dog in this class but the same person who handled each dog in the first five exercises must handle each dog in the Long Sit and Long Down exercises, except that if a person has handled more than one dog in the first five exercises he must have an additional handler for each additional dog, when more than one dog that he has handled in the first five exercises is judged in the same group for the Long Sit and Long Down. No dog may be entered in both Open A and Open B classes at any one trial.

Section 3. **Open Exercises and Scores.** The exercises and maximum scores in the Open classes are:

1. Heel Free	40 points
2. Drop on Recall	30 points
3. Retrieve on Flat	20 points
4. Retrieve over High Jump	30 points
5. Broad Jump	20 points
6. Long Sit	30 points
7. Long Down	30 points
Maximum Total Score	200 points

Section 4. **C.D.X. Title.** The American Kennel Club will issue a Companion Dog Excellent certificate for each registered dog, and will permit the use of the letters "C.D.X." after the name of each dog that has been certified by three

different judges of obedience trials to have received qualifying scores in Open classes at three licensed or member obedience trials, provided the sum total of dogs that actually competed in the regular Open classes at each trial is not less than six.

Section 5. **Heel Free, Performance and Scoring.** This exercise shall be executed in the same manner as the Novice Heel on Leash and Figure Eight exercise, except that the dog is off leash. Orders and scoring are the same as in Heel on Leash and Figure Eight.

Section 6. **Drop on Recall.** The principal features of this exercise, in addition to those listed under the Novice Recall, are the dog's prompt response to the handler's command or signal to Drop, and the dog's remaining in the Down position until again called or signalled to Come. The dog will be judged on the promptness of its response to command or signal and not on its proximity to a designated point.

Orders for the exercise are "Leave your dog," "Call your dog," an order or signal to Drop the dog, another "Call your dog" and "Finish." The judge may designate in advance a point at which, as the dog is coming in, the handler shall give his command or signal to the dog to Drop. The judge's signal or designated point must be clear to the handler but not obvious or distracting to the dog.

On order from the judge, the handler may give command and/or signal for the dog to Stay in the sit position while the handler walks forward about 35 feet to the other end of the ring, where he shall turn and stand in a natural manner facing his dog. On judge's order or signal, the handler shall give command or signal to Come and the dog must start straight in at a brisk pace. On judge's order or signal, or at a point designated in advance by the judge, the handler shall give command or signal to Drop, and the dog must immediately drop completely to the down position, where he must remain until, on judge's order or signal, the handler again gives command or signal to Come. The dog must come straight in at a brisk pace and sit straight, centered immediately in front of the handler's feet, close enough that the handler could readily touch the dog's head without moving either foot or having to stretch forward. The dog must not touch the handler nor sit between his feet.

The Finish shall be executed as in the Novice Recall.

Section 7. **Drop on Recall, Scoring.** All applicable penalties listed under the Novice Recall as requiring a score of zero shall apply. In addition, a zero score is required for a dog that does not drop completely to the down position on a single command or signal, and for a dog that drops but does not remain down until called or signalled.

Substantial deductions, varying with the extent, shall be made for delayed or slow response to the handler's command or signal to Drop, for slow response to either of the Comes, for extra command or signal to Stay if given before the handler leaves the dog, for the dog's standing or lying down instead of waiting where left in a sit position, for extra command or signal to Finish and for failure to finish.

Minor deductions shall be made for slow or poor sits or finishes, for touching the handler on coming in or while finishing, or for sitting between the handler's feet.

Section 8. **Retrieve on the Flat.** The principal feature of this exercise is that the dog retrieve promptly.

Orders are "Throw it," "Send your dog," "Take it" and "Finish."

The handler shall stand with his dog sitting in the Heel Position in a place designated by the judge. On order, "Throw it," the handler shall give command and/or signal to Stay, which signal may not be given with the hand that is holding the dumbbell, and throw the dumbbell. On order to send his dog, the handler shall give command or signal to retrieve. The retrieve shall be executed at a fast trot or gallop, the dog going directly to the dumbbell and retrieving it without unnecessary mouthing or playing with the dumbbell. The dog must sit straight to deliver, centered immediately in front of the handler's feet, close enough that the handler can readily take the dumbbell without moving either foot or having to stretch forward. The dog must not touch the handler nor sit between his feet. On order from the judge to take it, the handler shall give command or signal and take the dumbbell.

The finish shall be executed as in the Novice Recall.

The dumbbell, which must be approved by the judge, shall be made of one or more solid pieces of one of the heavy hardwoods, which shall not be hollowed out. It may be unfinished, or coated with a clear finish, or painted white. It shall have no decorations or attachments but may bear an inconspicuous mark for identification. The size of the dumbbell shall be proportionate to the size of the dog. The judge shall require the dumbbell to be thrown again before the dog is sent if, in his opinion, it is thrown too short a distance, or too far to one side, or too close to the ringside.

Section 9. **Retrieve on the Flat, Scoring.** A dog that fails to go out on the first command or signal, or goes to retrieve before the command or signal is given, or fails to retrieve, or does not return with the dumbbell sufficiently close that the handler can easily take the dumbbell as described above, must be scored zero.

Substantial deductions, depending on the extent, shall be made for slowness in going out or returning or in picking up the dumbbell, for not going directly to the dumbbell, for mouthing or playing with or dropping the dumbbell, for reluctance or refusal to release the dumbbell to the handler, for extra command or signal to finish and for failure to sit or finish.

Substantial or minor deductions shall be made for slow or poor sits or finishes, for touching the handler on coming in or while finishing, or for sitting between the handler's feet.

Section 10. **Retrieve over High Jump.** The principal features of this exercise are that the dog go out over the jump, pick up the dumbbell and promptly return with it over the jump.

Orders are "Throw it," "Send your dog," "Take it" and "Finish."

This exercise shall be executed in the same manner as the Retrieve on the Flat, except that the dog must clear the High Jump both going and coming. The handler must stand at least eight feet, or any reasonable distance beyond

8 feet, from the jump but must remain in the same spot throughout the exercise.

The jump shall be as nearly as possible one and one-half times the height of the dog at the withers, as determined by the judge, with a minimum height of 8 inches and a maximum height of 36 inches. This applies to all breeds with the following exceptions:

The jump shall be once the height of the dog at the withers or 36 inches, whichever is less, for the following breeds—

Bloodhounds	Mastiffs
Bullmastiffs	Newfoundlands
Great Danes	St. Bernards
Great Pyrenees	

The jump shall be once the height of the dog at the withers or 8 inches, whichever is greater, for the following breeds—

Spaniels (Clumber)	Norwich Terriers
Spaniels (Sussex)	Scottish Terriers
Basset Hounds	Sealyham Terriers
Dachshunds	Skye Terriers
Welsh Corgis (Cardigan)	West Highland White Terriers
Welsh Corgis (Pembroke)	Maltese
Australian Terriers	Pekingese
Cairn Terriers	Bulldogs
Dandie Dinmont Terriers	French Bulldogs

The jumps may be preset by the stewards based on the handler's advice as to the dog's height. The judge must make certain that the jump is set at the required height for each dog. He shall verify in the ring with an ordinary folding rule or steel tape to the nearest one-half inch, the height at the withers of each dog that jumps less than 36 inches. He shall not base his decision as to the height of the jump on the handler's advice.

The side posts of the High Jump shall be 4 feet high and the jump shall be 5 feet wide and shall be so constructed as to provide adjustment for each 2 inches from 8 inches to 36 inches. It is suggested that the jump have a bottom board 8 inches wide including the space from the bottom of the board to the ground or floor, together with three other 8 inch boards, one 4 inch board, and one 2 inch board. A 6 inch board may also be provided. The jump shall be painted a flat white. The width in inches, and nothing else, shall be painted on each side of each board in black 2 inch figures, the figure on the bottom board representing the distance from the ground or floor to the top of the board.

Section 11. **Retrieve over High Jump, Scoring.** Scoring of this exercise shall be as in Retrieve on the Flat. In addition, a dog that fails, either going or returning, to go over the jump, or that climbs or uses the jump for aid in going over, must be scored zero. Touching the jump in going over is added to the substantial and minor penalties listed under Retrieve on the Flat.

Section 12. **Broad Jump.** The principal features of this exercise are that the dog stay sitting until directed to jump and that the dog clear the jump on a single command or signal.

Orders are "Leave your dog," "Send your dog" and "Finish."

The handler will stand with his dog sitting in the Heel Position in front of and at least 8 feet from the jump. On order from the judge to "Leave your dog," the handler will give his dog the command and/or signal to Stay and go to a position facing the right side of the jump, with his toes about 2 feet from the jump, and anywhere between the lowest edge of the first hurdle and the highest edge of the last hurdle.

On order from the judge the handler shall give the command or signal to jump and the dog shall clear the entire distance of the Broad Jump without touching and, without further command or signal, return to a sitting position immediately in front of the handler as in the Recall. The handler shall change his position by executing a right angle turn while the dog is in mid-air, but shall remain in the same spot. The dog must sit and finish as in the Novice Recall.

The Broad Jump shall consist of four hurdles, built to telescope for convenience, made of boards about 8 inches wide, the largest measuring about 5 feet in length and 6 inches high at the highest point, all painted a flat white. When set up they shall be arranged in order of size and shall be evenly spaced so as to cover a distance equal to twice the height of the High Jump as set for the particular dog, with the low side of each hurdle and the lowest hurdle nearest the dog. The four hurdles shall be used for a jump of 52″ to 72″, three for a jump of 32″ to 48″, and two for a jump of 16″ to 28″. The highest hurdles shall be removed first. It is the judge's responsibility to see that the distance jumped is that required by these Regulations for the particular dog.

Section 13. **Broad Jump, Scoring.** A dog that fails to stay until directed to jump, or refuses the jump on the first command or signal, or walks over any part of the jump, or fails to clear the full distance, with its forelegs, must be scored zero. Minor or substantial deductions, depending on the specific circumstances in each case, shall be made for a dog that touches the jump in going over or that does not return directly to the handler. All other applicable penalties listed under the Recall shall apply.

Section 14. **Open Group Exercises, Performance and Scoring.** During Long Sit and the Long Down exercises the judge shall stand in such a positioin that all of the dogs are in his line of vision, and where he can see all the handlers in the ring, or leaving and returning to the ring, without having to turn around.

These exercises in the Open classes are performed in the same manner as in the Novice classes except that after leaving their dogs the handlers must cross to the opposite side of the ring, and then leave the ring in single file as directed by the judge and go to a place designated by the judge, completely out of sight of their dogs, where they must remain until called by the judge after the expiration of the time limit of three minutes in the Long Sit and five minutes in the Long Down, from the time the judge gave the order to "Leave your dogs." On order from the judge the handlers shall return to the ring in single file in reverse order, lining up facing their dogs at the opposite side of the ring, and returning to their dogs on order from the judge.

Orders and scoring are the same as in the Novice Group exercises.

CHAPTER 5
UTILITY

Section 1. **Utility Class.** The Utility class shall be for dogs that have won the title C.D.X. Dogs that have won the title U.D. may continue to compete in this class. Dogs in this class may be handled by the owner or any other person. Owners may enter more than one dog in this class, but each dog must have a separate handler for the Group Examination when judged in the same group.

Section 2. **Division of Utility Class.** A club may choose to divide the Utility class into Utility A and Utility B classes, provided such division is approved by The American Kennel Club and is announced in the premium list. When this is done the Utility A class shall be for dogs which have won the title C.D.X. and have not won the title U.D. Obedience judges and licensed handlers may not enter or handle dogs in this class. Owners may enter more than one dog in this class but the same person who handled each dog in the first five exercises must handle the same dog in the Group Examination, except that if a person has handled more than one dog in the first five exercises he must have an additional handler, who must be the owner or a member of his immediate family, for each additional dog, when more than one dog he has handled in the first five exercises is judged in the same group for the Group Examination. All other dogs that are eligible for the Utility class but not eligible for the Utility A class may be entered only in the Utility B class to which the conditions listed in Chapter 5, Section 1 shall apply. No dog may be entered in both Utility A and Utility B classes at any one trial.

Section 3. **Utility Exercises and Scores.** The exercises, maximum scores and order of judging in the Utility classes are:

1. Signal Exercise	40 points
2. Scent Discrimination Article No. 1	30 points
3. Scent Discrimination Article No. 2	30 points
4. Directed Retrieve	30 points
5. Directed Jumping	40 points
6. Group Examination	30 points
Maximum Total Score	200 points

Section 4. **U.D. Title.** The American Kennel Club will issue a Utility Dog certificate for each registered dog, and will permit the use of the letters "U.D." after the name of each dog that has been certified by three different judges of obedience trials to have received qualifying scores in Utility classes at three licensed or member obedience trials in each of which three or more dogs actually competed in the Utility class or classes.

Section 5. **Signal Exercise.** The principal features of this exercise are the ability of dog and handler to work as a team while heeling, and the dog's correct responses to the signals to Stand, Stay, Drop, Sit and Come.

Orders are the same as in Heel on Leash and Figure Eight, with the additions of "Stand your dog," which shall be given only when dog and handler are walking at normal pace, and "Leave your dog." The judge must use signals for directing the handler to signal the dog to Drop, to Sit and Come, in that sequence, and to finish.

Heeling in the Signal Exercise shall be done in the same manner as in Heel Free, except that throughout the entire exercise the handler shall use signals only and must not speak to his dog at any time. On order from the judge, "Forward," the handler may signal his dog to walk at heel, and on specific order from the judge in each case, shall execute a "Left turn," "Right turn," "About turn," "Halt," "Slow," "Normal" and "Fast." These orders may be given in any sequence and may be repeated as necessary, but the judge shall attempt to standardize the heeling pattern for all dogs in the class.

On order from the judge, and while the dog is walking at heel, the handler shall signal his dog to Stand in the heel position near one end of the ring. On further order, "Leave your dog," the handler shall signal his dog to Stay, go to the other end of the ring and turn to face his dog. On separate and specific signals from the judge, the handler shall give his signals to Drop, to Sit, to Come and to Finish as in the Recall. During the heeling part of this exercise the handler may not give any signal except when a command or signal is permitted in the Heeling exercises.

Section 6. **Signal Exercise, Scoring.** A dog that fails, on a single signal from the handler, to stand or remain standing where left, or to drop, or to sit and stay, or to come, or that receives a command or audible signal from the handler to do any of these parts of the exercise, shall be scored zero.

Minor or substantial deductions depending on the specific circumstances in each case, shall be made for a dog that walks forward on the Stand, Drop or Sit portions of the exercise.

A substantial deduction shall be made for any audible command during the Heeling or Finish portions of the exercise.

All the penalties listed under the Heel on Leash and Figure Eight and the Recall exercises shall also apply.

Section 7. **Scent Discrimination.** The principal features of these exercises are the selection of the handler's article from among the other articles by scent alone, and the prompt delivery of the right article to the handler.

Orders are "Send your dog," "Take it" and "Finish."

In each of these two exercises the dog must select by scent alone and retrieve an article which has been handled by its handler. The articles shall be provided by the handler and shall consist of two sets, each comprised of five identical objects not more than six inches in length, which may be items of everyday use. One set shall be made entirely of rigid metal, and one of leather of such design that nothing but leather is visible except for the minimum amount of thread or metal necessary to hold the object together. The articles in each set must be legibly numbered, each with a different number and must be approved by the judge.

The handler shall present all 10 articles to the judge, who shall designate one from each set and make written note of the numbers of the two articles he has selected. These two handler's articles shall be placed on a table or chair within the ring until picked up by the handler, who shall hold in his hand only one article at a time. The judge or steward will handle each of the remaining 8 articles as he places them on the floor or ground about 15 feet in front of the handler and dog, at random about 6 inches apart. The judge must make sure that the articles are properly separated before the dog is sent, so that there may be no confusion of scent between the articles.

Handler and dog shall turn around after watching the judge or steward spread the articles, and shall remain facing away from those articles until the judge has taken the handler's scented article and given the order, "Send your dog."

The handler may use either article first, but must relinquish each one immediately when ordered by the judge. The judge shall make certain that the handler imparts his scent to each article only with his hands and that, between the time the handler picks up each article and the time he gives it to the judge, the article is held continuously in the handler's hands which must remain in plain sight.

On order from the judge, the handler will immediately place his article on the judge's book or work sheet. The judge, without touching the article with his hands, will place it among those on the ground or floor.

On order from the judge to "Send your dog," the handler may give the command to Heel before turning, and will execute a Right about Turn, stopping to face the articles, the dog in the Heel Position. The handler shall then give the command or signal to retrieve. Handlers may at their discretion on orders from the judge to "Send your dog," execute with their dog a Right about Turn to face the articles, simultaneously giving the command or signal to retrieve. In this instance the dog shall not assume a sitting position, but shall go directly to the articles. The handler may give his scent to the dog by gently touching the dog's nose with the palm of one open hand, but this may only be done while the dog and handler have their backs to the articles and the arm and hand must be returned to a natural position before handler and dog turn to face the articles.

The dog shall go at a brisk pace to the articles. It may take any reasonable time to select the right article, but only provided it works continuously. After picking up the right article the dog shall return at a brisk pace and complete the exercise as in the Retrieve on the Flat.

These procedures shall be followed for both articles. Should a dog retrieve a wrong article in the first exercise, that article shall be placed on the table or chair. The correct article must be removed, and the second exercise shall be conducted with one less article on the ground or floor.

Section 8. **Scent Discrimination, Scoring.** Deductions shall be the same as in the Retrieve on the Flat. In addition, a dog that fails to go out to the group of articles, or retrieves a wrong article, or fails to bring the right article to the handler, must be scored zero for the particular exercise.

Substantial deductions shall be made for a dog that picks up a wrong article, even though he puts it down again immediately, for any roughness by the handler in imparting his scent to the dog, and for any excessive motions by the handler in turning to face the articles.

Minor or substantial deductions, depending on the circumstance in each case, shall be made for a dog that is slow or inattentive, or that does not work continuously. There shall be no penalty for a dog that takes a reasonably long time examining the articles provided the dog works smartly and continuously.

Section 9. **Directed Retrieve.** The principal features of the exercise are that the dog stay until directed to retrieve, that it go directly to the designated glove, and that it retrieve promptly. The orders for the exercise are "One," "Two" or "Three," "Take it" and "Finish." In this exercise the handler will provide three predominantly white, cotton work gloves, which must be open and must be approved by the judge. The handler will stand with his back to the unobstructed end of the ring with his dog sitting in the Heel Position midway between and in line with the two jumps. The judge or steward will then drop the three gloves across the end of the ring, while the handler and dog are facing the opposite direction, one glove in each corner and one in the center, about 3 feet from the end of the ring and for the corner gloves about 3 feet from the side of the ring. All three gloves will be clearly visible to the dog and handler, when the handler turns to face the glove designated by the judge. There shall be no table or chair at this end of the ring.

The gloves shall be designated "One," "Two" or "Three" reading from left to right when the handler turns and faces the gloves. The judge will give the order "One," or "Two," or "Three." The handler then must give the command to Heel and turn in place, right or left to face the designated glove. The handler will come to a halt with the dog sitting in the Heel Position. The handler shall not touch the dog to get it in position. The handler will then give his dog the direction to the designated glove with a single motion of his left hand and arm along the right side of the dog, and will give the command to retrieve either simultaneously with or immediately following the giving of the direction. The dog shall then go directly to the glove at a brisk pace and retrieve it without unnecessary mouthing or playing with it, completing the exercise as in the Retrieve on the Flat.

The handler may bend his knees and body in giving the direction to the dog, after which the handler will stand erect in a natural position with his arms at his sides.

The exercise shall consist of a single retrieve, but the judge shall designate different glove numbers for successive dogs.

Section 10. **Directed Retrieve, Scoring.** A dog must receive a score of zero for the following: not going out on a single command, not going directly to the designated glove, not retrieving the glove, anticipating the handler's command to retrieve, not returning promptly and sufficiently close so that the handler can readily take the glove without moving either foot or stretching forward.

Depending on the extent, substantial or minor deductions shall be made for a handler who over-turns, or touches the dog or uses excessive motions to get the dog in position.

All other deductions listed under Retrieve on the Flat shall also apply.

Section 11. **Directed Jumping.** The principal features of this exercise are that the dog go away from the handler in the direction indicated, stop when commanded, jump as directed and return as in the Recall.

The orders are "Send your dog," the designation of which jump is to be taken, and "Finish."

The jumps shall be placed midway in the ring at right angles to the sides of the ring and 18 to 20 feet apart, the Bar Jump on one side, the High Jump on the other. The judge must make certain that the jumps are set at the required height for each dog by following the procedure described in Retrieve over the High Jump.

The handler, from a position on the center line of the ring and about 20 feet from the line of the jumps, shall stand with his dog sitting in the Heel Position and on order from the judge shall command and/or signal his dog to go forward at a brisk pace to a point about 20 feet beyond the jumps and in the approximate center. When the dog has reached this point the handler shall give a command to Sit; the dog must stop and sit with his attention on the handler but need not sit squarely.

The judge will designate which jump is to be taken first by the dog, and the handler shall command and/or signal the dog to return to him over the designated jump. While the dog is in mid-air the handler may turn so as to be facing the dog as it returns. The dog shall sit in front of the handler and, on order from the judge, finish as in the Recall. The judge will say "Exercise finished" after the dog has returned to the Heel Position.

When the dog is again sitting in the Heel Position the judge shall ask, "Are you ready?" before giving the order to send the dog for the second part of the exercise. The same procedure shall be followed for the second jump.

It is optional with the judge which jump is taken first, but both jumps must be taken to complete the exercise and the judge must not designate the jump until the dog is at the far end of the ring. The dog shall clear the jumps without touching them.

The height of the jumps shall be the same as required in the Open classes. The High Jump shall be the same as that used in the Open classes, and the Bar Jump shall consist of a bar between 2 and 2½ inches square with the four edges rounded sufficiently to remove any sharpness. The bar shall be painted a flat black and white in alternate sections of about 3 inches each. The bar shall be supported by two unconnected 4 foot upright posts about 5 feet apart. The bar shall be adjustable for each 2 inches of height from 8 inches to 36 inches, and the jump shall be so constructed and positioned that the bar can be knocked off without disturbing the uprights.

Section 12. **Directed Jumping, Scoring.** A dog must receive a score of zero for the following: anticipating the handler's command and/or signal to go out, not leaving the handler, not going out between the jumps, not going at least 10 feet beyond the jumps, not stopping on command, anticipating the handler's command and/or signal to jump, not jumping as directed, knocking the bar off the uprights, climbing or using the top of the High Jump for aid in going over.

Substantial deductions shall be made for a dog that does not stop in the approximate center of the ring; for a dog that turns, stops or sits before the handler's command to Sit, and for a dog that fails to sit.

Substantial or minor deductions, depending on the extent, shall be made for slowness in going out or for touching the jumps. All of the penalties listed under Recall shall also apply.

Section 13. **Group Examination.** The principal features of this exercise are that the dog stand and stay, and show no shyness or resentment.

All the competing dogs take this exercise together, except that if there are 12 or more dogs, they shall be judged in groups of not less than 6 nor more than 15 dogs, at the judge's option. The handlers and dogs that are in the ring shall line up in catalog order, side by side down the center of the ring, with the dogs sitting in the Heel Position. Each handler shall place his armband, weighted with leash or other article if necessary, behind his dog. The judge must instruct one or more stewards to watch the other dogs while he conducts the individual examinations, and to call any faults to his attention.

On order from the judge, "Stand your dogs," all the handlers will stand or pose their dogs and on further order, "Leave your dogs," will give command and/or signal to Stay and walk forward to the side of the ring where they shall turn and stand facing their respective dogs. The judge will approach each dog in turn from the front and examine it, going over the dog with his hands as in dog show judging except that under no circumstance shall the examination include the dog's mouth or testicles.

When all dogs have been examined and after the handlers have been away from their dogs for at least three minutes, the judge will promptly order the handlers, "Back to your dogs," and the handlers will return, each walking around and in back of his own dog to the Heel Position, after which the judge will say, "Exercise finished." Each dog must remain standing at its position in the line from the time its handler leaves it until the end of the exercise, and must show no shyness or resentment. The dogs are not required to sit at the end of this exercise.

Section 14. **Group Examination, Scoring.** There should be no attempt to judge the dogs or handlers on the manner in which the dogs are made to stand. The scoring will not start until after the judge has given the order to leave the dogs, except for such general things as rough treatment of a dog by its handler, or active resistance by a dog to its handler's attempts to make it stand. Immediately after examining each dog the judge must make a written record of any necessary deductions, subject to further deductions for subsequent faults.

A dog must be scored zero for the following: displaying shyness or resentment, moving a minor distance from the place where it was left, going over to any other dog, sitting or lying down before the handler has returned to the Heel Position, growling or snapping at any time during the exercise, repeatedly barking or whining.

Substantial or minor deductions, depending on the circumstance, must be made for a dog that moves its feet at any time during the exercise, or sits or lies down after the handler has returned to the Heel Position.

CHAPTER 6

TRACKING

Section 1. **Tracking Test.** This test shall be for dogs not less than six months of age, and must be judged by two judges. With each entry form for a licensed or member tracking test for a dog that has not passed an AKC tracking test there must be filed an original written statement, dated within six months of the date the test is to be held, signed by a person who has been approved by The American Kennel Club to judge tracking tests, certifying that the dog is considered by him to be ready for such a test. These original statements cannot be used again and must be submitted to The American Kennel Club with the entry forms. Written permission to waive or modify this requirement may be granted by The American Kennel Club in unusual circumstances. Tracking tests are open to all dogs that are otherwise eligible under these Regulations.

This test cannot be given at a dog show or obedience trial. The duration of this test may be one day or more within a 15 day period after the original date in the event of an unusually large entry or other unforeseen emergency, provided that the change of date is satisfactory to the exhibitors affected.

Section 2. **T.D. Title.** The American Kennel Club will issue a Tracking Dog certificate to a registered dog, and will permit the use of the letters "T.D." after the name of each dog which has been certified by the two judges to have passed a licensed or member tracking test in which at least three dogs actually participated.

The owner of a dog holding both the U.D. and T.D. titles may use the letters "U.D.T." after the name of the dog, signifying "Utility Dog Tracker."

Section 3. **Tracking.** The tracking test must be performed with the dog on leash, the length of the track to be not less than 440 yards nor more than 500 yards, the scent to be not less than one half hour nor more than two hours old and that of a stranger who will leave an inconspicuous glove or wallet, dark in color, at the end of the track where it must be found by the dog and picked up by the dog or handler. The article must be approved in advance by the judges. The tracklayer will follow the track which has been staked out with flags a day or more earlier, collecting all the flags on the way with the exception of one flag at the start of the track and one flag about 30 yards from the start of the track to indicate the direction of the track; then deposit the article at the end of the track and leave the course, proceeding straight ahead at least 50 feet. The tracklayer must wear his own shoes which, if not having leather soles, must have uppers of fabric or leather. The dog shall wear a harness to which is attached a leash between 20 and 40 feet in length. The handler shall follow the dog at a distance of not less than 20 feet, and the dog shall not be guided by the handler. The dog may be restrained by the handler, but any leading or guiding of the dog constitutes grounds for calling the handler off and marking the dog "Failed." A dog may, at the handler's option, be given one, and only one, second chance to take the scent between the two flags, provided it has not passed the second flag.

Section 4. **Tracking Tests.** A person who is qualified to judge Obedience Trials is not necessarily capable of judging a tracking test. Tracking judges must be familiar with the various conditions that may exist when a dog is required to work a scent trail. Scent conditions, weather, lay of the land, ground cover, and wind, must be taken into consideration, and a thorough knowledge of this work is necessary.

One or both of the judges must personally lay out each track, a day or so before the test, so as to be completely familiar with the location of the track, landmarks and ground conditions. At least two of the right angle turns shall be well out in the open where there are no fences or other boundaries to guide the dog. No part of any track shall follow along any fence or boundary within 15 yards of such boundary. The track shall include at least two right angle turns and should include more than two such turns so that the dog may be observed working in different wind directions. Acute angle turns should be avoided whenever possible. No conflicting tracks shall be laid. No track shall cross any body of water. No part of any track shall be laid within 75 yards of any other track. In the case of two tracks going in opposite directions, however, the first flags of these tracks may be as close as 50 yards from each other. The judges shall make sure that the track is no less than 440 yards nor more than 500 yards and that the tracklayer is a stranger to the dog in each case. It is the judges' responsibility to instruct the tracklayer to insure that each track is properly laid and that each tracklayer carries a copy of the chart with him in laying the track. The judges must approve the article to be left at the end of each track, must make sure that it is thoroughly impregnated with the tracklayer's scent, and must see that the tracklayer's shoes meet the requirements of these regulations.

There is no time limit provided the dog is working, but a dog that is off the track and is clearly not working should not be given any minimum time, but should be marked Failed. The handler may not be given any assistance by the judges or anyone else. If a dog is not tracking it shall not be marked Passed even though it may have found the article. In case of unforseen circumstances, the judges may in rare cases, at their own discretion, give a handler and his dog a second chance on a new track. A track for each dog entered shall be plotted on the ground by one or both judges not less than one day before the test, the track being marked by flags which the tracklayer can follow readily on the day of the test. A chart of each track shall be made up in duplicate, showing the approximate length in yards of each leg, and major landmarks and boundaries, if any. Both of these charts shall be marked at the time the dog is tracking, one by each of the judges, so as to show the approximate course followed by the dog. The judges shall sign their charts and show on each whether the dog "Passed" or "Failed," the time the tracklayer started, the time the dog started and finished tracking, a brief description of ground, wind and weather conditions, the wind direction, and a note of any steep hills or valleys.

The Club or Tracking Test Secretary, after a licensed or member tracking test, shall forward the two copies of the judges' marked charts, the entry forms with certifications attached, and a marked and certified copy of the catalog pages or sheets listing the dogs entered in the tracking test, to The American

Kennel Club so as to reach its office within seven days after the close of the test.

CHAPTER 7
NONREGULAR CLASSES

Section 1. **Graduate Novice Class.** The Graduate Novice class shall be for C.D. dogs that have not been certified by a judge to have received a qualifying score toward a C.D.X. title prior to the closing of entries. Dogs in this class may be handled by the owner or any other person. A person may handle more than one dog in this class, but each dog must have a separate handler for the Long Sit and Long Down exercises when judged in the same group. Dogs entered in Graduate Novice may also be entered in one of the Open classes.

Performances and judging shall be as in the Regular classes, except that the Figure 8 is omitted from the Heel on Leash exercise. The exercises, maximum scores and order of judging in the Graduate Novice class are:

1. Heel on Leash (no Figure 8)	30
2. Stand for Eaxmination	30
3. Open Heel Free	40
4. Open Drop on Recall	40
5. Open Long Sit	30
6. Open Long Down	30
Maximum Total Score	200

Section 2. **Brace Class.** The Brace class shall be for braces of dogs of the same breed that are eligible under these Regulations and capable of performing the Novice exercises. The dogs need not be owned by the same person, but must be handled by one handler. Dogs may be shown unattached or coupled, the coupling device to be not less than six inches over-all length; whichever method is used must be continued throughout all exercises. A separate Official Entry Form must be completed in full for each dog entered.

Exercises, performances and judging shall be as in the Novice class. The brace should work in unison at all times. Either or both dogs in a brace may be entered in another class or classes at the same trial.

Section 3. **Veterans Class.** The Veterans class shall be for dogs that have an obedience title and are eight or more years old prior to the closing of entries. The exercises shall be performed and judged as in the Novice class. Dogs entered in the Veterans class may not be entered in any Regular class.

Section 4. **Versatility Class.** The Versatility class shall be for dogs that are eligible under these Regulations and capable of performing the Utility exercises. Owners may enter more than one dog. Dogs in this class may be handled by the owner or any other person, and may be entered in another class or classes at the same trial.

Six exercises will be performed, two each from the Novice, Open and Utility classes, except that there will be no Group exercises. The exercises will be performed and judged as in the Regular classes. The exercises to be performed by each dog will be determined by the handlers drawing one of a set of cards listing combinations of the six exercises totaling 200 points. These cards will be furnished by the trial-giving clubs. Each handler shall provide a dumbbell, Scent Discrimination articles and Directed Retrieve gloves.

Novice	exercise No. 1.	25
Novice	exercise No. 2.	25
Open	exercise No. 1.	35
Open	exercise No. 2.	35
Utility	exercise No. 1.	40
Utility	exercise No. 2.	40
Maximum Total Score		200

Section 5. **Team Class.** The Team Class shall be for teams of any four dogs that are eligible under these Regulations. Five dogs may be entered, one to be considered an alternate for which no entry fee shall be required. However, the same four dogs must perform all exercises. Dogs need not be owner-handled, need not be entered in another class at the same trial, and need not have obedience titles. A separate Official Entry Form must be completed in full for each dog entered.

There shall be two judges, one of whom will call commands while the other scores the teams' performances. The teams will be judged one at a time, except for the Long Sit and Long Down exercises which shall be done with no more than four teams (16 dogs) in the ring.

The dogs on a team will perform the exercises simultaneously and will be judged as specified for the Novice class, except that a Drop on Recall will be used in place of the Recall exercise. In all exercises except the Drop on Recall, the teams have the option of executing the judge's commands on the team captain's repeat of the command.

In the Figure Eight portion of the Heel on Leash exercise, five stewards will be used. The stewards shall stand eight feet apart in a straight line. One dog and his handler shall stand between two stewards, all members of the team facing in the same direction. On orders from the judge, the team shall perform the Figure Eight, each handler starting around the steward on his left and circling only the two stewards between whom he had been standing.

In the Drop on Recall exercise, the handlers will leave their dogs simultaneously on command of the judge. The dogs shall be called or signalled in one at a time on a separate command from the judge to each handler. The handler shall, without any additional command from the judge, command or signal his dog to drop at a spot mid-way between the line of dogs and the handlers. Each dog shall remain in the Down position until all four have been called and dropped, whereupon the judge shall give the command to call the dogs, which shall be called or signalled simultaneously. The finish shall be done in unison on command from the judge.

Section 6. **Team Class, Scoring.** Scoring of the Team class shall be based on the performance of the dogs and handlers individually plus team precision and coordination. Each dog and handler will be scored against the customary maximum, for a team total of 800 maximum available points. Individual dog's scores need not be recorded. The exercises and maximum scores are:

1. Heel on Leash	160
2. Stand for Examination	120
3. Heel Free	160
4. Drop on Recall	120
5. Long Sit	120
6. Long Down	120
Maximum Total Score	800

SUGGESTED CONSTRUCTION OF HIGH JUMP

FRONT VIEW OF HIGH JUMP

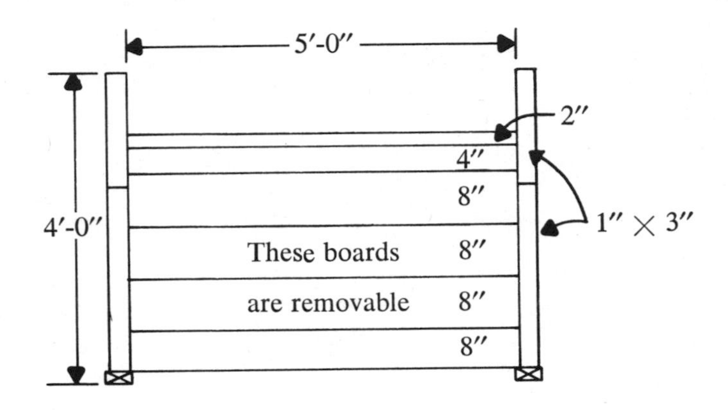

SIDE VIEW OF HIGH JUMP

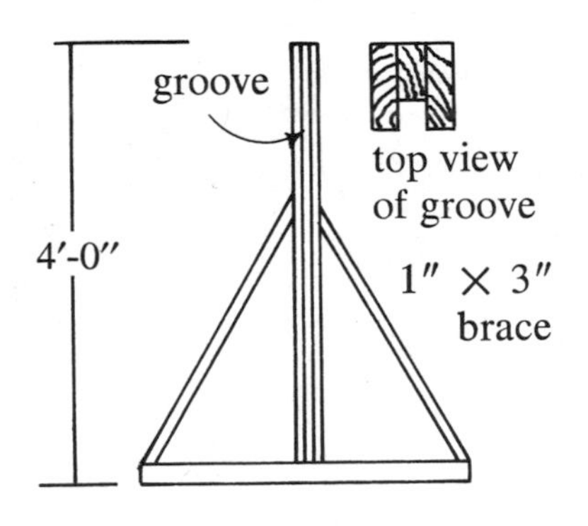

This upright consists of two pieces of 1″ × 3″ and one piece 1″ × 2″, nailed together, with the 1″ × 2″ forming the groove for the boards to slide in.

The high jump must be painted a flat white.

SUGGESTED CONSTRUCTION OF BROAD JUMP

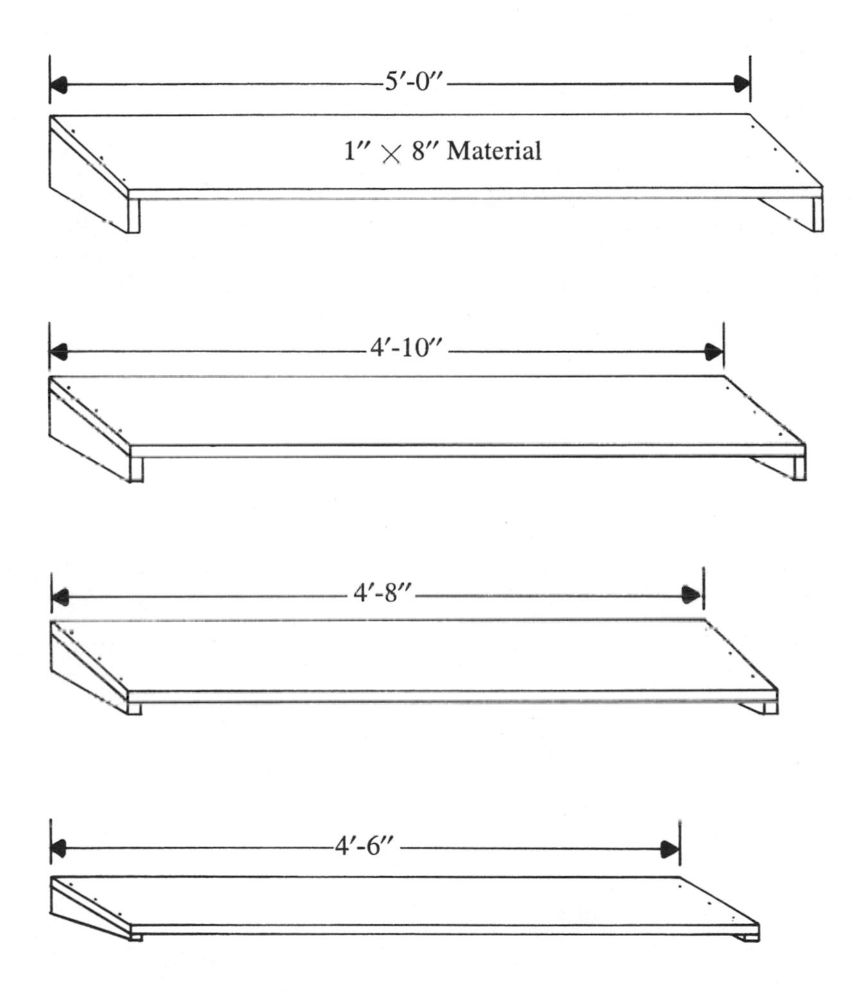

END VIEW OF FOUR HURDLES

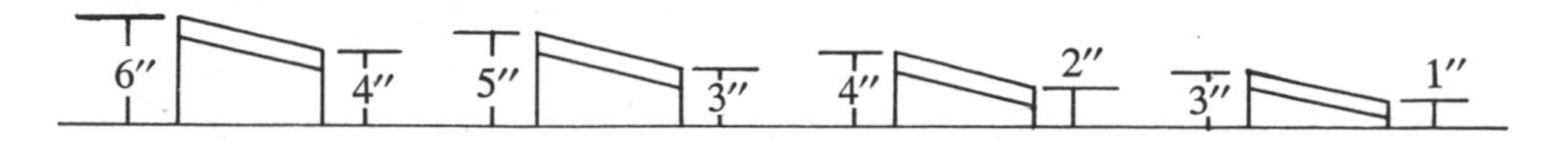

This jump must be painted a flat white.

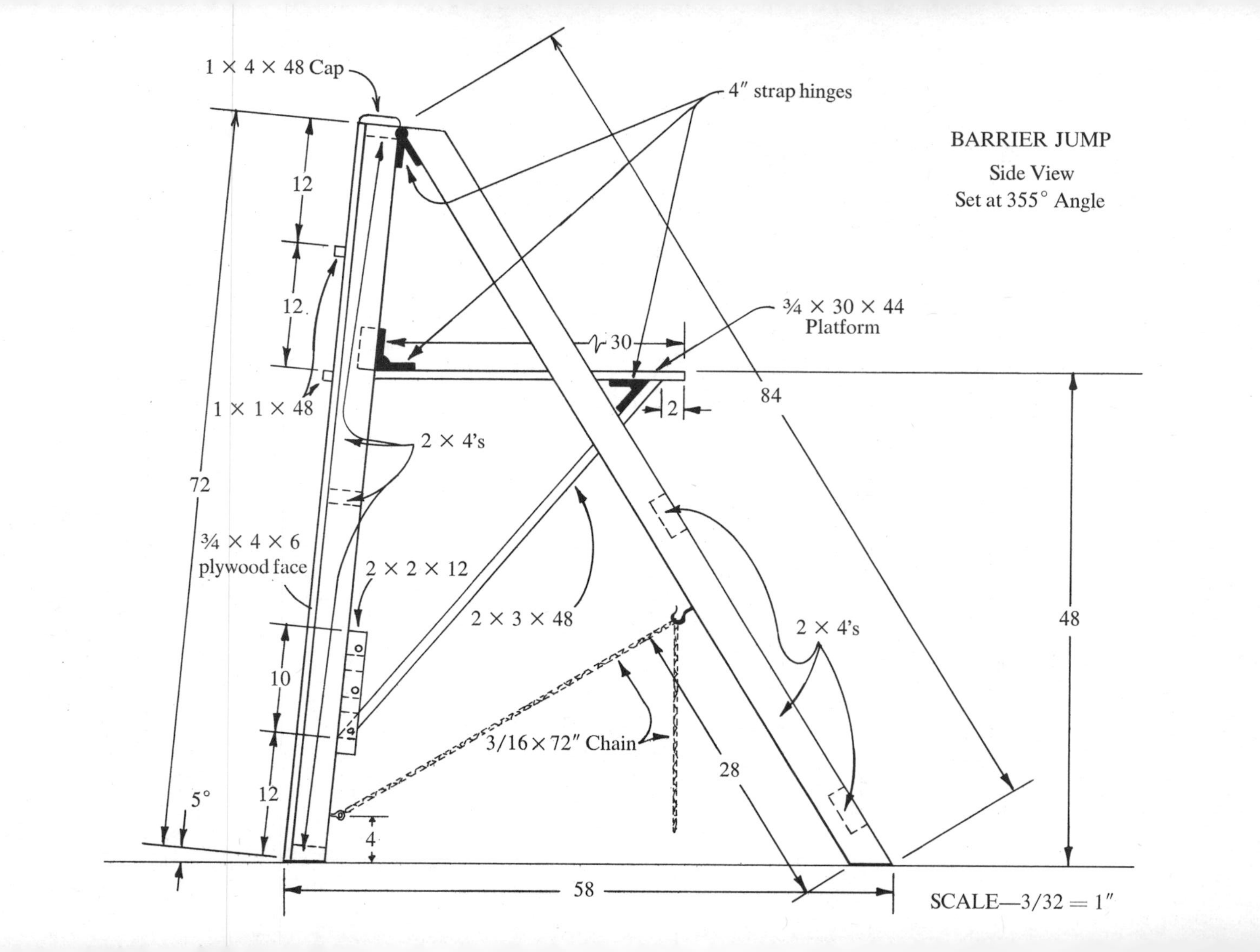
BARRIER JUMP
Side View
Set at 355° Angle
1 × 4 × 48 Cap
4″ strap hinges
¾ × 30 × 44
Platform
30
2
84
12
12
1 × 1 × 48
2 × 4’s
72
¾ × 4 × 6
plywood face
2 × 2 × 12
2 × 3 × 48
2 × 4’s
48
10
3/16 × 72″ Chain
28
12
5°
4
58
SCALE—3/32 = 1″

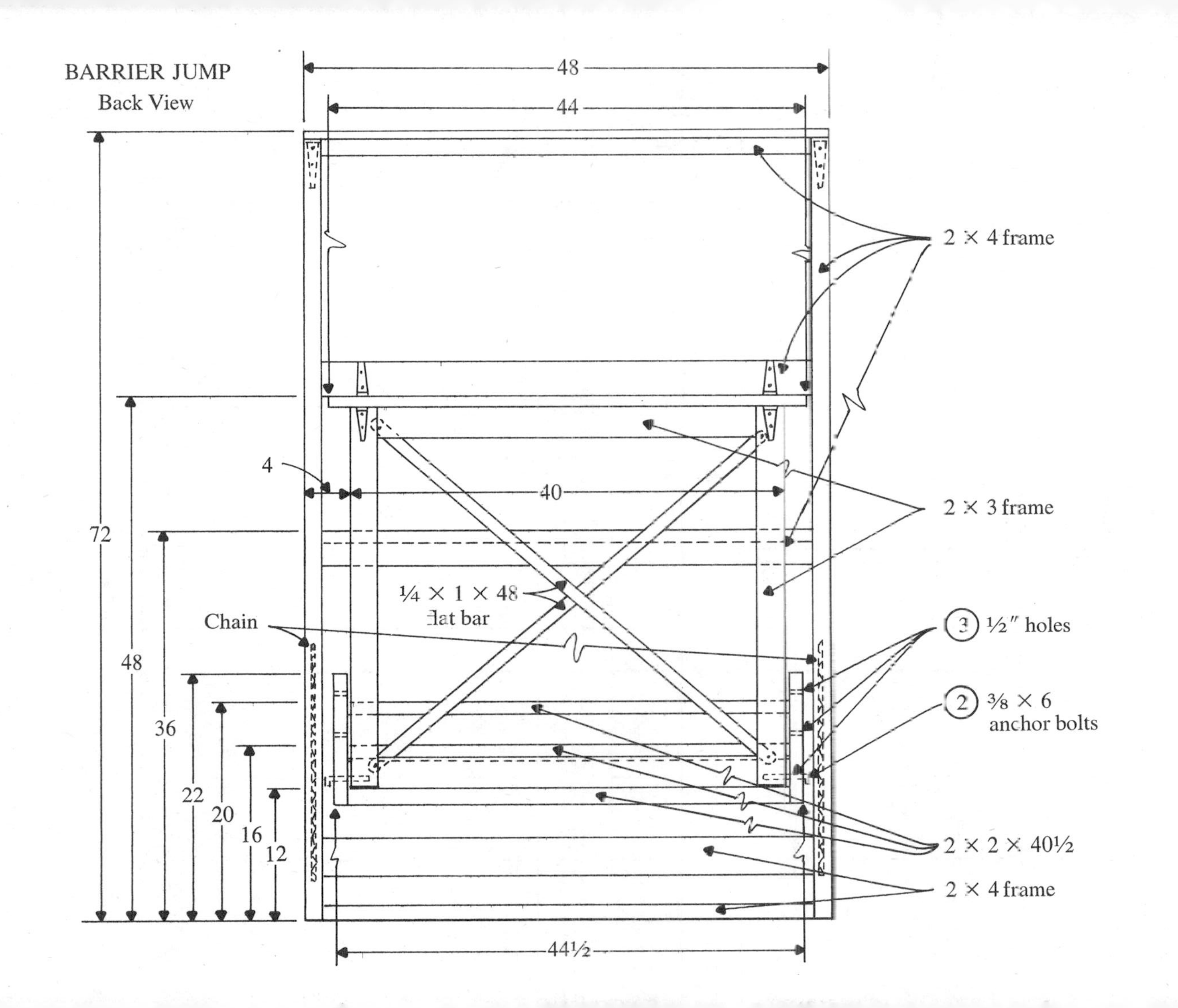
BARRIER JUMP
Back View
48
44
2 × 4 frame
4
40
72
48
36
2 × 3 frame
1/4 × 1 × 48
flat bar
Chain
3 1/2″ holes
2 3/8 × 6
anchor bolts
22
20
16
12
2 × 2 × 40 1/2
2 × 4 frame
44 1/2

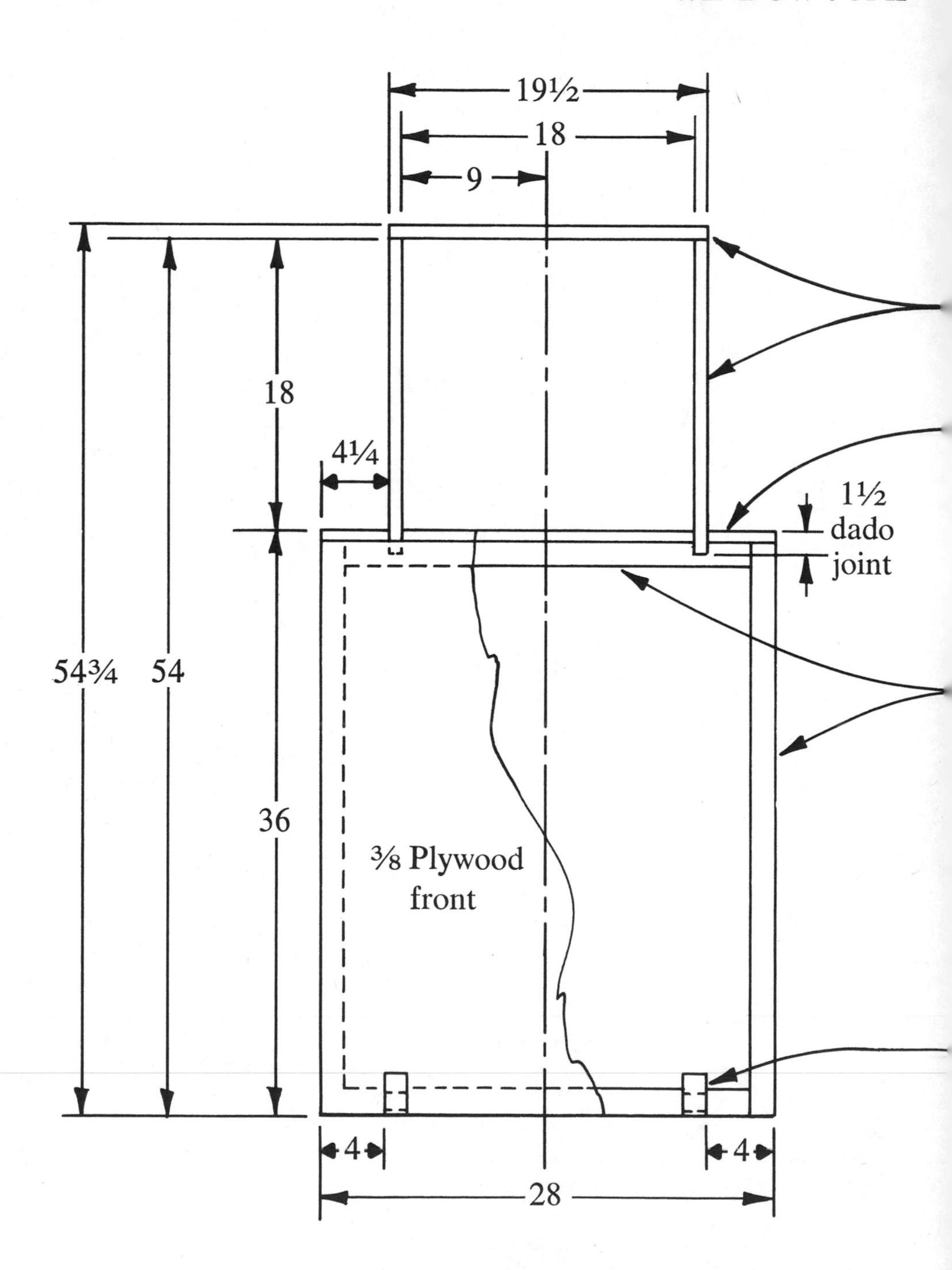

FRONT VIEW

Scale 3/32 = 1 inch

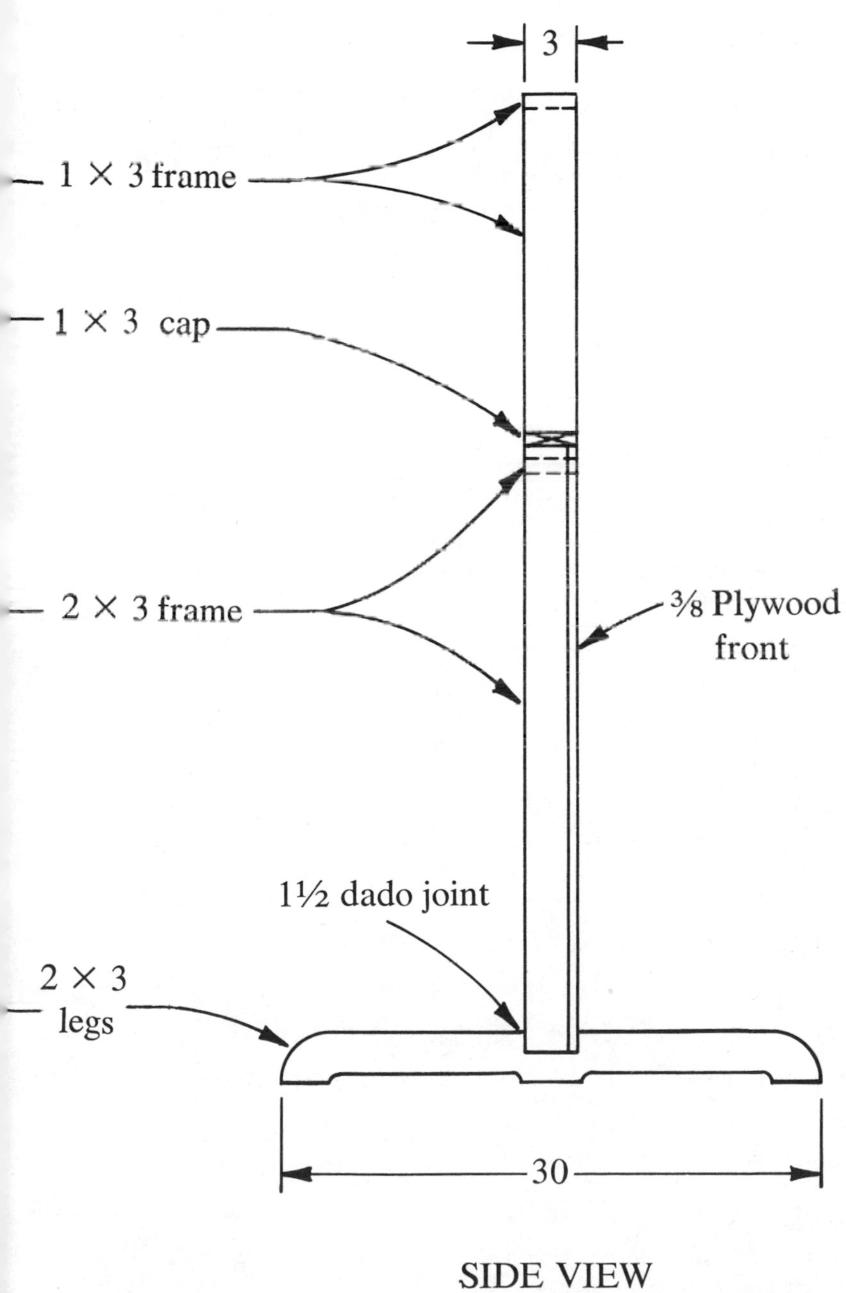

SIDE VIEW

LONG JUMP

Front View of Long Jump

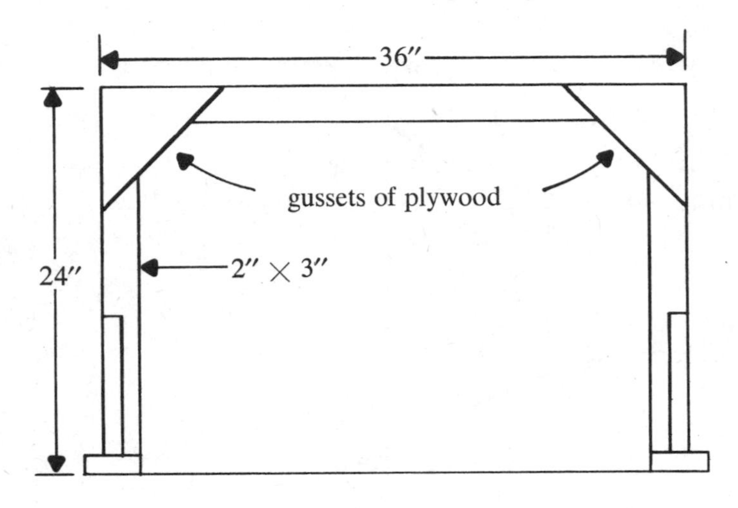

Side View of Long Jump

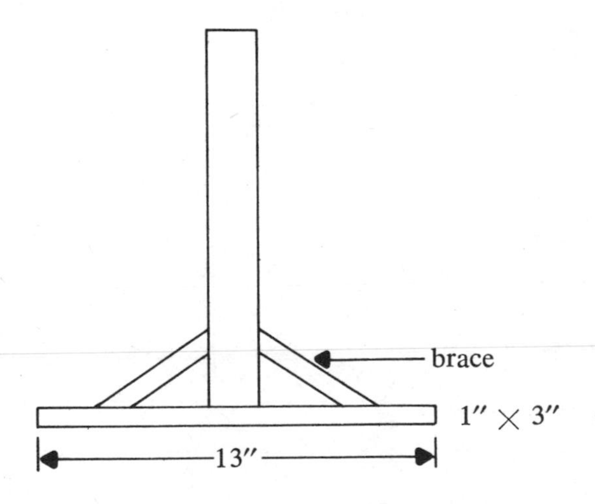

5 ft. set 4 ft. set